FULL HOUSE

The Definitive Guide
for Successfully Promoting
School and Community Theater

by George E. Chartier

DRAMATIC
CONCEPTS
PUBLISHING

FULL HOUSE

The Definitive Guide for Successfully Promoting School and Community Theater

Copyright © 1992 by George E. Chartier

All rights reserved. No part of this book may be reproduced in any manner whatsoever without the expressed written consent of the author or publisher, except in the form of brief excerpts or quotations for the purposes of review. The information contained may not be duplicated in other books, databases or other media without written consent of the author or publisher. Making copies of this book, or any portion of this book for any purpose other than the purchaser's personal use is a violation of United States copyright laws.

Publishers Cataloging in Publications Data
Chartier, George E., 1955–
Full House.
Bibliography:
Includes index.
1. Theater — Management.
2. Arts publicity.
I. Chartier, George   II. Title.
PN3160.P8C43   92-71038
ISBN 1-881237-00-1

The paper used in this publication meets the minimum requirements of the National Standard for Information Sciences (ANSI) Permanence of Paper for Printed Materials.

Cover design concept by Rodney Baker

Desktop publishing production by Michael Dulac

First Printing October 1992

Printed in the United States of America
Braceland Brothers Inc., Philadelphia, PA 19153

DRAMATIC CONCEPTS PUBLISHING

Dramatic Concepts Publishing
1101 North Kenilworth St #2
Arlington VA 22205
(703) 532-0279

DRAMATIC
CONCEPTS
PUBLISHING

DEDICATION

To
George H. Merritt
vice president–advertising and public relations,
Milton Bradley Company,
who taught me that publicity is
the greatest game there is.

Je me souviens.

Contents

Acknowledgments

Introduction

The Spell of Theater

The Deadly Dozen Publicity Errors

Chapter 1 Questions and Answers

>A review of the most frequently asked questions about promoting theater—and some quick answers to get started on the road to success.

Chapter 2 How Promotion Works

>Hidden benefits of promotion. Competing attractions. Using emotion and details. Picturing your audience.

Chapter 3 The Company Publicist

>Establishing responsibilities. Determining lines of authority. Combining tasks for maximum promotion.

Chapter 4 Getting Started

>Setting a goal. Selecting tools. Locating sources. Getting organized.

Chapter 5 The Master Battle Plan

>Tracking multiple tasks. Scheduling deadlines. Using the plan to communicate.

Chapter 6 The Publicity Team

>Recruiting help. Dividing tasks. Training assistants.

Chapter 7 Budgeting and Money Management

>Lobbying for a budget. Predicting costs. Soliciting bids. Keeping records. Getting reimbursed.

Chapter 8 The News Release

>Misconceptions. Proper form. Newspapers, radio and TV. News releases vs. advertising. Variations and timing. Writing style.

Chapter 9 Dramatic Photos

>Posing dramatic pictures. Finding a photographer. Creative uses for photos. Writing captions.

Chapter 10 Media Relations

>Newsroom organization. When the media ignores you. News kits. Reviews vs. previews. Dealing with radio and TV. The news conference.

Chapter 11 Working With Printers

>Selecting a printer. Saving money at the print shop. Glossary of printer's terms.

Chapter 12 Posters

>What makes a good poster. Working with your designer. Timetable for poster production.

Chapter 13 Leaflets, Brochures and Other Handouts

>Purposes and uses. Content and design. Methods and distribution.

Chapter 14 Signs and Displays

Creating effective indoor displays. Designing and producing outdoor signs.

Chapter 15 The Power of the Playbill

Mining promotional gold. Making money and influencing audiences. A useful layout system. Advertising and billing.
Tips for production management.

Chapter 16 Advertising

Advertising's role. Location and timing. Calculating costs. Measuring success. Design for newspapers. Ads for radio and TV. Reality-check.

Chapter 17 Publicity Stunts

Creating legends—not jokes. Working with police and journalists. Tying into your production's theme. Evaluating risks.

Chapter 18 School Promotion

Taking advantage of the system. The problem of recruitment. Organizing and teaching.

Chapter 19 Building Group Recognition

The value of name recognition. Elements of an identity program. Developing a communications plan.

Chapter 20 The One-Person Publicity Shop

Setting priorities. Basic equipment. Acquiring skills. Keeping organized.

Chapter 21 Self-Promotion

Getting recognition you deserve. Being—and looking—prepared. Get credit by giving credit. Inform, reward and cheer others first

Chapter 22 Final Words

Why we do what we do: a pep talk about The Big Picture.

Appendix A: The Master Battle Plan

Appendix B: Budget Work Sheets

Appendix C: Playbill Work Sheets

Appendix D: Biography Questionnaire

Appendix E: Journalism Style Guide

Suggested Reading

Index

About the Author

Acknowledgments

The knowledge distilled in this book most recently comes out of my head. By this I mean the thoughts and words are the product of my experiences.

Many people showed me or led me or pushed me into these experiences, however, so their presence, their guidance and their knowledge flows through me as the ink flows along these pages. It is impossible, then, to entirely separate my ideas from theirs.

Yet, as rivers that converge still retain their individual and identifiable sources, so does my stream of consciousness. The greatest sources of my thoughts on dramatic promotion for the theater spring from these great founts of inspiration:

Edgar C. Alward, my English and speech teacher at Westfield State College, who taught me the power of words; George H. Merritt, vice president-advertising and public relations at Milton Bradley Company, who showed me the power of promotion; Daniel Flynn, vice president for development at Fitchburg State College, who taught me the importance of establishing priorities and keeping in mind The Big Picture; George O'Brien, editor of *The Evening News* in Westfield, Mass., who trained me to think as a journalist; Karen Grava Williams, director of public relations at The University of Connecticut, who taught me the necessity of team-building.

Also, master magician George Perrin, who taught me how to produce dramatic publicity on a lean budget; Robert Lehan, my drama teacher at Westfield State College, who helped me look critically at theater; Ed Radding owner of Radding Signs in Springfield, Mass., who taught me about marketing and encouraged me to pursue my dreams; the Suffield Players of Suffield, Conn., who have given me endless theatrical challenges, joy, and pride; Chet Makoski Jr., vice president of Gamble Bradshaw Makoski: Design, in Farmington, Conn., my graphic design mentor; Robert Thomas, media specialist at the Medical Center of Central Massachusetts, in Worcester, who continues to teach me more and more about publicity photography; and Lyle W. Pearsons, an award-winning playwright, actor, designer and director who lured me into theater work and inspired me to write this book.

Many people granted permission for their promotional materials to be reproduced in this book. I have given them credit when their samples appear, but I thank them here at the outset for their generosity. Theater people have big hearts as well as big ideas.

Before this manuscript was published in book form, several people with expertise in writing and theater generously agreed to review every word to be sure the ideas were clear and sound: Susan Conaty-Buck, George O'Brien, Lyle W. Pearsons, Ed Radding, Bart. P. Roccoberton Jr., and Robert Thomas. Also, Kay Janney, Mary Norris, Margie Secora and Jim Stidfole contributed their expertise to review specific chapters.

My friend David Pesci, a powerhouse of a writer and a person, painstakingly edited this book. Two people gave me invaluable counsel as I struggled to bring this book from manuscript to press: Konrad Rogowski, a superb director, actor, playwright and printing expert; and Candace Hall, who walked the road to publication before me. You hold this book in your hands because they helped make it so.

Michael Dulac, whose friendship goes back 20 years now, executed the desktop publishing throughout this book. He patiently interpreted and modified my design ideas, and suffered through thousands of changes I made in the six drafts that led to the final manuscript. Frankly, I'm amazed that he's still speaking to me.

Finally, I will be forever grateful to my parents, Georgette and Charles Chartier, who gave me perspective. They were the voices in my life that always, always told me to slow down, get more rest, eat regular meals and cut out all that theater stuff. Although I fought them every step of the way, they managed to turn out a rather acceptable product, if I do say so myself.

These people—a flood of talent and generosity—give true meaning to my daily efforts to "go with the flow."

Introduction

Nothing thrills me like getting a phone call from the director of a play I've been promoting for two months, and hearing three magic words: "We're sold out."

Mingling with the actors as they apply their makeup on opening night, I love passing around copies of advance stories appearing that day in the local papers. The stage manager comes by and announces "15 minutes" and the actors ask "How's the crowd?" The stage manager pauses in mid-run to say, "Full house — and we're sold out tomorrow night and next Saturday too."

The actors whistle and hoot and applaud. They throw themselves at the costume rack, energized with a tangible purpose: "There's an audience out there waiting for us to perform!"

In the house itself, I greet familiar customers in the audience — but I'm always looking for the newcomers, too.

"I was afraid I wouldn't get in," someone tells me, looking bewildered. "I never imagined I'd need reservations to see a community theater play!"

"How did you hear about the show?" I ask, ever surveying the market. The newcomer says he found a flier in his mailbox, saw the article in the newspaper, and received a reminder with his monthly bank statement.

In the lobby, customers line up at the snack bar. Ushers scramble to seat people holding tickets at the door.

Full house.
Sold out.
I love it.

At intermission, I note newcomers signing up to be put on the mailing list. Others are showing friends their favorite actors in photographs of previous shows hanging in the lobby.

"Oh, look at the play they're doing next!" someone says, pointing to the notice in the playbill. "We have to come back for that show!"

A shy teenager approaches an usher and says she's read the handout about all the free on-stage and back-stage training the theater offers. She wants to join the group — hurrah! (Maybe I can convince her to join the publicity team.)

After the show, the ticket manager tells me that people at this show have ordered fifteen more tickets for next Friday night — they're coming back and bringing friends. It looks like we will be sold out for the entire run.

The production manager asks me if we should take down the sign on the town green, since sales are flush. No, I say; leave it up. We may add an extra performance.

Welcome to the world of promotion.

Whether you are an experienced publicist looking for a few new ideas (see the chapter on Publicity Stunts), a newly elected board member (see the chapter on building The Publicity Team), a brave newcomer who said "Sure, I'll do publicity" in a moment of weakness (see the chapter on Getting Started), or the publicity manager for your own traveling show (turn to the chapter on The One-Person Publicity Shop), this book is for you.

The ideas in this book address the needs of community theater, but can easily be applied to children's theater, secondary school, college theater or professional theater. While these groups sometimes appeal to different audiences, the promotional need of any theatrical enterprise is ultimately the same: to fill the house.

As a community theater actor, I have stood on stage and squinted into the darkness to hear the sound of an uneasy audience clapping in a half-empty theater. It is a terrible, hollow sound. I have attended wonderful plays where the performers and backstage crew outnumbered the people holding tickets, and heard the lament "I didn't see any announcements in the paper, there were no posters downtown — did anyone do any publicity? What a shame!"

Shame indeed. It's a shame when actors and crew rehearse for weeks and hardly anyone turns out to see the show. It's a shame when a reviewer says nice things in the newspaper the day the show closes, and the production is called a critical success but a financial disaster because ticket sales were so poor. It's a shame when 25 people are seated in a 125-seat house, straining smiles and shifting in their seats, when they would have been screaming with laughter at the comedy on stage if instead the house were at least two-thirds full.

It's your party and you can cry if you want to, or you can try the ideas in this book and sing "There's no business like show business!" These ideas are the result of my experience in business, journalism and theater. You now have what I've learned in twenty years of testing, rejecting and refining promotional strategies designed for one purpose: to fill show seats with eager, paying customers.

The ideas in this book are not complicated. They do not require a degree in marketing or journalism to execute. Best of all, most do not cost much money. Every time a publicist spends $10 (the cost of a ticket to most community theater performances), a customer gets in free —and that's money the rest of the production never sees. Every $10 spent on publicity is $10 less in the budget for costumes, makeup, set construction and dressing, and $10 less in the company treasury to pay royalties, rental and insurance.

In one key instance, this book shows you how to make money — through advertising in the playbill. Of course, the best way to make money in the theater is to create the kind of publicity campaign that will create a full house.

The publicist who can fill a house night after night, show after show, using but a small budget and big ideas, is invaluable to a struggling theater. The people who work to put on a show invest their time, their energies, their skills and their hearts. It is in your power, as the company publicist, to see that these hearts are emboldened by the cheers and applause of a robust audience.

Please write to me and let me know how these ideas work for you and do add suggestions of your own. If I use your ideas, I'll give you credit in a future edition. Let's share the wealth of our knowledge and together bring the drama of live theater to people everywhere.

May all your houses be filled, your shows sell out in advance, and your phones stay busy with volunteers asking how they can help with publicity!

—*George E. Chartier*

The Spell of *Theater*

It's a prickly question for theater publicists: do we spell it *theater* or *theatre*?

The artistic director of one of the most prominent drama schools in the United States once said that while he managed to overcome many daunting administrative and directorial challenges during his tenure, he had to admit defeat when he tried to change the school's pervasive use of the European spelling of *theatre* for the American spelling, *theater*.

"I found that it would have taken an act of Congress" to change the company's name from *theatre* to *theater*, he said.

Webster's New Collegiate Dictionary lists both versions, but cites the American spelling first, indicating that this is the way the majority of people in the U.S. spell *theater*.

The Oxford American Dictionary also cites *theater* as the preferred spelling and the *Associated Press Stylebook and Libel Manual*, followed by journalists nationwide as their guide of choice, directs writers to use the spelling *theater* "except in some proper names," such as Shubert Theatre. My computer spell-checker doesn't even recognize *theatre* as a legitimate spelling choice.

Yet the majority of announcements and articles and book titles that I see written by people working in American theater reveals that practitioners of the dramatic arts in the U.S. prefer using the European spelling—*theatre*. This is odd, as few people in the U.S. use the British spelling for other words—*colour, flavour, grey* and *jaol* (jail), for example.

This practice of using the continental spelling when an American word exists suggests to me that many people working in American theater harbor feelings of inferiority when comparing their nation's efforts to Europe's—and especially English theater. Indeed, while Harry Shaw's trusty *Dictionary of Problem Words and Expressions* notes that "*Theater* is much the more common spelling," he adds, "some writers and some persons in theatrical professions seem to feel that *theatre* has more appeal and dignity."

There's no need to feel this way. American playwrights O'Neil, Williams, Albee and August Wilson have found great favor among European audiences, while productions of plays by Shakespeare, Moliere, Ibsen and other giants of European theater have found new life on this continent when performed in the distinctly American style of acting.

Throughout this book and in my work promoting community theater on American shores, I use the American spelling—except, as the *AP Stylebook* recommends, when writing about a building or organization that clings to the old European spelling in its formal name.

The Deadly Dozen Publicity Errors

Easy steps to certain doom:

1. Don't plan ahead. Wait until five weeks or less remain before opening night to begin publicity.

2. Expend the minimum effort possible. Send one news release to one journalist and wait for it to get printed.

3. Don't bother with interesting publicity photos.

4. Exaggerate about the quality of the production and go for the hard sell—but don't give useful details about the show.

5. Leave off your phone number on news releases so that journalists have to hunt for you when they have questions.

6. Ignore journalism standards. Print your news releases single space on both sides of the paper. Don't bother checking spelling, grammar or punctuation.

7. Don't update your mailing list regularly.

8. Don't plan and follow a budget.

9. Give up easily. Don't try new ideas.

10. Hide or obfuscate information on posters and other publicity. Minimize or conceal the name of your group and the phone number for tickets. Don't reveal what the play is about.

11. Avoid speaking with journalists who receive your news releases. Don't ask their opinions—tell them yours. Expect them to drop everything when you phone.

12. Assume people want to see your show. Don't look objectively for the news value in your production.

FULL HOUSE

Questions and Answers

Chapter 1

1 *The town newspaper won't print any of my press releases. I think the editor hates theater or something. What can I do to get better news coverage of my show?*

First, you must be sure that you're doing everything right: Are your releases written in a factual, journalistic style that's easy for an editor to use—or in a hyped-up or too clever advertising manner that doesn't match the newspaper's style?

Are your releases brief and to the point? Are they mailed at least 10 days before you'd like to see the news in print? Are your releases typed and do they indicate whom to contact for more information?

Do your releases always present critical information that answers the questions who? what? when? and where?—in logical order?

If you answered "no" to any of these questions, turn to Chapter 8 in this book to learn how to write effective news releases.

2 *My releases are fine. Still, other theater groups get attention all the time in the newspaper. Why isn't the publicity I send ever used?*

Do you ever send attention-getting photographs of actors in dramatic poses? Do you try to stir a journalist's curiosity with a phone call? Have you ever spoken to or met journalists who cover your area? Does you publicity clearly attempt to educate people about what your show is about and why audiences need to see the performance?

See Chapter 2 on **How Promotion Works**, Chapter 9 on **Dramatic Photos**, and Chapter 10 on **Media Relations** for tips on improving your publicity efforts in these areas. Don't overlook Chapter 17 on **Publicity Stunts** for ways to attract attention.

3 *Newspapers in town won't send a reviewer to write about my show—they say they have a policy of only reviewing professional theater. What can I do to change their minds?*

Are you sure you need a reviewer? A bad review by an unqualified writer can be damaging to ticket sales and hurtful to actors and crew. I don't believe in reviews for primary and secondary school theater — a bad review does too much damage. For community theater, consider asking the newspaper to write a preview article to appear before opening night that will inform the public about what's in store.

If you're representing a college theater, the acting students need to be reviewed as part of their training.

See Chapter 10 on **Media Relations** to learn how to prepare a reviewer for your show.

4 *Ticket sales are always slow on opening night, but then pick up by the third or fourth performance. How can I get more people to come to the first shows without buying a lot of expensive advertising?*

Your theater staff must offer enticements that can be publicized. Offer two-for-one tickets to student organizations. Have actors, designers or the director talk about the show on radio and in free lectures to civic groups (See Chapter 10 on **Media Relations**). Invite a popular local radio, TV or civic personality to lead an after-show discussion. Offer a discount price, free snacks, a wine and cheese reception or other special amenities to people who patronize the opening weekend—and spread the word everywhere that these benefits are available. Try **Publicity Stunts** (Chapter 17), and consider promoting your show with public access cable TV (Chapter 18).

5 *My theater group doesn't have a permanent location in town. How can you build audience loyalty if you're moving around so much?*

Make sure you have large, clear, readable signs in front of where you'll be performing. Include on your posters and fliers a reliable phone number that people can call for directions — Chapter 13 on **Leaflets, Brochures and Other Handouts**, and Chapter 14 on **Signs and Displays** show how. Emphasize the name of your group in all publicity so that it becomes familiar to the public. Chapter 19 discusses **Building Group Recognition**.

6 *Publicity is such a headache. How can I find people to help get the job done?*

College students majoring in business, English, communications, and theater management often need the volunteer experience for college credit. Let actors and crew members know you're looking. Mention on-the-job training opportunities in all your publicity, including the playbill. See Chapter 6 on building **The Publicity Team** for more ideas.

7 *What do you do if you don't have anyone who knows how to take decent publicity photos?*

Talk to the owner of the local camera shop for recommendations of talented customers. Seek out the head of the local school's photography club. Have your group pay for someone to take a short evening course in photography. See Chapter 10 on **Dramatic Photos** for details and more suggestions.

8 *Advertising is so expensive! How can I cut costs and still get my ad where people will see it?*

Choose strategic days when people already interested in theater are apt to look for your ad. See Chapter 16 on **Advertising** for a sample diagram and explanation of timing in advertising. Consider giving away tickets on the radio or to civic groups doing fund raisers.

9 *When the producer asks me what kind of publicity budget I need, what do I say?*

Chapter 7 on **Budgeting and Money Management** shows how to estimate costs and how to explain the need for adequate funding. Appendix B is a blank form you can follow to work out a budget.

10 *Elaborate playbills seem like they're more work than they're worth. What's wrong with handing out a one-page playbill with just the essential information?*

First, the proliferation of home computer desktop publishing has conditioned people to expect a quality product with interesting information.

Second, your audience will appreciate your show, take more interest in your group, and fall more deeply in love with theater if you take time in the playbill to educate your audience. Provide details about the playwright, the script's themes, and production efforts such as costume and set design.

Third, a good advertising program will bring in profitable revenue. See Chapter 15 on **The Power of the Playbill** to learn how to convince someone to manage advertising.

11 *Aaaaaagh! Opening night is three weeks away and the publicity job has just been thrown into my lap. I have no help and no clue where to begin! What do I do?*

Calm down and turn to Chapter 20 on **The One-Person Publicity Shop**. The chapter shows you how to set priorities and launch a campaign quickly.

12 *Posters are expensive. Do they really convince people to come see a show?*

News releases, posters, advertising, fliers — none of these alone are usually enough to bring in audiences. It's the combination of these techniques, all designed to communicate the same strategic message, that combine to form an effective campaign. Chapter 2, on **How Promotion Works**, gives examples.

Still, an attractive poster is essential, although it doesn't need to be costly. See Chapter 11 on **Working With Printers** for tips on how to save money on posters and all your other printed publicity.

13 *The actors and the director never get me information on the show on time, and then I have to rush like crazy to get the publicity done. How can I get people to give me what I need when I need it?*

Make a list early of what you need, when, and from whom. Make copies of the list for everyone involved. Use the biography questionnaire in **Appendix D** to solicit information. Set deadlines and make it clear to everyone what the consequences will be of their failing to meet your deadlines ("no information = no publicity, no ticket sales, no audience, no profit").

14 *What's the biggest mistake publicists make?*

There are two: Failure to plan with adequate time to execute the plan, and failure to recruit enough assistance. Chapter 5 on designing the **Master Battle Plan** and Chapter 6 on building **The Publicity Team** show how to avoid the classic pitfalls.

Okay, I'll add one more: Posters. It pays to create really good ones that merge psychology and design. See Chapter 12 on **Posters** to learn why good posters work and where to find affordable designers.

For a more complete list of mistakes, see **The Deadly Dozen Publicity Errors**. The list appears right before this chapter.

15 *Publicity often seems like all work and no fun for the people involved. Does it have to be that way?*

Publicity is a lot of work, but planning and knowledge turn drudgery and panic into exhilaration as you learn how to improve your odds of success. Chapter 6 on building **The Publicity Team** suggests ways to inject joy into the teamwork, and Chapter 21 on **Self-Promotion** shows how to gain acclaim for your efforts.

Practice these techniques and, after a show or two you'll find yourself able to relax on opening night while standing in the back of the theater and admiring the most beautiful thing in the world to a theater publicist: a Full House!

Is Anybody There?

When I spoke to a friend recently about a play, he asked me, "What's it about?"

"It's about success and failure..."

"No," he shook his head; "What is it *about*?"

"—patriotism, commitment, conviction—"

"But," my friend persisted, "what is the play *about*? Is it about a man and a woman, or about a group of children in school, or about a pirate with a wooden leg...?"

The modern artist Josef Albers taught that the purpose of Art (read: Theater) is to *open eyes*, to reveal to others some observation the artist has made about the world. The artist does this through metaphor, parable, and symbolism.

The Glass Menagerie was not about a family and a gentleman caller. These elements were there, but they were symbols the playwright used to tell the audience about love and the ways we show it; about loneliness and the ways we deal with it; about memory, and the ways we preserve it. The playwright took an observation about life and polarized it with conflict, symbolized it with characters, vocalized it with speech — and created A Play.

There is a priest I know who speaks of the *Ah-ha experience* — a moment of realization when we have learned something which so moves us to understanding that we react by saying "Ah-ha!" He uses this expression in his lectures on solving problems, but the "Ah-ha" experience can also be applied to that moment in theater, during the performance, when a member of the audience sees beyond the makeup and the action, and realizes what the play is truly *about*. Sometimes this does not occur until the very last line of the play; sometimes the audience is told from the very beginning what to look for. Whichever way it occurs, the "Ah-ha" experience is why the playwright has created the little drama. He wishes to share his vision about the world with the world.

The sentiments of the playwright are clearly expressed in the words of John Adams, in the musical 1776, when, standing alone on the stage, he pleads, "Is anybody there? Does anybody care? Does anybody see what I see?"

"— Ah-ha!"

Your theater promotion works best when it communicates what the musical or play is truly about.

How Promotion Works

Chapter 2

- Hidden benefits of promotion
- Competing attractions
- Using emotion and details
- Picturing your audience

My first professional publicity job was working in the advertising department of that great game manufacturer, Milton Bradley Company, in Springfield, Massachusetts. On the wall behind my boss's chair hung an oak plaque emblazoned with gold letters. That plaque read: UNSEEN, UNTOLD, IS UNSOLD.

Unless news gets out about your theater's play, no one will show up. The publicist's principal job is to see that an audience shows up. If people don't learn about your show, no one will buy tickets, the actors will go home, the crew will pack up, bills won't get paid, everyone will call you a lousy publicist, and you may find yourself forced to take a truly ignoble job, such as spending the rest of your life writing the copyright notices that appear on the inside front page of theater scripts.

But you know that already. What you may not realize is that publicity accomplishes many other things for a theater group beyond filling seats during plays. It's important to understand the far-reaching effects of good promotion so that, when you are planning your campaign, these other needs will be filled:

Vital function

Promotion is vital to a theater group because it helps to

- ▲ sell tickets and bring in audiences, providing the theater company with income and a reason to perform
- ▲ attract good stage directors, performers, technical crew members and administrators
- ▲ create a positive impression that pleases current donors and helps attract new ones
- ▲ establish a good reputation that attracts advertisers
- ▲ build goodwill in the community that, in turn, will help the theater company survive occasional bad publicity.

Be honest, but be exciting

To build goodwill for the theater company and to attract repeat audiences, the publicist must be honest with the press and the public. Your promotion must not exaggerate what the show has to offer. Your publicity photos, the biographies in the program, and your news releases must be true representations of the production or the public will find you out and never again trust your theater group's word on anything.

On the other hand, the publicist must communicate enthusiasm if the public is to be persuaded that the show is worth supporting. This is accomplished by promoting the show's attractive qualities—the selling points, as they call these in advertising.

If your group is bravely mounting a production of *The Tragedy of Macbeth*, for example, one of the selling points is that the audience can expect to see lots of blood and mayhem. People love mayhem in a play or movie or novel, and when they know they can get to see it, they'll line up for tickets, money in hand.

If your play is a thriller, you'll want to emphasize the fun of being scared. If it's a musical with lots of costumes and popular songs, your publicity should announce these details.

With every play you do, stop and think of the last play like this that you attended and ask yourself: Why did I go to see that show? What is it about this kind of show that appeals to me? At intermission and at the end of the show, as the audience was filing out, what things stuck in my mind and what were others talking about?

Facing the competition

Talking about selling points may seem like an obvious part of promoting a show, but it's amazing how this fundamental strategy is often ignored. Many people who are new to public relations genuinely believe that all they have to do is send out one news release two weeks before opening night, announcing that The Middlesex Thespians will present *Euripides and Umendidies, Terrorist & Tailor*, and everyone in the neighborhood should surely cancel their plans to go grocery shopping and instead find a baby-sitter, rush through dinner, call a dozen friends and dash to the theater.

Others new to publicity think a few well-placed advertisements in the local paper should send people screaming to the telephone to order tickets right away.

Friends, we're in a competitive game here. As publicists, we're competing with household chores, tight family budgets, favorite TV shows, videos, movies, pool halls, bowling lanes, bars, concerts, sales at the local shopping mall, office and school homework, plays presented by neighboring theater groups, PTA meetings, craft shows, fatigue or plain old laziness, and a score of other distractions and excuses people can turn to instead of choosing to attend your play.

So, in the face of all this competition for your audience, your publicity must be inspired.

Think psychologically

When I worked in an in-house advertising agency I saw firsthand how a company conducts elaborate tests before it puts a product on the market. The testing ensures that the product will be well received by its intended audience. The company employed an entire department of psychologists and statisticians to test new product ideas with people grouped by age and gender. Then the company tested commercials with still more groups before fine-tuning promotion for TV, radio and the print media.

While you don't have to go to such elaborate and expensive lengths to plan your theater promotion, you should spend time thinking about what motivates your audiences. The successful theater publicist is a psychologist who understands why people attend certain kinds of shows, and why some shows are likely to be less popular than others.

Although there are lots of books and seminars available on general principles of marketing, there are only a few that focus on the theater, and fewer still that focus on how audience psychology affects theater publicity.

Let's do some focusing of our own right now with some generally accepted assumptions about the average American audience's tastes.

Comedies are easier to sell than tragedies. Musicals are more popular with audiences than straight plays. Mysteries and thrillers are more likely to draw audiences than political and social dramas.

The reason for these trends in audience tastes is that most people today go to the theater to relax and have a good time. After working all day, rushing through after-work errands, and struggling with kids and chores and bills at home, most audience members don't look forward to traveling out to your theater to watch a somber production. Your audiences want to be entertained. They want to experience something new, different and uplifting.

Now, this desire to be entertained doesn't mean that your group shouldn't do Arthur Miller's *Death of a Salesman* out of fear that it's too serious a play. It only means that you, the publicist, must adjust your promotional messages to meet and overcome a natural and predictable resistance that your audience may have to certain elements in plays.

Overcome any audience resistance to a play by communicating the entertaining elements of a production and the emotional benefits of attending the performance.

Let's get emotional

Remember this: Theater is an emotional experience. Aristotle, that great Greek granddaddy of all theatrical thinking (say this five times fast), wrote at some length about the *catharsis*, or emotional satisfaction an audience experiences from watching a drama played out in front of them. It's the feeling you recall experiencing while watching your annoying brother or sister get scolded by mom for being annoying. Didn't watching that dramatic scene give you a catharsis?

Think about plays you've seen a few years ago that impressed you. How many of the lines do you recall? Very few, surely. The plot? Hazy, most likely. What you probably recall with most certainty is that the play made you laugh, cry, get angry, jump with fear, or cheer with satisfaction.

When you read the script of the play you are going to promote:

▲ think about what emotions the play is designed to stir in the audience, and what emotions you experienced in reading the play;

▲ discuss with the director what emotional responses she or he intends to work toward in the current production;

▲ at the library, locate newspaper reviews published when the play first appeared to gather clues about how the critic and the audience reacted emotionally to the play.

Shakespeare is about as great as theater gets, yet it's amazing how many people are intimidated by the language and retain painful memories of struggling through a Shakespearean play studied in high school. If your group decides to do *King Richard III*, that's grea— but be prepared to design your publicity to overcome preconceptions and apprehensions about Shakespeare held by the general public. Remember, "The play's the thing."

Promote with the right details

Persuasive publicity designed to fill your theater with eager audiences does not mean saying in your news releases, fliers and posters, "This is an exciting play." Don't tell people what they're supposed to feel. Show

Communicate the entertaining elements and the emotional benefits of attending the performance.

them by description what the play offers that deserves an emotional response (look for examples of how to evoke emotional responses in Chapter 8, **The News Release**).

Here's a partial checklist of things that usually attract people to plays; your publicity should emphasize these things:

- ✓ music (well-known hit songs)
- ✓ comedy (physical stuff or witty words?)
- ✓ dancing
- ✓ costumes
- ✓ special effects (lightning storms, fog, flying bats)
- ✓ mystery
- ✓ thrills and suspense
- ✓ romance
- ✓ characters in danger
- ✓ heroic decisions
- ✓ controversial themes (it works for TV talk shows!)
- ✓ sex and nudity (which often are controversial)
- ✓ action (sword fights, frenetic farces)
- ✓ elaborate or unusual sets or props
- ✓ blood and guts

Secondary selling points include:

— if the play is an original script,

— if it stars popular local figures,

— if the production's proceeds benefit a local charity,

— if the play deals with a historic event that keenly interests the public (because it is connected with a coming holiday or is in the recent public memory),

— or if the play is a well-respected classic (Remember, however, that this can work for or against a production. Respect does not equal popularity).

Remember your broader audience

Your audience is larger than the gathering of people who come to your theater. As publicist, you must consider the following people when designing your publicity:

1. Regular theater-goers who come to most of your group's productions.

2. Audiences of nearby theaters who rarely or never attend your group's productions.

3. People in the area who never go to the theater.

4. Local businesses who currently advertise in your playbill or who should be advertising.

5. Current and potential donors.

6. People and groups in authority in your community (teachers, politicians, police officers and the fire marshall, religious leaders, members of the media, and anyone else who may lend either support to — or might be upset by — your theater's production).

In promoting your show, you must carefully select what you want to say about the production and weave the elements into strategic messages that will appeal to these groups. In some cases, you may wish to send

New 1989-90 Season!  SUFFIELD PLAYERS Presenting Entertaining Live Theater!

Surprises!   Thrills!   Suspense!

Being of Sound Mind

By Konrad J. Rogowski

A poignant, sometimes funny play written and directed by Suffield Player Konrad Rogowski. Four people invited to a New Hampshire summer home find themselves led by their unusual hostess along a roller coaster evening of games, challenges and revelations that change their lives forever. Join us for the surprises!

October 26-27-28 and November 3-4 & 10-11
Cabaret Seating at Mapleton Hall

Dr. Jekyll & Mr. Hyde

By George E. Chartier and Lyle W. Pearsons

Winner of 11 awards at the 1989 ACTConn drama festival, this new adaptation of Robert Louis Stevenson's classic thriller offers an evening of action and chills set against the backdrop of elegant Victorian London. Psychological terror directed by and starring Lyle Pearsons. Join us for the thrills!

March 8-9-10 and 16-17 & 23-24
Mapleton Hall

Sherlock's Last Case

By Charles Marowitz

This diabolically clever (and frequently funny) play illuminates little-noted aspects of the master sleuth's character. A murder plot, a perplexing question of identity, and romantic intrigue add up to a first-rate whodunit full of plot twists and theatrical sleight of hand. Join us for the suspense!

May 10-11-12 and 18-19 & 25-26
Cabaret Seating at Mapleton Hall

Ticket Reservations by telephone...

Pioneer Answering Service: (203)627-5749

Opening Thursdays & First Fridays $5
First Saturday Champagne Gala $10
All Other Nights $8

DISCOUNTS
$1 off all shows, all tickets for senior citizens, groups of 10 or more, and youths 18 years and under. Sorry, no multiple discounts.

RESERVE TICKETS EARLY
... for all shows at Mapleton Hall! Don't wait to hear "Sorry, we're sold out!" Reserve your tickets *early* and come to *opening night* on Thursdays.

LET US KNOW
... if you or a guest has a handicap that requires special attention. Our staff will be happy to make arrangements if you notify the operator when ordering tickets.

JOIN US
Consider supporting the players with a financial contribution, or by lending your special skills to our next production. We provide "on the job" training! Call:

(203) 668-0858
(413) 569-0318

THE SUFFIELD PLAYERS
P.O. BOX 101
SUFFIELD, CT 06078

Keep this information handy.

TO MAKE RESERVATIONS:
Call (203)627-5749 up to three weeks before opening night. Tell the operator:
- The *date* you wish to attend
- The *number* of tickets desired
- Your *name* and *phone number*
- Any special needs required by a guest with a handicap.

Note: Reservations will be accepted *until noon* on the day of the performance.

TO CHANGE RESERVATIONS:
Call (203) 627-5749 at least *24 hours in advance* of the performance. Give the operator all information about the old reservation, then provide complete information for the new date desired. Refunds or additional payment will be handled at the box office when tickets are picked up. We cannot guarantee exchanges made with less than 24 hours notice.

TO HOLD RESERVATIONS:
Your tickets will be held at the box office for you. Prompt payment will guarantee your reservation. Unpaid reservations will be held until one half hour before showtime.

All shows are performed in Mapleton Hall in Suffield, Connecticut.

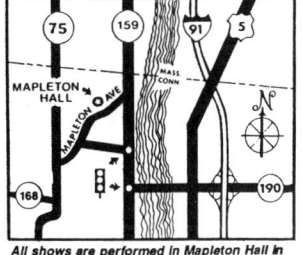

Suspense! Thrills! Surprises! Coming Soon To a Theater Near you!

Two sides of a season brochure. The information is organized with titles, dates and illustrations parallel to each other for a unified look. Note the appeal to emotions above the illustrations and on the cover. Surprises! Thrills! Suspense!

special fliers or write individual news releases targeted to specific groups. For example, a play about war might call for special promotion directed toward veterans' groups.

If your group is presenting *The Subject Was Roses*, you should consider working with a local flower store to create a shop window display, set up bouquets with an advertising card at the refreshment stand or in the theater's rest rooms, and place advertising in the playbill.

On the other hand, if you are doing *Agnes of God*, a controversial play concerning two nuns, you may want to consider how much to say in the local church bulletin. You will also want to consider what negative reactions you might expect from the local convent or rectory, and plan some opportunities that would give these people a chance to voice their views (such as after-show discussions where the audience, local authorities, the actors and the director can explore the issues in the play).

Okay. Now that we know that the secret (shhh!) to successful promotion is to use psychology to understand your theater group's many audiences, the next secret is to know what tasks you're expected to manage as a publicist. After that, you will learn how to assemble your tools and then organize and divide the promotional tasks among members of a publicity team.

But, before you turn the page too quickly, take a moment to chant the following chapter summary out loud:

Summary

- The publicist's job is to persuade people that a production promises a satisfactory experience that is worth the trouble of leaving home to see it.

- A publicist must be honest about what is written and said in promoting a theater group's productions.

- Promotion is more than news releases and posters; it's using psychology to predict what it is about a production that will appeal to audiences on an emotional level.

- An effective publicity campaign tells people what they will see and hear, but chooses details that will prompt an emotional response.

- When planning promotion, a publicist considers how to appeal to all constituents, including advertisers, community leaders, and people who never go to the theater.

The Company Publicist

Chapter 3

- Establishing responsibilities
- Determining lines of authority
- Combining tasks for maximum

Envy the actor. An actor has merely to learn lines, move to the right spots on stage and gesture appropriately, speak convincingly, perhaps perform a few physical stunts in an action scene, and then accept applause.

Well, perhaps that's oversimplifying things a little, yet the actor's job description seems brief and simple compared with what is expected of a company publicist. The list can range from a few items to a comprehensive full-time job, causing a newcomer's reaction to range from "Geez, all this?" to "Ohnowhathaveidoneandwhatamigonnado?!"

Do everyone a favor

Before you begin any publicity campaign, you owe it to yourself and the theater company to draw up an official list of duties that you are expected to carry out as company publicist. This avoids two problems: discovering too late that you were expected to handle tasks you weren't warned about, and getting stuck with additional chores later on that you were not expecting. Your official job will be busy enough without last-minute surprises.

Knowledge will give you confidence and skill. Know what you're supposed to do (ask the producer or company president) and learn how to do it.

Depending on how large, complex and advanced your theater company is, the publicist may be responsible for any or all of the following tasks:

Possible Duties of the Company Publicist

— Secures public announcements in local news media outlets (newspaper, radio, TV) for all the theater company's events, including auditions, casting decisions, performances, and public service affairs (annual open house, town fair, etc.).

— Establishes or updates a system for communicating with the news media, including updating media mailing lists.

— Establishes and supervises a publicity committee comprising persons who assist in promotion.

— Consults the director, producer, committee head or other project leaders to develop promotional themes, and communicates these ideas to artists designing playbills and posters, fliers and other promotional materials. Coordinates the promotion schedule with the director, producer and other persons in authority.

— Obtains cost estimates on projects from local printers and coordinates printing of promotional materials.

— Draws up a budget of anticipated expenses early in production. Operates within the budget approved by the general manager,* keeps records of expenses, and submits detailed expense reports with receipts on a timely basis. Notifies

---

* Throughout this book you'll see the term "general manager." Different groups, due to a variety of organizational structures, will use different terms for this person. In this book, "general manager" is a catch-all term for the person in charge of making the production run — the person supervising all other administrative people in the theater company working on a particular show.

The Company Publicist 3.1

production manager when expenses threaten to exceed the budget.

— Makes frequent and regular reports to the governing board of the theater company, details progress on promotional activities, and provides samples of work that include published publicity.

— Arranges news media interviews of key theater personnel.

— Provides the company ticket sales agent with promotional information on productions, to be used by ticket sales personnel to answer customer questions about the nature of the show. This includes a synopsis of the show's plot, dates and location of production, ticket prices, seating style, and other sales information.

— Maintains a history file of promotional materials related to the theater company's accomplishments.

— Suggests ways the theater company might improve publicity efforts in town and the surrounding communities.

— Manages the completion of these tasks:

• writing news releases, public service announcements, advertisements, brochures and other promotional literature;

• making calls to reporters and editors, as well as making other phone calls related to promotion;

• taking publicity photographs and arranging for the development, printing and distribution of these;

• printing, assembling and distributing news releases, posters, fliers, the playbill* and other promotional materials;

• painting or otherwise preparing, positioning, removing and storing outdoor signage;

• preparing, positioning, etc., indoor promotional displays at the theater** and elsewhere.

• developing and implementing methods of building audience attendance.***

Pretty scary, isn't it? You can easily be overwhelmed by all these responsibilities unless you understand the tasks, have a plan for carrying them out in an

■ ■

* The playbill may be a quasi-promotional item requiring a separate manager to handle advertising sales and preparation of display ads. Sometimes the publicist is in charge of producing the playbill, and coordinates this effort with the ad manager who supplies the ads. See the chapter in this book on producing the playbill.

** Lobby and other theater displays often fall under the authority of the house manager. The wise publicist will sit down with the house manager early in the production to agree on who will decorate the lobby. See the chapter on Signs and Displays.

*** A well-run theater group should have a marketing director who recruits people to join the company, and who maintains a mailing list of members, subscribers and supporters. The company publicist should work with the marketing director to ensure that public relations efforts are coordinated.

organized fashion, and can find plenty of helpers. As a matter of fact, the next few chapters will help you do just these things.

Determine lines of authority

But first of all, you need to know who in your organization calls the shots and pays the bills. To whom does the publicity director answer? How many supervisors do you have in your group? Get lines of authority clarified early, just as you establish your list of responsibilities. Then, when the general manager says "Do it this way," and the director says "Forget her, I'm the boss," you'll know who's who and who's boss.

Combining tasks for maximum promotion

Each of the responsibilities listed for the publicity director represents a different tool that can be used to bring attention to your production. Remember the lesson of the previous chapter: It's the combination of several promotional tools that makes a lasting impact on the public and works to deliver a full house.

That's what this book is all about. Ready? Good! Let's look at what basic tools you'll need to get going. Before turning the page, however, remember to chant each chapter's summary aloud.

Get lines of authority clarified early.

Summary

- Before beginning any campaign, the publicist should secure approval of an official list of duties.
- Determine lines of authority and know who has jurisdiction over which areas of a production.
- Publicity involves the coordination of many tools aimed at communicating with the public.
- A publicist keeps track of media progress and budgets, and keeps key people in the theater company informed.
- A publicist is creative, resourceful and informed!

Getting Started

Chapter 4

- Setting a goal
- Selecting tools
- Locating sources
- Getting organized

It's four weeks to opening night. The playbill is supposed to be at the printer's shop in a week and a half, and you've just realized that you don't have biographies about the actors yet.

You've written a news release about tickets going on sale, and you're supposed to look at photos later tonight, the artist designing the poster is waiting for you to call back with the name of the playwright and the ticket reservations phone number, and it just dawns on you that you've got to put together a whole new mailing list because the last list is nearly unreadable and hasn't been revised in five years.

Christopher Durang wrote the play *The Actor's Nightmare*, which describes an actor who can't remember his lines and doesn't know what play he's in.

The scene I've just described could be called *The Publicist's Nightmare*. No planning, no organization, no tools. Have you ever found yourself in this situation? No, wait: You don't have to tell me. It's happened to every publicist since Julius Caesar's publicist was given this assignment by the big boss: "Look, I'm invading six towns in the next four days and I'll need speeches, posters, some fancy medals and an article in the next issue of the *Roman Legion News*. Shake a sandal and get going."

Before the next show begins rehearsal, let's see how to get started on all the publicity tasks and stay on track:

Setting a goal

If you're a mountain climber, you begin to be good at your hobby by learning about what techniques you need to know. Then, you try out some of these techniques on some easy hills. Pretty soon, you want to climb some bigger mountains and your growing experience tells you that you'll need to prepare more for the greater challenges. You'll need to learn more about climbing, but you'll also need some equipment. You'll need provisions.

Publicity is like mountain climbing, and you've got to prepare yourself to climb your next theatrical mountain with care. First, you need to look at your mountain and decide a few things: how high to climb, from what side, and how much time you have to climb it.

Translation: If you're sitting down to plan your publicity campaign seven or eight weeks before opening night, you can afford to plan lots of promotional strategies: Radio, TV, newspapers, fliers, billboards, signs, a booth in the shopping mall — you name it. If, however, it's four weeks to the first curtain, you won't have time to do all these things. You'll need to concentrate on which ones will be most effective within your deadline.

Again, if you have a team of volunteers (see Chapter 6 on building **The Publicity Team**), you can divide up the tasks and climb that mountain together, everyone pulling everyone else up at record speed.

Bart. P. Roccoberton Jr., who directs the Puppetry Arts Program at The University of Connecticut, speaks of an equilibrium of time, people and money: The less of one you have, the more of the others you need.

So, begin by reviewing how much time, assistants and experience you have to work with. Factor in other variables such as how many promotional outlets are available and necessary. For example, if you live in a rural area with no nearby radio or TV station, where the only

> ### Basic tools for promotion
>
> ▲ a mailing list
>
> ▲ newspaper samples
>
> ▲ a large calendar
>
> ▲ publicity guidebooks
>
> ▲ writing guides
>
> ▲ box office information
>
> ▲ a script
>
> ▲ the play's history
>
> ▲ a personnel list
>
> ▲ biographies

way to get news out is in the one local paper published weekly, and the only three places everyone in town is sure to visit are the grocery store, the post office and church — well, then, your options are limited and you'll just have to use these opportunities the best way you can.

On the other hand, if you're operating out of a major city that can draw people from 10 or more surrounding towns, each of which has its own newspaper in addition to the two or three newspapers in the central city, and there's a library system that welcomes posters and displays, and there are radio stations with talk shows that need guests to interview, etc., etc., — the possibilities are broad.

One last consideration before starting out on your mountain climb. How much effort is necessary? Let's say, for example, you are in a small community with only about 15,000 people to draw from — men, women and children of all ages — and you know that it is considered a statistical miracle if any public event anywhere draws as much as one-tenth of a population. Then let's say that your theater holds 100 people and your group plans to present just three performances. How much effort do you need to invest in publicity to draw the maximum audience your theater production can hold?

Frankly, your job is fairly easy compared to the publicist in the same town with a 500-seat theater. The publicist with the 100-seat theater can probably draw a full house every night with some news releases published at the right time in the right newspapers and with a few posters strategically located around town. The publicist with the larger theater must expect a more challenging climb.

So, take an hour or two to measure your mountain. Then carefully select the tools you'll need to make the climb.

Basic tools and supplies for dramatic promotion

1 An up-to-date mailing list. Your goal is to get your news mentioned in places where your current and potential customers stop, look and listen for news. Your library, the mayor's office of community affairs, and your state arts organization can help you assemble these lists.

Your list should include your area's newspapers (names of arts reporters and arts editors), radio & TV news departments (you'll want to know the names of the news room assignment editors and news directors), arts groups (including state arts organizations and your area's other theater groups), and regional arts news publications (such as *New England Theater Digest*). Don't forget to include newsletters produced by your town government and other civic organizations that may list public events in town.

If your library doesn't have a directory of local and regional news media, look for the "Newspapers" and "Television and Radio Broadcasters" listings in the yellow pages of your town and regional telephone directories (your library should have copies of these directories). Write down the names, addresses and phone numbers. Then look under "Dance Instruction" and "Costumes — Retail and Rental" for names of businesses whose clients are naturally interested in theater; they may be willing to post news releases for their clients to see, and probably will take a poster.

You may also wish to send audition and ticket sales notices to the drama departments of neighboring high schools and colleges. The strategy here is to think of where your customers are, and where they look for news.

Next, check the white pages of the major city nearest to where your group performs to locate a listing for the local commission on the arts, arts council, or the like. A phone call to city hall may also lead you to locate the chief area arts support group. This group should help you compile a list of arts organizations interested in receiving news about your theater group's activities.

At the library, read over the arts pages in back issues of newspapers in your town and from neighboring towns. Look for news about theater groups and other arts organizations, and copy down the addresses and phone numbers of groups that might have members interested in knowing what your theater company is doing.

Once you've complied these lists, call these places to verify that the organizations are still in business and are at the address on your list. Find out when the deadline is for submitting news. Verify that someone there wants to receive news releases about your group. Write down that person's name so that you can address your news to a specific person. An envelope with someone's name is more likely to be opened than one addressed to "Arts Editor."

Sure, this is a lot of work, but you'll save a lot of time and money because a mailing list that has been "fact-checked" requires fewer releases and less postage than an out-of-date list. This fact-checking chore is ideal for a volunteer in your group that wants to help but can't get out of the house much.

2 Recent samples of area newspapers. Before you mail out news releases, you should study the places that will receive them. Become familiar with how theater stories are treated in different papers and tailor your releases accordingly. Some newspapers only print brief listings, while others accept long feature stories. If you're not sure what a newspaper accepts, call the editor and ask.

3 A large calendar. One of the big-as-life calendars with lots of room to list multiple deadlines is perfect to track your Master Battle Plan (**Chapter 5** and **Appendix A**). You'll probably want to post the two or three calendar months next to each other on the wall of your work area so you can see the entire production run all at once. Get a set of color markers or pencils, too, so you can mark deadlines for different publicity projects (posters, news releases, photos, fliers, signs, etc.) in different colors.

4 A handbook on publicity. The one you're reading right now is probably best for your specific needs. Also, see the list of suggested reading at the end of this book. You may wish to check your library or ask the publicity manager at a nearby university or a large corporation to recommend other material on publicity.

The material should cover the basics, including how to write a news release, how to work with the news media, and how to put together a news kit. All this information is in this book.

5 Writing guides. A good dictionary (*Webster's New World*, 2nd edition), thesaurus (*St. Martin's Roget's Thesaurus*), style guides (Associated Press Stylebook & Libel Manual, Strunk & White's *The Elements of Style*), grammar and

Publicity consists of an equilibrium of time, people and money: The less of one you have, the more of the others you need.

punctuation books (Edgar C. Alward's *Up Your Punctuation* is the best one I know; see **Appendix E** to order).

6 Box office information. As soon as the information is available, put together a fact sheet about the show for you and any assistants helping you (Chapter 6 tells you how to find volunteers). This way, the basic information is always handy. Carry this fact sheet with you everywhere.

The fact sheet should list the dates and location of the production that you're promoting; running time; how and where people can buy tickets, including rules regarding ticket reservations, ticket prices, minimum age of customers (in the case of plays with adult themes and rough language); and any discretionary warnings about controversial material in the show.

You'll want to include a brief description of the play (two or three sentences) with any fancy slogans you intend to use in your publicity, such as: "The award-winning play that inspired the award-winning movie" or "Tennessee Williams' masterpiece of stolen hearts and broken promises."

Give one copy of this fact sheet to the person in your group in charge of the box office ticket sales, who will think you're simply wonderful to have thought of this!

7 A copy of the script. Read it as soon as you can, because you'll refer to it many times as you discuss the play with the director, the poster designer, actors and crew, and reporters. You'll use it when writing news releases and drafting information for the playbill. You'll want to file the copy in your historical file after the show.

The library will help you find out facts about the play: when and where it was first produced, what critics said, who starred, what awards it won.

8 The play's history. This is certainly one of the most overlooked sources of publicity information. The reference desk of a large city or university library will help you find out facts about the play your group is producing: when and where it was first produced, what the critics said about it, who starred in it and who directed it, what awards it may have won, if it was ever made into a movie and who starred in it, etc.

When I publicized a local production of the musical *Jesus Christ Superstar*, my research revealed that the show was tested in a handful of towns just before opening on Broadway. One of those pre-Broadway towns bordered the town where the new production was being staged. My publicity played up the news that the musical was "coming back home" to the area where it started.

In a home town news release about a local production of *A Raisin in the Sun*, you could observe that the starring actor "is stepping into the role that has been played by many great actors, including Sidney Poitier who immortalized the role in the 1961 film."

You may discover that the play you are publicizing was first produced exactly 25 years ago. Anniversaries make great excuses for publicity. Yet, you'll never know, and you'll miss out on some interesting promotional possibilities, unless you do some research on your play.

9 Personnel list. Make a second fact sheet with the correct names, addresses and phone numbers (both home and work numbers) of your group's administrators, general manager, technical director, major crew members, the stage director, the cast members, and your assistants.

SUFFIELD PLAYERS
present
"DON'T TOUCH THAT DIAL!"

A live, old-time radio show

Directed by John Howland

Performance dates:

Thursday,	May 10, 1990	$5	
Friday,	May 11	$5	
Saturday,	May 12	$10	(price includes after-show gala with hors d'œvres, music)
Friday,	May 18	$8	
Saturday,	May 19	$8	

Showtime: Doors open 7 p.m., curtain at 8 p.m. all shows. Show ends approximately 10 p.m.

Theater: All shows at historic Mapleton Hall, 1305 Mapleton Ave., Suffield, Conn. Mapleton Avenue is located off Route 159, just over the Massachusetts line, one mile south of Riverside Park. Mapleton Ave. can also be reached from Route 75, just north of Suffield Center. Free parking.

Seating: Cabaret-style seating

Discount: $1.00 off each ticket in groups of 10 or more: $1.00 off for senior citizens & students. Sorry, only one discount per ticket.

Description of "Don't Touch That Dial!":
A fun-filled reenactment of an old-time radio show, featuring six sketches, a multitalented cast, and a host of imaginative sound effects performed the old-fashioned way. Intermingled with the comedy, mystery and dramatic sketches will be commercials from friendly "sponsors."

10 Brief biographies. As soon as they're named, arrange to get biographical information about the director and actors (also, the general manager, stage manager and designers if you intend to feature them in publicity). Use the profile questionnaire located in **Appendix D**.

Other useful information

If you plan to purchase advertising, you'll need to get prices and ad sizes early to do some comparison shopping.

You should prepare a list of likely printers for your posters, playbill, tickets and fliers (you may or may not be responsible for designing and printing all these items; see Chapter 3 on **The Company Publicist**; also see Chapter 11 on **Working With Printers**).

Early on, you will find it very handy to find someone who knows your town and surrounding towns. That person could assemble a checklist of likely locations to place posters. That checklist will help you decide how many posters to print (you can learn more about posters in Chapter 12).

Get a large plastic box with a handle, or a three-ring binder with pockets, to carry all your papers when you travel to the theater and the library. Put information in file folders labelled Fact Sheets & Phone Numbers, Master Battle Plan, News Releases, Poster, Playbill, Mailing Lists, Budget, Bills & Receipts, Script and Background Notes, Photographs, and so on.

At your desk you should place all your guide books, plenty of sharp pencils and red pens, stationery imprinted with your theater company's name, and a bowl filled with your favorite snacks.

Now that you're prepared, let's look at how everything fits together on your giant calendar. Following that, you'll learn how and where to find volunteer help to get the work done.

But first, take a moment to review the summary points for this chapter. There could be a quiz later!

Summary

☞ The first step in any publicity campaign is to gauge its complexity, based on how much time, experience, assistants and opportunities you have to work with.

☞ Next, orient yourself with the production. Do research on the history of the play. Gather facts about the present production. Find out who's involved with the show and how to contact them.

☞ Target your audiences by compiling an up-to-date mailing list. Know who are on your mailing list and why they want information on your show; don't just amass a long list of names and addresses.

☞ Keep organized. Post a giant wall calendar where you can refer to it constantly while executing the Master Battle Plan.

The Master Battle Plan

Chapter 5

- Tracking multiple tasks
- Scheduling deadlines
- Using the plan to communicate

Have you ever seen someone plan an itinerary for a trip? If you were a truck driver, a simple schedule might look like this:

> Sept. 3: Deliveries to customers A and B in Tucson.
>
> Sept. 4: Deliveries to C, D and E in Phoenix.
>
> Sept. 5: Deliveries to F and G in Albuquerque.
>
> Sept. 6: Deliveries to H and I in Amarillo.

Now, imagine you're the boss of a fleet of 20 trucks and you have the itineraries of each driver on a separate sheet of paper. If you want to keep track of all 20 agents at any given day of the week, you could create a calendar like this:

> **Sept. 3**
> Truck 1 - Tucson A, B
> Truck 2 - Duluth K, L, M
> Truck 3 - Jacksonville S, T...
>
> **Sept. 4**
> Truck 1 - Phoenix C, D, E
> Truck 2 - St. Cloud N, O
> Truck 3 - Orlando U, V...
>
> **Sept. 5**
> Truck 1 - Albuquerque F, G
> Truck 2 - Minneapolis P, Q...

This master calendar gives the manager an easy way to know each day what's happening everywhere. With a handy chart like this on the wall, this manager isn't flipping through stacks of papers for an answer when the company president asks "Customer O wants to know when his shipment is supposed to arrive." One glance allows the manager to say "Truck 2 arrives late this afternoon in St. Cloud."

Tracking Multiple Tasks

With the Master Battle Plan for theater promotion that comes with this book, combined with your wall calendar (one of the essential tools listed in the previous chapter), you have a similarly easy, organized way to know immediately what publicity tasks are supposed to be accomplished every day during the campaign leading through opening night and right up until the day the production crew strikes the set from the stage.

By following a series of schedules outlined in the various chapters in this book and summarized in the Master Battle Plan, you will be able to insert all the dates for all the tasks your publicity campaign requires.

Your Master Battle Plan summarizes the itineraries of each part of the campaign — news releases, posters, fliers, etc. — and allows you to quickly combine those dates onto your master wall calendar.

Without a plan, it's easy to get caught up in the details of one project and miss deadlines on the others. The Master Battle Plan teaches you the steps involved in accomplishing different parts of the promotional campaign. It builds in the time you'll need to get the jobs done. If you miss a single step along the way, your master calendar will serve as an early warning system that alerts you to get back on track.

After all, you got into the theater for fun, right? That, and to save the theater from perishing, of course! This is why you need a plan. Keeping on schedule eases anxiety and lets you enjoy the theater.

Scheduling deadlines

Here is how you prepare the Master Battle Plan.

Pick a task, such as producing the posters for your show. Then you write down in order all the steps needed to complete the task — how to go from concept to putting up the posters in shop windows. Then you assign sufficient time to complete each step in the project.

Trying to estimate how much time you'll need for each step is tricky, or as Hamlet would say, "Aye, there's the PUB" (Plan Uv Battle).

For the majority of publicity projects, the Master Battle Plan suggests the average number of days you can expect you'll need to complete a given step. If you are new to publicity, you may want to build in extra time for each step. If you're quite experienced, you may feel comfortable compressing the suggested schedule — but, I don't recommend it. Things go wrong in the best of campaigns, and you should always allow extra time to catch up should you fall behind. For example, you should allow extra time whenever you work with a new printer or an inexperienced assistant.

After you've tested the timing of each step over a couple of shows, you should be able to adjust the recommended schedule to suit your experience. As you develop other publicity ideas, you'll find it easy to design a schedule of your own.

Let's look at the schedule in the Master Battle Plan for posters:

Things go wrong in the best of campaigns, and you should always allow extra time to catch up should you fall behind

---

POSTERS

_____ - Get specs and copy from general manager and director and give to poster artist
[10 weeks before opening night].

_____ - Review artist's design. Get director's and general manager's approval
[8 weeks before opening night].

_____ - Proofread poster galleys and make corrections
[7 weeks before opening night].

_____ - Take completed paste-up of poster to printer
[6 weeks before opening night].

_____ - Pick up posters from printer
[4 weeks before opening night].

_____ - Distribute posters
[3 weeks before opening night].

_____ - Opening night.

In Chapter 12 on **Posters**, you'll learn about design and printing terms. The terms that may be new to you are "specs," "mechanical" and "paste-up." "Specs" is short for "specifics," and refers to the physical details of the poster to be printed: the size of the poster, the number of inks (colors) to be used, the kind of paper the poster will be printed on, and so on. "Copy" is advertising slang for the words. In this case, the copy you'll need is the actual wording on the poster — the name of the theater group, the title of the play, the names of the playwright and director, the production dates, the box office phone number, and all the rest.

"Mechanical" and "paste-up" mean the same thing: the original piece of artwork, with all the words and art glued into position, ready for the printer to duplicate.

Chapter 12 on **Posters** will explain the reasons for these steps, but for now, let's try filling in some dates. We start with opening night — say, May 5 — and work backwards using the suggested timing in the plan. Since we want to have posters on hand to distribute three weeks before opening night, we count back and write:

> *April 14* - Distribute posters
> [3 weeks before opening night].
>
> *May 5* - Opening night.

The plan calls for getting the posters back from the printer a week before the distribution date, and allows two weeks for the printer to produce the poster from the date you deliver the paste-up. Counting backwards, our schedule looks like this:

> *March 24* - Take completed paste-up of poster to printer
> [6 weeks before opening night].
>
> *April 7* - Pick up posters from printer
> [4 weeks before opening night].
>
> *April 14* - Distribute posters
> [3 weeks before opening night].
>
> *May 5* - Opening night.

If the printer produces the poster in just one week, you've saved a week. It's better to be early than late.

When you first sit down to work out your schedule, you'll only need to know the date for opening night to know when you should begin a project. You'll also know instantly if you're behind schedule. In our example, the first step is to gather the information for the poster copy (the words, remember?). Our plan tells us when we need to have this copy in hand under ideal conditions:

> *Feb. 24* - Get specs and copy from general manager and director and give to poster artist
> [10 weeks before opening night].

Let's say that your theater group decides on March 7 that it wants to produce Arthur Miller's *The Crucible*. Opening night is May 5 and the show will run two weekends.

Master Battle Plan: Posters

	Sun.	Mon.	Tues.	Wed.	Thurs.	Fri.	Sat.
10 weeks (before opening night)	FEB 20	21	22	23	24 Give poster specs to artist	25	26
9 weeks	27	28	MAR 1	2	3	4	5
8 weeks	6	7	8	9	10 Review poster design	11	12
7 weeks	13	14	15	16	17 Proofread poster gallies	18	19
6 weeks	20	21	22	23	24 Take poster to printer	25	26
5 weeks	27	28	29	30	31	APR 1	2
4 weeks	3	4	5	6	7 Pick-up posters from printer	8	9
3 weeks	10	11	12	13	14 Distribute posters	15	16
2 weeks	17	18	19	20	21	22	23
1 week	24	25	26	27	28	29	30
production week	MAY 1	2	3	4	★ 5 OPENING NIGHT	6	7

After you've used the Master Battle Plan you'll learn to anticipate problems

Yikes! Did I say it's March 7? Your schedule tells you that you're two weeks late starting. All right, take a deep breath. Being two weeks late at the beginning of a 10-week schedule isn't nearly as bad as being two weeks late half-way into the schedule. With eight weeks left to your poster plan, you have time to catch up (we have extra time built in, such as two weeks for the printer).

So, you obtain information on the show from the director and producer, recruit an artist and you're on your way, compressing the steps where you can to get on schedule.

Using your plan to communicate

Being a few days or a week behind schedule is no cause for a brain meltdown. It just means the pressure is on a little bit to keep things moving. After you've used the Master Battle Plan once or twice, you'll learn to anticipate problems before they happen, such as the temperamental artist who needs more than 3-1/2 weeks to design the poster, or the director who can't decide if he likes the design without mulling things over for two weeks. If you know from the beginning that these characters will strain your schedule, you can march up to them, wave your Master Battle Plan under their nose and say, "Look, Quasimodo, we're behind schedule. Let's get moving!"

If you have volunteers helping you with publicity, you will refer to your Master Battle Plan to check on their progress. "How's it going?" you may ask your volunteer who's in charge of getting the poster printed. "Do we have posters back from the printer?" If you have this conversation on Apr. 13 and the answer is "no, not yet," you'll know it's time to apply some persuasion.

Just don't call your volunteer helpers "Quasimodo." I have a hunch they won't like it.

The master calendar

The master calendar works wonders after you've completed your projected schedule for all parts of the Master Battle Plan. Let's say you have these dates filled in for the following tasks:

POSTERS
April 7 - Pick up posters from printer
  [4 weeks before opening night].

PLAYBILL
April 7 - Deliver final galleys to playbill artist
  and proofread later that week
  [4 weeks before opening night].

SIGNS
April 7 - Begin painting exterior signs
  [4 weeks before opening night].

ADVERTISING
April 7 - Deliver display ads to newspapers
  [4 weeks before opening night].

If you've faithfully transferred all your dates from your Master Battle Plan onto your master wall calendar, you will see that four tasks have deadlines arriving on the same day. While getting dressed on the morning of Apr. 4, you'll look at your calendar and say, perhaps, "Hmm. I think I'll call the printer and see if the posters are ready. Then, tonight after dinner, I'd better stop at the theater and see if there's any fresh paint and brushes for the signs. I should check to be sure the signs are in shape to paint, too. Let's see, the schedule also says I have three more days to finish editing the playbill before bringing it to the typesetter. I'm a little behind with the playbill, so I shouldn't spend too much time at the theater tonight. Have to keep on schedule!"

The Full House
Master Battle Plan
for successful school and community theater publicity.

Weekly summary of tasks

4 weeks before audition:
- ▲ Send out audition announcement

10 weeks before opening night:
- ▲ Set up publicity committee, including photographer, artist and writer

8 weeks before opening night:
- ▲ Review artist's poster design

7 weeks before opening night:
- ▲ Send news media calendars a listing of show dates, times, location, and ticket ordering information.
- ▲ Proofread galleys for poster
- ▲ Deadline for all playbill advertising orders and playbill editorial copy
- ▲ Get general manager's approval to give away tickets on radio
- ▲ Research advertising costs

6 weeks before opening night:
- ▲ Announce cast selections
- ▲ Take black and white publicity shots
- ▲ Bring completed poster mechanical to printer
- ▲ Deliver playbill copy to typesetter
- ▲ Send advance sales notice to patrons and VIP's
- ▲ Contact radio for ticket give-aways
- ▲ Lay out advertising campaign and get budget approved

5 weeks before opening night:
- ▲ Announce when tickets go on sale
- ▲ Order photos from contact sheet
- ▲ Proofread playbill galleys and give one set to artist with corrections
- ▲ Prepare radio information packs for ticket give-aways
- ▲ Design display ads and radio ads; place insertion orders
- ▲ Prepare list of special display locations in town and secure permission

4 weeks before opening night:
- ▲ Mail Home Town Actor announcement
- ▲ Mail invitations, news kits to reviewers
- ▲ Pick up posters from printer
- ▲ Deliver final galleys to playbill artist and proofread later that week
- ▲ Mail invitations to patrons and VIP's
- ▲ Paint road signs
- ▲ Mail information packs to radio for ticket give-aways
- ▲ Deliver display ads to newspapers
- ▲ Assemble materials for special pisplays and arrange

3 weeks before opening night:
- ▲ Mail feature stories
- ▲ Make follow-up calls to reviewers and call box office to reserve seats
- ▲ Call radio and TV to book guests
- ▲ Distribute posters
- ▲ Deliver playbill mechanical to printer
- ▲ Post road signs
- ▲ Sit in on radio advertising recording
- ▲ Monitor newspaper advertising
- ▲ Set up promotional displays

2 weeks before opening night:
- ▲ Send reminder photo
- ▲ Listen to radio for ticket give-aways
- ▲ Monitor radio advertising
- ▲ Pitch story ideas and photo opportunities to newspapers

1 week before opening night:
- ▲ Put spare news kits and reviewer information packs in box office
- ▲ Mail information to TV news
- ▲ Pick up playbills from printer
- ▲ Obtain list of ticket winners from radio

During week leading to opening night:
- ▲ Take action and cast photos
- ▲ Confirm reviewers
- ▲ Make follow-up calls to TV news

After opening night:
- ▲ Send second reminder photo
- ▲ Distribute news clips to VIP's, post reviews
- ▲ Review list of radio ticket winners with box office to verify who showed up

After show closes:
- ▲ Take down and store signs and displays
- ▲ Review publicity budget and file report

copyright © 1992 George E. Chartier. All rights reserved.

Thus, you skip merrily off to work, content with the knowledge that you know exactly how well you're progressing in getting your publicity done. In fact, you're so content and skipping so merrily that you forget to bring your lunch to work with you.

When this happens, please don't write to me and say you took one look at your Master Battle Plan and it made you lose your lunch.

A blank copy of the Master Battle Plan is in the back of this book, in **Appendix A**. Keep the original in the book and copy the form each time you start a new project.

For each set of tasks (posters, news releases, signs), you may want to assign a different color marking pen to note deadlines on your wall calendar. Then, when you're studying your calendar, it's easy to track the poster schedule because you've marked all the poster steps in, say, a green marker.

The Master Battle Plan does more than remind you of your publicity schedule. It serves as a substitute memory. It frees you from having to remember all those deadlines and trying to keep the process straight in your mind. Think of your brain as a house with lots of furniture. Your Master Battle Plan is like an extra room that you've added to store your publicity furniture. The furniture in the spare room is there when you need it, but it isn't cluttering up the living room all the time!

See Chapter 21 on **Self Promotion** to learn what else the Master Battle Plan does for you. You'll be surprised.

SUMMARY

- ☞ The Master Battle Plan lays out each step of a project and suggests the average amount of time needed for completion.

- ☞ The Master Battle Plan tells you instantly when you're behind schedule.

- ☞ It's a good idea to anticipate delays by building extra time into your publicity schedule.

- ☞ After you use the Master Battle Plan on just one or two shows, you'll learn how to refine the schedule and to anticipate delays before they happen.

- ☞ Check your Master Battle Plan and wall calendar every day to keep track of your progress. Use your plan to let others know when their delays are putting publicity off schedule; but, be careful whom you call "Quasimodo."

The Publicity Team

Chapter 6

- Recruiting help
- Dividing tasks
- Training assistants

Promoting a single stage production, even in a small community with limited news outlets, is a big job. There are posters to design, print, and put up around town; news releases to write, copy and mail; photographs to snap, develop and send out; signs to paint and post; and fliers to design, print and send to your patron mailing list.

The way to avoid wearing yourself out trying to accomplish all these tasks is to form a publicity committee. Sharing promotional duties makes good business sense. What good to the theater company is a creative publicist who's burned out after one show?

Beyond the obvious divide-and-conquer rationale, there are other reasons to build a publicity committee. A team of people will come up with more ideas than one person could alone, and new ideas are the lifeblood of successful promotions. A team of individuals, each working in an assigned area, can put a lot of creative energy into details.

The point of joining a non-profit group is to participate, and in the theater, it's as true as ever that "many hands make light work." Why keep all the fun to yourself? Let other people join in.

There is still another reason to form a publicity committee. From that team, one or more people may emerge as leaders to take over the job in future productions. Experienced leaders are vital to any organization, and promoting from within the ranks is best achieved by giving people opportunities to try small, manageable tasks to start.

Here's a possible division of tasks:

Publicity Manager — Board or staff position. The person in charge. Keeps checklists, decides how to divide up the allotted promotional budget, and supervises and trains the publicity team.

Media Director — Supervises writing and distribution of news releases and feature stories. Need not be a writer if there is also a media writer. Also arranges TV, radio and newspaper interviews.

Media Writer — Writes the news releases, public service anouncements, biographies and notices in the playbill, synopsis of the play and other information for the phone ticket reservation service, and other promotional writing for brochures and advertising.

Artist — Designs posters, fliers, the playbill, special brochures, road signs, and even the tickets and covers of news kits if necessary. Could be three people: One designs and pastes up the playbill, another paints the road signs, a third does the poster and miscellaneous graphic art.

Playbill Supervisor — Oversees details of assembling all elements of the playbill, including a typesetter, if the playbill is elaborate.

Advertising Agent — Solicits businesses to buy display advertising in the playbill, and follows up on billing.

Poster and Flier Manager — Sees that posters, fliers, bank stuffers, handouts and other printed promotional materials are posted, placed, mailed, stuffed and distributed.

Photographer — Takes publicity photos to send to newspapers, including "head shots" of actors for the playbill and the theater lobby. Takes color and black and white photographs for special presentations and theater archives.

Display Manager — Sets up and takes down photo displays, window displays, lobby displays and lawn signs.

Special Promotions Manager — Arranges for free tickets to be given away by radio, TV, businesses and civic organizations in exchange for publicity. Buys and places advertisements. May also double as Poster and Flier Manager.

These divisions of labor are not hard and fast, and will change according to the tastes of the board of directors and the publicist. The main thing is to be sure that all publicity jobs are assigned, and that no one person is stuck with too much to do.

As publicity manager, you owe it to your team to understand the tasks of each of your team members so you can match up talents with tasks.

Recruiting help

Here's the section you've been searching for, isn't it? Where do you recruit all these wonderful people? In general, building your crack promotion team takes a little planning, but strategic announcements can pay off with quick responses. Here are some of my favorite ways of recruiting assistants:

1 Post notices in your playbills that your group offers on-the-job training and welcomes people with a willing heart.

2 Place brief, pre-printed forms and pencils in the lobby, by the snack bar, at the box office — even in the rest rooms — inviting people to check off which activities they would like to learn more about, such as ushering, painting, costume design and, of course, publicity.

3 Add a paragraph to your news releases — especially audition notices — announcing that volunteer back stage and theater management trainee positions are open by contacting you or some other responsible person in your group, and include a phone number.

4 Include a check-off box on the information forms that actors fill out at auditions, asking those auditioning whether they'd be willing to join the back stage or management team if they are not selected for a role.

5 Pose and send to newspapers a funny picture showing members of your theater group in military gear and watching the publicity leader point to a large wall map of your town labelled "Publicity battle plan for Springfield." The caption would indicate that your group is looking for a few good publicity helpers.

6 Ask the English, journalism, photography, art and business teachers at your local high school or college if you could speak to classes for ten minutes about the opportunities to gain experience in marketing that you can offer students if they are willing to give a few hours to working on the publicity team. Mention how good this looks on their school record when applying to college or employers. Look for an arts management course. Contact the school art club, photography club and school newspaper.

7 Ask your librarian if you can post a small, three-sided tent card on a shelf next to theater books, announcing that real-life involvement in theater — on stage and behind the scenes — is as close as your theater company's phone number.

8 Post ushers at the exit to your theater after the show to thank people leaving for attending and to distribute fancy invitations to become active members of your group. List as many activities as you can think of, including publicity of course.

9 Hold an open house at your theater and recruit boldly.

10 Ask friends in your theater group and especially the president of your theater company to recommend people who have expressed an interest in getting involved.

11 Contact senior citizen volunteer associations.

12 Get a member of the theater group to dress up as a mime and perform on street corners where people loiter — er — congregate. At the end of a brief performance, the mime hands out invitations to come to a party to learn how to get involved in theater.

Once you have a list of potential publicity team members, the next step is to throw a party.

The first meeting

About two to two and a half months before opening night*, you should have made your calls and provided your team members with some background on the production: a plot synopsis, dates and location of the production, and audition dates.

If the script is readily available in the library, encourage your team members to seek out a copy to review. If the script is new or hard to locate, and there's time to send around a copy of the script, start with your media director. Mail her or him the script with instructions to read it and in 3-5 days pass it on to the next team member on the list. Otherwise, plan to have your team meet with the cast during the first rehearsal when the script will be read aloud. You might even wish to conduct a partial reading among your team members at the first publicity team meeting.

I think it's a great idea to get the producer or the theater company president to host a get-acquainted party for everyone involved in the show. At that party, the president introduces key people in the organization and should introduce all newcomers and guests. Everyone should feel welcomed and wanted. The director can talk about the plot of the show and introduce the cast. The publicist should stand up and make a blatant advertisement: Invite people to join the publicity team where people can learn about posters, playbills, news releases and lots of other fun things. Over on one side of the room should be a large board with tasks

Be sure all publicity jobs are assigned and that no one person has too much to do.

---

*If you're reading this when opening night is only a few weeks away, don't panic! Less lead time means you may have to accelerate your schedule a little and probably cut some promotional activities, that's all. See Chapter 20 on **The One-Person Publicity Shop**.

marked down (props, costumes, lights, ushering, publicity) and room for people to sign up.

Whether or not this meeting happens, the publicist should plan a separate meeting to initiate the publicity team.

Where do you hold that all-important first meeting? You can meet at the theater where the play will be presented, but you can set a friendly, relaxed tone right from the start if you instead meet at your home, the theater company president's home, or at the home of one of the publicity team members. Bring plenty of refreshments.

At your first publicity meeting, plan to accomplish three goals:

— Get everyone acquainted with each other.

— Inspire confidence: Let everyone know they can turn to you for any guidance they need. Convince everyone that being on the publicity team will be interesting and fun.

— Make sure everyone leaves with an assignment.

If any of the following activities did not take place at a previous get-acquainted gathering for everyone in the theater company, plan to do these at your first publicity meeting:

▲ Show slides of previous productions.

▲ Pass around scrapbooks and samples of promotion done for earlier shows.

▲ Provide each member of the team with an information kit, consisting of a list of all team members' names, titles, phone numbers, brief job descriptions, information about the production (dates, ticket prices, names of cast and crew), and a copy of a completed Master Battle Plan for publicity (described in the last chapter).

▲ Give each person who is new to the theater group a packet of information describing a brief history of the company, a list of past productions, sample news clips, and a list of the company officers with phone numbers.

▲ Use name tags if you have several newcomers.

▲ Give each team member some little gift that says, in effect, "thank you" and "you're a member of the team," such as a note pad, badge or T-shirt with the theater's logo. Ahead of time, ask management if you can budget a small amount of funds for this expense as part of the cost of membership development.

▲ Read parts of the script aloud if most people have not read it yet. If it's a musical and a recording of some of the music is available, play selections as you discuss plans.

▲ Invite the show's director and the theater company president to stop by to say a few words.

Okay. The cheese and crackers are moving fast, you're on your third bottle of wine or soda pop, everyone's made witty remarks about what the actors are really saying in those posed pictures during the slide show, all the VIP's have made their speeches about how wonderful the show is going to be — and now it's time to talk about the work ahead.

Discuss the principles of promotion as outlined in Chapter Two, emphasizing the many benefits of publicity and the multi-pronged approach to getting publicity: print and electronic media, posters and displays, fliers, playbills and other promotional devices.

Review the job descriptions and ask for volunteers. Offer to be a mentor to anyone who looks interested but apprehensive. After positions are filled, review the basic duties so that everyone knows what everyone is doing. You can be somewhat general at this first meeting and avoid getting bogged down in details if you promise members to give individual training in the coming days and weeks. Be sure your team understands how each job fits into the publicity plan, how everyone relates to each other, and when things need to get done.

Before reviewing the Master Battle Plan, go over anticipated expenses with your team. Explain what purchases team members may make without notifying you ahead of time and what expenses must first have your approval. Instruct your team to keep meticulous track of expenses and to notify you regularly so you can record expenses and monitor your budget.

For more information on budgeting, handling money, tracking expenses and getting reimbursed, see Chapter 7 on **Budgeting and Money Management**.

Introduce the Master Battle Plan

As the last chapter explained, the Master Battle Plan is a list of duties and dates for completion of all promotion for the production. It serves as a clear map to follow along the promotional road to the opening night of the play, and works as a faithful reminder of what needs to be done today, tomorrow and next week.

Using the instructions in the last chapter, fill out the dates for the Master Battle Plan *before* the first publicity meeting and at the meeting hand out copies to your team. Stress to them how to read the plan and how important it is to get tasks done on time. Clearly state what will happen when deadlines are missed.

Instruct your team members to make several copies of this plan: They should carry one copy in a purse or wallet, and post copies at home and at work along with the names and phone numbers of publicity team members.

Take several breaks during the meeting. Remember to keep things festive. It's a good point to remind members and potential members of your publicity team that the management and promotional skills that they will develop over the few weeks before opening night will come into use in just about any job they hold, in any walk of life.

The last three things to do before the meeting breaks up are:

▲ Ask everyone to announce what tasks each is scheduled to accomplish during the next week.

▲ Schedule a second meeting to review progress in one or two weeks.

▲ Thank everyone from the bottom of your theatrical heart for volunteering and for coming to the meeting.

Provide each member of your publicity team with an information kit, and some little gift that says, in effect, "thank you."

Be generous in giving credit to your volunteers when things go right — and accept all the blame when things go wrong.

Reward your troops

Throughout the coming weeks, please remember to frequently "speak in couplets" with your team members. Say "thank you," "well done," "nice job," "thank you," "good thinking," "great idea," "thank you," "need help?" "any questions?" "thank you," "call me" and "thank you."

Keep your weekly meetings brief if you can — an hour and a half should do it if you're organized and the chatter is restrained. Before each meeting, check with the play's director, production manager and the box office for news on progress of the production and any problems involving publicity. Report this news to your crew. If you meet at the theater and these people are available, invite them in at the end of the publicity meeting to hear a summary progress report.

Volunteers join an organization for love, not money. Pay them back with praise. Praise costs you nothing, yet it's precious to your team members.

When you meet with the play director, the theater company board of directors and other VIP's during the production, be generous in giving credit to your volunteers when things go right — and accept all the blame when things go wrong.

Find tangible ways to thank your volunteers, too. Feed them goodies. Invite your team members to join you to watch rehearsals. Give them each a thoughtful but inexpensive gift — coffee mugs, T-shirts, or badges with funny or flattering slogans.

After the production closes, schedule a celebration Sunday brunch to thank everyone for helping. Review how effective the publicity was and what improvements should be made for next time. As you pick up the check, give everyone a souvenir photo from the show, and then look sincerely and gratefully at your team members: This is the time to ask them to stay on to help you promote the next show.

Summary

- ☛ Don't try to do the whole job yourself. Aggressively recruit people to join your publicity team and divide up the tasks.
- ☛ As early as possible, throw a publicity planning party to acquaint your team members with each other and the Master Battle Plan.
- ☛ Schedule and hold brief weekly meetings to advance the plan and to keep your team active.
- ☛ Reward your team members with thanks and praise, food and gifts, encouragement and recognition. Make sure they're having fun.

Budgeting and Money Management

Chapter 7

- Lobbying for a budget
- Predicting costs
- Soliciting bids
- Keeping records
- Getting reimbursed

Oh, dear. Here is an unpleasant subject that we artistic people don't like to talk about. Haggling over costs and keeping track of money.

Volunteer organizations such as community theater groups go through cycles of being casual about tracking costs and then turning miserly and suspicious about every request for funds. Everyone in the theater company at one time or another gets a call from the general manager or (uh-oh!) the treasurer to tighten the money belt:

◆ To costume designers — "Can't we borrow some costumes from the museum? Tell the curator we'll be careful."

◆ To set designers — "If you can't talk the lumber yard into giving us the wood, maybe we can find some stuff at the town dump. It's all going to get painted anyway."

◆ To the people running the snack bar — "Can't we buy a cheaper brand of coffee? No one will know the difference."

◆ To the lighting crew — "Geez, I thought you replaced some bulbs last year — two years ago at the most. We gotta buy more?"

◆ To the publicist — "Instead of printing big posters, let's save money and just, you know, run off something on a mimeograph machine. As long as the information goes out, it doesn't have to be fancy or anything, does it?"

My response to that last question might be, "We aren't counting on bringing in a big audience or anything, are we?" or alternatively, "People shouldn't get the idea that this show is worth seeing or anything, should they?" and then again, "You don't suppose the quality of our publicity has any effect on ticket sales, do you?"

Before you can spend money on publicity, you must be ready to defend your budget. When finances are tight, the first thing many businesses do is cut the promotion budget. Some people never realize that this action only digs a deeper grave.

Alternatives to budget cuts

Nearly every chapter in this book suggests ways to trim costs, and as a publicist you should be on the lookout all the time for ways to *maintain quality* without paying top dollar. However, you must realize — and make others in your theater group understand — that sacrificing quality is a dangerous measure that the public is quick to detect, whether the deficiency is in construction, design, house management or publicity.

If you're not allowed a budget sufficient to do your job right, you're being set up to fail. Refuse to be set up. Work with others in your group to develop ways to raise funds. Survey audiences as well as people at the bus stop to find out why people aren't breaking down the doors to your theater to see one of your shows. (see Chapter 19 on **Building Group Recognition**) Check with other theater groups of comparable size to see if your prices are in line. Talk with the Chamber of Commerce. Seek advice from your state's commission on the arts. Read this book.

— Oh, pardon me. You *are* reading this book!

Master Publicity Budget

Publicity budget for _____
NAME OF SHOW

News releases—postage and printing

# ___ general release(s) x # ___ mailings x $ ___ postage per piece	= $ ___
# ___ feature story(s) x $ ___	= $ ___
# ___ hometown releases x $ ___	= $ ___
# ___ reminder releases x # ___ mailings x $ ___	= $ ___
# ___ letters inviting reviewers x $ ___	= $ ___
# ___ news kits @ $ ___ x $ ___ postage per piece	= $ ___
photocopying charge: # ___ copies @ $ ___	= $ ___
# ___ mailing lables (___ -count per pack) @ $ ___	= $ ___

.... Total = $ ___ $ ___ Estimate $ ___ Final

Photography and displays

# ___ rolls of B&W film for press pictures	= $ ___
$ ___ cost of developing film x # ___ B&W rolls	= $ ___
# ___ regular-sized reprints @ $ ___ each	= $ ___
# ___ enlargements @ $ ___ each	= $ ___
# ___ rolls of color slide film @ $ ___ each	= $ ___
$ ___ cost of developing slides x # ___ rolls	= $ ___
$ ___ cost of bulletin board materials	= $ ___

.... Total = $ ___ $ ___ Estimate $ ___ Final

Road signs and banners

| white opaque base paint, colors | = $ ___ |
| cost of wood $ ___ ; cost of cloth $ ___ | = $ ___ |

.... Total = $ ___ $ ___ Estimate $ ___ Final

Master Publicity Budget (from Appendix B) — a shopping list to predict expenses.

Predicting costs

It's a lot easier to know if the publicity budget you're given is adequate if you know how to predict what your expenses will be. In fact, it's likely that before rehearsal begins, the general manager may ask you how much you expect to spend.

What every theater publicist needs is a budget work sheet that lists most of the standard kinds of promotional items along with a method of calculating their costs. Fill in the blanks, total the costs, and — boom! — you have a budget.

The *Master Publicity Budget* in **Appendix B** of this book is a model I designed for my own budgeting. This worksheet includes most of the expense categories you'll encounter when planning publicity. After you've used it for one or two shows, you'll quickly discover how to refine the subjects to reflect your situation.

In other words, this blank budget sheet is a shopping list. You may not need all the items on the list, but by starting off with this list, you're less apt to forget some essential items that could cause you to budget too low for publicity. It's always better to budget a little *high* to cover expenses you can't foresee.

There are no prices on the work sheet because prices vary from rural to urban regions. You'll need to visit a few places to accurately estimate costs. For example, you can visit camera stores or talk to your volunteer photographer to find out what publicity photography materials and services will cost. You may need to stop at a hardware store to price paint for signs. An experienced printer can show you samples of posters and give you a price range to choose from.

Postage and printing (including copying) are likely to be your biggest expenses if your theater group is in a densely populated area with many news media to contact. Photography will be very expensive if you use a lot of pictures and can't work a cost-cutting deal with a photographer.

My budget work sheet includes a listing for long-distance telephone charges because I've used my phone a lot to direct teams of publicity volunteers living as far as 30 miles apart. On these occasions, each member worked on one aspect of publicity, and during the week I would communicate with them by phone. On weekends we would all meet at the theater to review progress, and then head out with our individual plans until meeting the next weekend. I kept a clipboard by my telephone and logged each theater-related call, then submitted the itemized telephone bills to my theater group's board of directors. I was entitled to be reimbursed for this expense as much as construction crew members were for their lumber expenses.

In a non-profit organization like community theater, you are expected to volunteer your time, energy and talent; you shouldn't have to volunteer your wallet, too.

Well, sometimes you volunteer that, too. If you hold a victory dinner for your publicity team after the show closes, you might feel generous and pick up the tab. We publicity people have soft hearts.

Learning curve

After each show is done and all bills are paid, it will be educational to compare your estimated budget with the real-life total. It is a great satisfaction to find after a few tries that your estimate can come within just five or ten percent of the actual costs. Budget managers in Hollywood, where blockbuster movies routinely run 30, 40, 50 percent and more over budget, dream of being able to make accurate cost predictions.

Remember the Hollywood example if you ever find yourself defending a budget that comes in way over the final costs: Clear your throat, look your accuser in the eye and say in a bored voice, "Oh, come now, Jasper; surely you're familiar with the Hollywood method? The budget assumes that we'll make up our expenses on the next production."

But seriously, even if you come in over budget, an analysis of cost and revenue may reveal that the added expenses were worth it to produce outstanding publicity, added public goodwill or increased ticket sales.

Susan Conaty-Buck, an arts management consultant in Harrisburg, Va., says "You can aid your learning curve by keeping

```
       PROPOSED BUDGET FOR "CRIMES OF THE HEART"

       Submitted by Norma Wood
       to general manager Rich Zwicker Jan. 5, 19__


       POSTAGE ............................... $   75.00

       PHOTOGRAPHY ...........................    110.00

       PRINTING .............................    1010.00

            News releases  $ 25.00
            Posters          100.00
            Fliers            35.00
            Playbill         500.00
            Bank stuffers    100.00
            Cafe placemats   250.00

       NEWSPAPER ADVERTISING .................    200.00

       OTHER .................................     45.00

            Sign paint        15.00
            Phone calls       30.00
       _____

       Total promotional expenses ......... $1,440.00

       Anticipated playbill revenue .......     30.00

       PROJECTED NET PROMOTIONAL EXPENSE

       (expenses less revenue) ............ $  610.00
```

In a proposed budget, don't forget to include anticipated revenue from playbill advertising.

```
PRINTING BID REQUEST              Feb. 10, 19__

From:  Muriel Hiernaux
       Inner Circle Playhouse
       1234 Merritt Circle

       Phone: 404-12XX
─────────────────────────────────────────────────
JOB NAME:    Crimes of the Heart Playbill
QUANTITY:    1000 playbills consisting of:
             9 pages printed both sides
             plus 1 cover printed both sides
SIZE:        8-1/2" x 14" before folding
PAPER:       COVER: 60# offset canary, pebble
             finish
BODY:        50# offset white, smooth finish
INK:         COVER: black, both sides, no bleed
             BODY:  black, both sides, no bleed
PRE-PRESS:   7 photographs, 4 x 5" (head shots
             of actors) to be reduced to
             1-1/4" x 1-3/4" and converted to
             halftones. May be gang shot, as
             reduction size will be identical.
             Printer to position halftones where
             indicated on the mechical.
FINISHING:   saddle stitch (2 staples)
             1 center fold
DELIVERY:    mechanicals (camera-ready except
             for halftones) will be delivered to
             printer April 15; need printed
             playbills ready for theater
             representative to pick up April 29.
TERMS:       net 30 days
```

To compare estimates on printing projects, prepare a sheet of specifications and ask several printers for prices.

detailed notes on how end-figures were determined. It helps a lot for future budgeting to know that the 'cost of wood' was determined by 10 feet of 3/4" ply @ $2.00 per foot = $20.00."

Notes are especially important for advertising expenses so that specific costs can be checked when bills come in weeks later.

Soliciting bids

For printing jobs, you'll probably want to compare estimated costs with several printers to determine which will give you the best price. (Chapter 11 on **Working with Printers** discusses other factors, such as quality and reliability in printers.) To fairly compare estimates, you need to prepare a bid sheet.

A bid sheet lists the specifications for the job in as much detail as possible. Show the same list of specifications to each person you're considering doing business with, and ask each one to write out an estimated cost without seeing what price the others have bid. When you compare the bids, they may be close. If they're not, you'll need to find out whether all bidders understand the job or if a lower bid reflects plans to take some financial shortcuts that could sacrifice quality.

Avoid doing business with someone who routinely under-bids the competition but manages to come up with unanticipated expenses that result in costs which match the original bids by the competition. This is an unreliable merchant.

Be wary of someone who can't or won't make an estimate even after you've presented a bid sheet with the specifications of the job clearly detailed. If you don't know what someone's services are going to cost, you probably can't afford them.

Presenting your budget

If you present the board of directors or the production manager a detailed budget before the first rehearsal, you'll earn a reputation as someone who's organized and knows how to plan. This inspires confidence in your expertise and can eliminate a lot of haggling over your budget request.

"Well," the production manager is likely to say, "if the publicist already has a budget figured out, she must know what she's talking about!"

Later, when you submit bills for reimbursement, the production manager and treasurer are likely to handle the paperwork and cut you a check much more quickly than if they never saw your budget and didn't know these expenses were coming.

Keeping records

Most likely, you'll find yourself paying for small publicity expenses out of your own pocket and then submitting bills to the production manager for reimbursement.

If this is the case, develop the habit early of keeping your receipts together in an envelope, in a file folder with your budget work sheet and bid sheets. Mark your receipts clearly: Circle the date on each, underline the total cost, and write a note on the receipt explaining the purpose of the expense. On a separate sheet, called an expense log, copy down this information so that you can keep a running tally.

Check with management to receive a copy of a formal document stating that your organization is non-profit. When you or your team members make purchases for your theater group, you can avoid paying any sales tax.

If you are supervising a team of publicity volunteers, they should follow the same procedure and hand you copies of their tally sheets along with their receipts at each weekly meeting. Reimburse them as quickly as possible. Date and mark their tally sheets "paid."

Do the same for your printer and other merchants; don't make them wait too long to be reimbursed. *Prompt payment ensures good business relations in the future.*

Expenses should be categorized according to accounts or departments agreed on with the production manager and the company treasurer. Typical accounts include Advertising, Photography, Postage, Printing, Supplies, and Telephone.

Getting reimbursed

If publicity team members can afford to spend money out of their own pockets and wait for reimbursement until after opening night, great! Otherwise, be prepared as publicity manager to advance funds or reimburse your team members as expenses come up.

Ideally, members should submit receipts and itemized explanations of expenses at least once a month. Keep copies of these and submit originals to the general manager, who in turn submits receipts and notes to the treasurer. The treasurer should reimburse you with one check, accompanied by a copy of the itemized expense report you originally submitted.

About every two weeks, submit your receipts and tally sheets along with a summary page of expenses listed by accounts. Keep a copy of the tally sheets and summary page until the accounting books are closed on the season in case anyone questions the expenses. Besides, you'll use these sheets to compare final expenses with your proposed budget and to draft future budgets.

The first thing many businesses do is cut the promotion budget; this action only digs a deeper grave.

```
EXPENSE REIMBURSEMENT REQUEST

Production: "CRIMES OF THE HEART"

Submitted by: Domenico Seren Gay
April 2, 19__
_____

Attached are receipts for the following expenses
which I have incurred while promoting this show:

PRODUCTION EXPENSES:

Postage                                $  50.00
2 coils of stamps @ $25.00 each

Photography                               15.71
2 rolls B&W film. Total $7.59
developing rolls: $8.12

Printing                                  62.70
300 audition announcements: $15.45
900 Bank stuffers: $47.25

Other                                     31.11

    signs  1 gal white ext latex $11.32
           1 qt red latex $4.28
           1 qt gloss black latex: $3.89

    phone  long distance bills itemized
           for Jan. and Feb.: $11.62

CAPITAL EXPENSES (not show-related)       99.83

Archives: 25-sheet packe of plastic sleeves
for color slides: $11.81

General promotion: two 3x4' bulletin boards for
displays in bank lobby and library: $88.02
_____
TOTAL REIMBURSEMENT REQUEST            $259.35
```

Don't wait too long to submit your bills for reimbursement. Brief, periodic submissions are easier for the general manager and treasurer to handle. On the other hand, wait until you've accumulated a few bills before filing for reimbursement. In most volunteer groups, each check a treasurer writes costs the organization a bank fee.

Getting reimbursed: submit receipts with a formal itemized request. List expenses by account categories determined by your treasurer.

Summary

☛ To maintain a sufficient budget for publicity, you need to accurately predict expenses. Make a shopping list of items you expect to spend money on, consult experts to determine estimates, and make a budget.

☛ Present your budget as early in the production run as you can — even before the first rehearsal if possible. You'll quickly earn a reputation for being organized and knowledgeable.

☛ Keep good records of expenses and submit bills regularly. Don't keep merchants or volunteers waiting to be reimbursed.

☛ Compare preliminary budgets with final expenses. Aim in future shows to keep expenses within five or ten percent of the original budget.

The News Release

Chapter 8

- Misconceptions
- Proper form
- Newspapers, radio & TV
- News releases vs. advertising
- Variations and timing

The news release is the cornerstone of your publicity campaign. A release is an easy way to get information out to the news media, and it is by far the method preferred by all reporters and news editors.

I used to use the old name, "press release," until a radio reporter testily reminded me that not all people employed in the news media disseminate the news with a printing press; so now I say "news release."

Misconceptions

Most people think they know how to write a news release. Most people are wrong, which is why most news releases don't do their job. Show me someone who laments "Newspapers never use my news releases" and I'll lay odds 10-1 that the problem is the way the release is structured or written.

Let's begin by dispelling two major misconceptions about news releases right away. These misconceptions are so widespread that they are held even by some people with years of public relations experience:

✗ False notion number one

Newspapers are supposed to print your news release word-for-word.

I don't know where some people get this idea, unless they believe that they are perfect writers. Big city newspapers with seasoned editors will never allow a news release's words to appear in the newspaper without some fact-checking and rewriting that makes the story fit the newspaper's style and the editor's judgement of what is news.

Small, home town newspapers aren't so persnickety, so it is very likely that a well-written news release will run as is. Still, you should emulate the writing style of big city newspapers. Notice how they change your words. Work to imitate the big-city style so well that your releases eventually undergo very little rewrite when the news appears in print.

✗ False notion number two

The news media are obliged to report everything going on, or at least everything submitted to them.

Nope, nope, nope. Reporters report what they believe the majority of the public wants to learn about. The key word in that last sentence is *majority*.

This leads us to a third false notion (I know I said I would tell you about only two false notions, but I just changed my mind). This third notion is related to writing news releases but really exists as *the fundamental challenge of all theater publicity:*

✗ False notion number three

The majority of the public is interested in the arts and especially theater news.

Sigh. I wish this were so, but the ugly truth (we can take it — the theater was created to deal with ugly truths!) is that most people don't go out of their way to see an art exhibit or a theatrical performance. For fires and auto accidents, people will leave their homes willingly. For a play, people have to be convinced. To convince editors that you have something happening which is as interesting as a fire or a car crash, you need to write a good news release.

Wait! I just thought of another one:

✘ False Notion Number Four

The same news release can be sent to all newspapers, TV and radio stations.

Not so. See the end of this chapter for special news release needs of radio and TV. Their news needs are vastly different from newspapers, and if you want the attention of the electronic news media, you need to learn the accepted format. That's what this chapter is all about: Writing for the news media.

First, some basics:

Ten Golden Rules For Writing News Releases

All types of news releases follow these common rules (see the end of this chapter about special needs for radio):

1 *Type your releases.* All news releases should be typed, double-spaced, upper- and lower-case (that is, not all capital letters) on *only one side of a page.* Valuable information will be lost when an editor misses printing on the back side of a news release. Don't take that chance! Also, for all releases but the long feature story, keep your news releases to two pages. Indent each paragraph except the first one. Don't skip an extra line between paragraphs; you're already typing double-spaced.

2 *Leave room for the editor's notes.* Leave a one-inch margin at the top, bottom and sides of each page of your release. Big daily newspapers often edit your release to conform to their own style, and editors use the margins to make notes here and between the lines. Also, leave space on the first page for an editor to indicate notes to the typesetter. Begin the body of your release about *halfway down the first page.*

3 *Identify the organization sending the release.* The best way is to use stationery imprinted with your group's logo. Otherwise, type the name of your organization in capital letters across the top of the first page. White paper is best because it's easy to read, but stationery with a light pastel tint can add distinction to your releases. Be consistent with your choice, however. Stick to one style paper and logo so editors will learn to quickly recognize news releases from your group.

4 *Identify the news media contact.* Editors need to know whom to phone when they want to get more information on the show or to clarify information in the release. Make it easy for editors to find you: Type your name and phone number — day and evening numbers if they're different, and include your area code if you are near a border — at the top of the first page, either above or just below the name of your group. To avoid having your name and phone number accidentally published, which would result in three zillion calls from the public seeking tickets, identify yourself as MEDIA CONTACT and add the note: Do not publish these numbers. (See Rule 9 regarding tickets.)

5 *Date the news release.* Some times a release is held for a few days in the newspaper office or radio studio when the news business is extra busy. When this happens, imagine the confusion when a busy editor days later has to look up, down, and every which place in your release to decipher how new or old the release is. When in doubt, the editor will assume the release is old and will pitch it. Save everyone a lot of trouble and indicate at the top of the first page FOR IMMEDIATE RELEASE. Type the date you are mailing the release, or write FOR RELEASE ON OR AFTER... with the date if your news is specially timed.

6 *Write a headline.* Editors face an unbelievable mountain of mail every day. They need to know instantly what your release is about when looking at the first page. Your headline should summarize without being cute. Keep it plain and direct, and let the editor think she or he is clever by improving it!

7 *Write "top to bottom."* Put the critical news first, then add details of diminishing importance. Your first two sentences should answer the classic, eternal news questions: WHO? WHAT? WHERE? and WHEN? You may also wish to answer a fifth question, WHY? here or later in the release.

WHO? Who is putting on the show? Although your group is identified at the top of the page, identify the group again in the body of the news release. Who is directing it? Who is acting in it?

WHAT? What is going on? What is the name of the play? What is the occasion — auditions? Tickets going on sale? Change of performance dates?

WHEN? When does the event happen?

WHERE? Where does the event take place?

WHY? Is the event a fund-raiser? Is it the first or last show of the season? Does the event mark an anniversary? Was it selected to coincide with the season (a murder-mystery for Halloween)?

If you can't fit even an indication of all this information into the first two lines (and you probably can't) without making your sentences three miles long, you must prioritize. Give the information in a logical order that the reader can follow. Give the basic news first, then fill in details in later paragraphs.

8 *Keep sentences and paragraphs short.* Sentences shouldn't have multiple clauses or go on for more than 25 words. Average about 15 words per sentence. Paragraphs in news writing are different than in books. Limit paragraphs to no more than two or three sentences. Look at how your newspaper does this.

9 *Put the ticket phone number last.* This seems to violate Rule 7, but editors skimming a news release about a public event always jump to the last line of the release to see who the public should contact for more information about the event. And don't bury this all-important phone number in the middle of the last sentence. Write, "Tickets for 'Our Town' may be reserved by calling 736-XXXX."

10 *Indicate the end of the release.* Releases of more than one page may become separated as they are passed from the desks of the city editor to the arts editor and then to the harried typesetter in the news room. Type "###" or "-30-" or "END" on a separate line following the last line of your news release.

Bonus rule:

11 *Number the pages.* On the first page of a multiple-page release, type "MORE" or "Page 1 of 2" (of a two-page release), and at the top of the second page type the date, your group's name, and "Page 2 of 2" on one line.

Editors need to know instantly what your release is about when looking at the first page.

The radio news release

Radio news is brief — very brief. The news hole on most stations is three minutes on the hour, including the sponsor's commercial, weather forecast, traffic report, and news of local politics and crime. In the face of all this essential news ahead of your story and with the news reporter's limited time to report it all, you're not likely to get your show mentioned by mailing the kind of news release you'd send to a newspaper.

But there is a way to get on the air — and I'm not talking about paid commercials.

You're more likely to get your news on the air if you submit it not as a news release but as a PSA — a public service announcement. PSA's are read between the music selections all day long. DJ's fill these gaps with a little chatter, some commercials, and a few bits of news about local events which they announce as a public service.

PSA's follow almost all the same rules as news releases: You must identify the organization, the contact and the date of the release at the top of the notice; you must indicate the end of the story; and you should type the release double-spaced on one side of a page.

Many DJ's prefer to receive PSA's on postcards. They're easy to handle, don't take much room at the radio console, and won't rattle like paper.

The one modification you need to know is that radio PSA's are typed in ALL CAPITAL LETTERS. This makes it easier for announcers to read on the air.

Keep your sentences extra short so that announcers won't run out of breath in mid-sentence. You can test the pronounceability of your PSA by reading it aloud. If you find that you have created some accidental tongue-twisters — several s's and f's close

Many DJ's prefer to receive PSA's on postcards.

```
Community News:    Public Service Announcement
Press Contact:     David Pesci 727-2727
Please Announce:   Jan. 26 - Feb. 5, 19xx
_____

—THE BASEMENT PLAYERS WILL PRESENT THE ROMANTIC STORY OF "CYRANO
DE BERGERAC" ON STAGE FEBRUARY 3, 4 AND 5. PERFORMANCES WILL BE
AT 8 P.M. EACH NIGHT AT BERNIE'S BAR AND GRILL, 12 MAIN STREET,
SPRINGDALE. "CYRANO" FEATURES A CAST OF 30 IN THE STORY OF A FAMOUS
SWASH-BUCKLING POET AND HERO WHO HIDES HIS LOVE FOR A BEAUTIFUL
WOMAN. TICKETS CAN BE RESERVED BY CALLING 246-8000.

_____

Announcer: "Cyrano de Bergerac" is pronounced like this:
"SIH-ruh-no dih ber-sher-RACK" (A French accent helps!)
```

ICMT

Inner City Music Theater
12 Garage Alley Lane
Chicago IL 60605

April 18, 19xx

Liz King
News Director
WDRA TV-37
1 Drake Plaza
Chicago IL 60614

Dear Ms. King,

Despite what local florists may say, DON'T FEED THE PLANTS!

At least, not until the public sees the consequences firsthand in Inner City Music Theater's hororticultural production of the musical "Little Shop of Horrors."

The musical comedy features a four-foot-tall, four-foot-wide plant that looks at first like your average, garden-variety bean pod that has overdosed on steroids.

Then it opens its mouth, which has teeth and a tongue, and the actors become, uh, plant food—!

The plant, which grows on stage from a tiny, innocent-looking table sprout into a voluminous vegetable during the wacky musical show, is really a series of clever puppets hand-made by a team of theater crew members.

A reporter from WDRA TV is welcome to meet the designers and their creation, the singers and dancers, and the heroes and victims, during rehearsals this weekend or Monday, Tuesday or Wednesday next week. Rehearsals are 7-10 p.m. in our Garage Alley Lane Theater. "Little Shop of Horrors" opens next Friday, April 26 with a live band and a lively company of performers. The accompanying fact sheet has details.

I should warn you that the monster plant might try to swallow one of your reporters if she or he gets too close, but perhaps you'll think it worth the risk to send someone from your station to record a few preview moments of the show for your viewers.

I hope you'll say "yes" when I phone in a day or two to ask if a camera crew might be available to come to a rehearsal.

Until then, please — DON'T FEED THE PLANTS!

Best wishes,

John Webster

John Webster
Publicist 424-9810

A letter to a TV program's producer has a more personal touch than a news release. See also Chapter 10 on Media Relations.

together, or too many p's and b's that could trip up an announcer — rewrite the trouble spots.

Limit your PSA to one page and time it to no more than 30 seconds. PSA's contain only the absolutely critical information, and like news releases, they are written in a matter-of-fact journalism style, not as a breathless advertisement. Do not write "For the time of your life, come see the Basement Players' production of..." Similarly, no radio announcer will read "Surprise, surprise! Don't miss..." If your PSA sounds like a hyped-up commercial, the radio station will ask you to buy advertising time. You want the station to announce your event as a service to the public, so keep the tone under control, no matter how excited you are about the show.

Write your PSA like this: "The Basement Players will present the romantic story of 'Cyrano de Bergerac' on stage February 3, 4 and 5. Performances will be at 8 p.m. each night at Bernie's Bar and Grill, 12 Main St., in Springdale. 'Cyrano' features a cast of 30 and tells the story of the famous swash-buckling poet and hero who hides his love for a beautiful woman. Tickets can be reserved by calling 246-8000."

There's plenty of details in that brief announcement to entice people to attend. Sentences are short. The ticket information was not written as a directive but as a piece of information: Not "Call today!" but "Tickets can be reserved..."

Type a note (in upper and lower case, single spaced, like a regular letter) at the top of the PSA and address it to the radio station's news director. Indicate in the note that you would appreciate it if your news could be announced throughout the week preceding opening night.

If the radio station has a habit of featuring guests for live interviews, include a separate note in an envelope with your PSA that indicates your willingness to supply a guest. On that note include your name, phone number, whom you recommend (the director, an actor), and the name and production dates of the show. By supplying a separate note, the station's news director can pass on the PSA to the morning news DJ and then hand your note to the host of the talk show.

If you have access to professional audio equipment, you can produce your own PSA complete with music background. Most radio stations will consider using a professional-sounding, brief PSA.

See Chapter 10 on **Media Relations** for more information on working with radio and TV people.

News releases for television

Most regions now offer a TV channel with a 24-hour on-screen community calendar listing events in town. If your community has cable TV, you probably have a whole channel devoted to area events listings.

Most TV stations automate the process of putting news onto calendars by requiring all announcements to be submitted on a special form available to the public by calling or writing to the station. Make copies of the blank forms and file the original. Note the deadline for submitting the community calendar news.

Begin the message with the name of the show, unless your group is better known than the play. Write in sparse telegram form with a few, choice adjectives and articles, but avoiding wasteful uses of "a" "an" or "the." End the message with "Tickets: call 987-9000."

Beyond the community calendar, you may want your TV station to feature your theater group's production. If the station has a special talk show or non-news program, send a letter suggesting what you have in mind to the program's producer and follow up with a phone call. This has a more personal touch than a news release.

When communicating with the newsroom, however, a news release is appropriate. The evening news anchor isn't likely to read your release on the air (unless your local news show makes a practice of announcing events), but a properly written release could prompt the station to send a camera crew to your theater to videotape a few moments of rehearsal and a brief interview with the director and an actor. It's a long shot, but the right show and the right news release could attract the interest of someone in the news room.

When dealing with TV, understand that the news release is only the initial step to get the news room's attention. You will need to phone the station a few days after mailing the release to close the sale. Again see Chapter 10 on **Media Relations** for a longer discussion on working with TV news.

Your news release for TV should emphasize *visual elements*: movement, color, costumes, flashy special effects, a huge cast dancing and singing its heart out, a well-known personality in the cast (a town selectman), or dramatic action, including duels and death scenes. Mention these in your lead sentence to catch the reader's eye.

The reader, by the way, is either the news director (in a small TV station) or the assignment editor (the news director's assistant at big TV stations) who assigns the stories to be covered each day by the various camera crews. Send that person a news release one week before you would like a camera crew to visit your theater.

Add a single-spaced message positioned about two lines above your lead sentence. The message, addressed to the news director, should indicate where and when rehearsals are held. Invite the news director to send a camera crew and include the phone number at the theater along with your daytime phone number. Even if your daytime phone number is at the top of the news release, repeat it in the note to the news director so both numbers are easily found and are not confused. The news director or assignment editor will call you before sending a crew. You should include the phone number of the theater in case the crew needs to contact you if it gets lost or is delayed on the way.

Concentrate on newspapers

The information in the rest of this chapter is most appropriate to working with newspapers. This is where the publicist has the most opportunity to be seen and heard, and to be creative with the written word. Newspapers as the news medium of choice for the arts are still so dominant that it's not unusual for a theater company publicist in a large metropolitan area to send out a dozen or more different news releases over two months to a mailing list of 20 or more daily and weekly newspapers.

By contrast, radio and TV don't want to see more than one or two releases about any single production. With this in mind, you can begin to direct your publicity efforts where they'll do the most good and where theater news is most welcome. Let's look at how to break into the pages of your local newspapers:

News comes in many forms

Even if your group operates in a small area with only one or two newspapers, you'll find yourself sending several kinds of news releases:

▲ announcing auditions

▲ announcing the director & cast

▲ announcing show dates

▲ one or more stories featuring the director, cast or crew

While you may choose not to send out every one of these different types of releases, you should be familiar with the purpose of each one and understand how, when mailed approximately a week apart, they can build ever-increasing interest in a show before opening night.

When dealing with TV, the news release is only the initial step to get the news room's attention.

To match the security of a paid advertisement, a publicist must write a good news story and strategically time when the media should receive it.

Here's the theory behind sending so many kinds of releases, each giving just a little more information about your show than the previous news release:

The smaller the newspaper and the fewer the number of other theater groups, the greater the likelihood that a newspaper will publish several news stories about your play.

You want to keep reminding the public about your play so that, as opening night approaches and tickets are still on sale, people who haven't yet bought tickets will be reminded frequently to purchase.

In a moment, we'll look at what kinds of newspapers are most likely to accept several news releases. But first, let's consider a classic question in promotion:

News releases vs. advertising

The easy, expensive way to remind the public about your show is to buy a lot of advertising. Look for Chapter 16 in this book that will help you buy **Advertising**.

By far, the more economical, creative promotion method calls for composing interesting news releases that are strategically timed to arrive in the newsroom just as the news value is at its peak — not too early, not too late.

The fact that a good news story is cheaper than an ad, and takes up much more space in the newspaper than a theater company can afford to buy, is only two of many reasons to concentrate your efforts on writing and sending news releases.

News releases have a greater effect on the public than advertisements. Published news stories educate the public with many more facts about your show than any ad could hope to do.

Moreover, a news story based on your news release gives the appearance that the newspaper endorses your show (the editor thought enough of your show to publish news about it, right?). No advertisement can match a newspaper's endorsement.

So, mailing news releases has every advantage over taking out a paid advertisement, save one: *When you buy an ad, you positively know that your announcement will appear when and where you want it.*

To match the security of a paid advertisement, a publicist must write a good news story and strategically time when the media should receive it.

Types and timing of news releases

Different kinds of news releases need to be mailed at different times. The timing is based mostly on when the information is of peak interest to the public. Here is a guide to the timing and content of various news releases. As you read the descriptions of the different kinds of releases, refer to the examples that follow this section.

1. Audition notice

Four weeks before auditions, mail an announcement. Name the theater group, the proposed play, and where and when auditions are to take place. Name the director if she or he has been chosen. Describe how many males and females are needed, what age range they should be able to portray, and whether actors should come prepared to sing, dance, or present a comic or serious monologue. Indicate who to contact if anyone is unable to attend auditions but would like to try out at another time.

Give a brief description of the play (playwright, plot synopsis, other interesting elements); two short sentences will suffice. Indicate where copies of scripts are available for preview. (Lend your local library 6-10 copies and arrange for scripts to be on file for the public to look at or borrow briefly.)

Indicate the general time when the show is planned to open, but avoid giving specific production dates. Say "The Guilford Players plan to present *The Iceman Cometh* during the last two weekends in November." If you state specific production dates, I guarantee you that at least half the public and news media will confuse these dates with the audition dates! If an editor calls you and asks for the specific production dates, explain your concern about confusing the public. Most editors will agree with your strategy.

2. Announce show dates

Seven weeks before opening night, announce the dates of the production. This allows newspaper and TV community calendars ample time to include these dates in previews of monthly events.

Announce where the show will take place, the name of the director, and when and where tickets go on sale. Give only a one-sentence description of the plot of the play, perhaps emphasizing one aspect of the play that should interest the public (such as a suspenseful plot, or elaborate costumes).

Tease the public on one point: Don't reveal for another week or two who has been cast. Dole out the information a little at a time.

3. Announce cast

Six weeks before opening night, announce the major members of the cast. In a large musical, announce the top six or seven actors only because no newspaper or radio station will announce 15 or more cast members in a preview story.

Announce what towns these cast members come from and, if the cast is small or the play is well known, what characters they will play. Give a two-sentence description of the play, emphasizing the selling elements ("the play features Noel Coward's famous wit applied to a hilarious case of mistaken identity"). Mention the production dates and when tickets go on sale.

4. Announce when tickets go on sale.

Whether or not your group has a season subscription program, tickets for individual shows usually go on sale about three weeks before opening night. If this is the case, time the release to appear in newspapers a few days to a week before this date, or about 5 weeks before opening night.

This is the time to go into detail about discounts for groups of ten or more, senior citizens, and student and children's prices. Also note at this time if the theater company advises parental discretion due to violence or adult themes in the show.

Reveal any special seating arrangements (cabaret style, theater style, theater in the round). Repeat the synopsis of the play's plot from the last release along with the selling features, but now add a sentence about the play's history: "The play first appeared on Broadway in 19xx,"

Types and timing of news releases

1. **Auditions**
   Four weeks before event

2. **Show dates**
   Seven weeks before opening

3. **Announce cast**
   Six weeks before opening

4. **Tickets on sale**
   Five weeks before opening

5. **Feature stories**
   Four weeks before opening

6. **Home town news**
   Three weeks before opening

7. **Reminder photo**
   Two weeks before opening

8. **Added reminder**
   Right after opening weekend

"...won a Tony Award," "It was made into a movie starring famous actress X."

5. Feature stories

Mail these four weeks before opening night. If you have a home town weekly shopping news that prints everything, try sending a feature story. This is longer than a regular news release and emphasizes an interesting aspect of the show.

Interview the director and print quotes about his or her unique vision of the play. Detail the production aspects that make the show especially appealing. Mention the 30 costume changes in Act I, how the show features a record cast of 40, describe how a cosmetician has been brought in to help design unusual makeup, explain that the play is an original script written by local playwrights, reveal that the lead actress has a background amazingly similar/opposite to her character, proclaim that the play will feature special magic effects to make Dracula appear and vanish and make bats fly — *details!*

The point of a feature story is to give the public more details than a straight news release has room for. You may wish to submit different features for different newspapers.

There are two other purposes for mailing feature stories: to arouse the interest of news editors who may wish to use your feature story as a jumping-off point for assigning a reporter to write an original feature; and to educate the newspaper reviewer before she or he arrives on opening night (more on this later).

6. *Home town releases*

Mail these three weeks before opening night. Here is one of the most effective and most underused kinds of news releases! If your cast members come from a variety of towns (which is very likely in urban areas with many suburbs), take advantage of the fact that just about every one of these towns probably has its own small newspaper.

Use a "shell" news release that has perhaps six paragraphs of basic information on the show, and then personalize the release by changing the lead sentence to feature the actor or actors in your show who reside in one town (Jacqueline Dillard and Amos Green, both of Suffolk Meadows, will appear in the Daylight Theater production of..."). About a third of the way into the release, plug in one paragraph each about the actors — where they went to school, where they work, what community activities they're known for, and recent acting credits. A computer or memory typewriter makes the task of retyping shell paragraphs easy.

Home town papers know their readers love to read about local citizens. That's why they will use your specially tailored releases. For each town you send a home town release to, simply change the lead sentence and the personalized paragraph, include a black and white portrait (known as a "head shot"), and you're bound to get free publicity.

When writing news releases for different home town newspapers, group all the performers from one newspaper's readership into a single release. If you have three actors from towns covered by Newspaper A, and four actors from various towns covered by Newspaper B, you'll write two news releases — each tailored to the readership of a specific newspaper. Be

---

When writing news releases for different home town newspapers, group all the performers from one newspaper's readership into a single release.

sure to talk this over with the director when preparing to set up poses for photographs.

This may appear to be a lot of work for only a little coverage, but don't underestimate home town news stories. Friends of actors mentioned in a home town newspaper will come out in great numbers to see the show and cheer on the performers.

Home town releases are likely to be published in all but the largest metropolitan newspapers, where too many arts groups competing for too little space make such stories impractical to use.

There's another side to this, however. Large cities tend to be home to large companies. If any of your actors work for a large company, ask if the company has its own weekly or monthly corporate newsletter. If so, the editor is likely to welcome a news release (or even a feature story) about one of its employees. As with other news releases, remember to include a photograph.

7. Reminder photo

Two weeks before opening night, you may find that you need some last-minute publicity to push ticket sales, but you've run out of new things to say about your show. The major newspaper in your area may have already run a feature story and a home town story and isn't likely to publish a third story about the play. What to do?

Don't send a news release. Send a dramatic black and white photograph with a one- or two-sentence description, called a *caption*. All newspaper photos have captions, and you can learn how to write one and prepare you photo for mailing by looking at the end of Chapter 9 on **Dramatic Photos**. Briefly, the caption should name who is in the picture, what they're doing, what play they're performing, what group is producing the show, where and when the show appears (list dates and curtain times), and how to get tickets.

If your show runs several weekends, send a second photo and caption a week later. Send different newspapers different photos because no newspaper wants to look the same as its competition.

8. Reminder that tickets are still available

If your show runs more than one weekend and ticket sales are sluggish on opening night, you may wish to quickly send news releases to select newspapers announcing that good seats are still available for your show. The fax machine makes it easy to send quick announcements, but call your newspapers first to be sure your fax will be accepted and that someone will be waiting at the receiving end.

The needs of different newspapers

If you live in a medium-sized, suburban community, your local news stand offers several kinds of newspapers. Not all of them print the same news or take the same slant on a news story. It follows that not all news releases about your theater group's activities should be mailed to every newspaper in your area.

You have to tailor your news releases to fit the needs of the key newspapers that will draw your audience. The more locally a newspaper is based, the more details about your show will be published. Also, certain details will interest certain newspapers more than others.

The more locally a newspaper is based, the more details about your show will be published.

— Show dates —

FOR IMMEDIATE RELEASE
March 13, 19XX

NEWS MEDIA CONTACT:
George Chartier
(203)123-456X days
(203)123-246X eves
(DO NOT publish
these numbers)

CALENDAR NOTICE

The Suffield Players present "Crimes of the Heart," Beth Henley's Pulitzer Prize-winning play, Thursday through Saturday, May 5-6-7 and Fridays and Saturdays, May 13-14 and 20-21.

Performances will be at Mapleton Hall, 1305 Mapleton Ave. Doors open 7 p.m., curtain at 8 p.m. for all performances.

A warm and zany play about three sisters suddenly reunited by a family crisis. Directed by Konrad Rogowski of Chicopee Falls, Mass.

Tickets go on sale April 11. Reservations: (203)765-432X. Prices: $5.00 for bargain opening nights Thursday and Friday, May 5 and 6; $10.00 for Saturday, May 7 performance, including after-show gala reception; $7.00 all other performances.

-30-

The Suffield Players, Inc, Box 101, Suffield, Connecticut 06078

— Audition announcement —

FOR IMMEDIATE RELEASE
January 10, 19XX

NEWS MEDIA CONTACT:
George Chartier
(203)123-456X days
(203)123-246X eves
(DO NOT publish
these numbers)

AUDITIONS SET FOR "CRIMES"

SUFFIELD, CONN.—The Suffield Players will hold auditions Sunday and Monday, January 25 and 26, for a production of the Pulitzer Prize-winning play, "Crimes of the Heart."

The show is scheduled to run three weekends in May. Auditions begin at 7 p.m. Sunday and 7:30 p.m. Monday at Mapleton Hall, 1305 Mapleton Ave. Four women and two men are needed to cast the warm and zany Beth Henley play about three sisters suddenly reunited by a family crisis.

Actors should be able to portray characters in the age range of 25-35 years old. The roles offer both comic and dramatic moments. Copies of the script are available at Kent Memorial Library, 50 North Main Street in Suffield. More information is available by calling the play's director, Konrad Rogowski at (413)123-122X between 7 and 9 p.m.

-30-

The Suffield Players, Inc, Box 101, Suffield, Connecticut 06078

8.12 Full House

— Announce cast —

FOR IMMEDIATE RELEASE
March 20, 19XX

NEWS MEDIA CONTACT:
George Chartier
(203)123-456X days
(203)123-246X eves
(DO NOT publish
these numbers)

ACTORS CAST TO PERFORM "CRIMES"

SUFFIELD, CONN.—Six area actors will star in the Suffield Players production of the Pulitzer Prize-winning play, "Crimes of the Heart." The show opens May 5 at Mapleton Hall, 1305 Mapleton Ave.

Cast in the warm and zany play about three sisters suddenly reunited by a family crisis are: Mark LaFlamme of Granby, Lee Little of Farmington, Mary K. Makoski of West Suffield, Lisa Dieli Parker of Enfield, and Kelly Seip and Tim Talbot of Springfield, Mass.

Konrad Rogowski of Chicopee Falls, Mass., a veteran actor, playwright and director with the Suffield Players, will direct the play featuring unusual saxophone playing, compromising photographs, and half-hearted (and hardly dangerous) suicide attempts. Rogowski says the scenes will be played for "maximum fun mixed with a few bittersweet tears." "Crimes of the Heart," by Beth Henley, won a Pulitzer Prize and became an Academy Award-winning movie.

The Suffield Players' production will be presented Thursday, May 5, and runs Fridays and Saturdays, May 6-7, 13-14 and 20-21. Doors open 7 p.m., curtain 8 p.m. for all performances.

Seats are cabaret style. Tickets on sale April 11: (203)765-432X.

-30-

The Suffield Players, Inc, Box 101, Suffield, Connecticut 06078

— Tickets on sale —

FOR IMMEDIATE RELEASE
March 27, 19XX

NEWS MEDIA CONTACT:
George Chartier
(203)123-456X days
(203)123-246X eves
(DO NOT publish
these numbers)

TICKETS ON SALE APRIL 11 FOR "CRIMES"

SUFFIELD, CONN.—Mississippi love and laughter will come to Suffield beginning Thursday, May 5, when the Suffield Players present Beth Henley's Pulitzer Prize-winning play, "Crimes of the Heart."

Tickets go on sale April 11 for the Players production running May 5-6-7, 13-14 and 20-21 at Mapleton Hall, 1305 Mapleton Ave., Suffield. Doors open 7 p.m., curtain 8 p.m. for all performances.

The warm and zany play, directed by Konrad Rogowski of Chicopee Falls, Mass., presents the story of three sisters suddenly reunited by a family crisis. "Crimes of the Heart" won the 1981 Pulitzer Prize and the New York Drama Critics Circle Award as best American play. It was made into an Oscar-winning 1986 film starring Tess Harper, Diane Keaton, Jessica Lang, Sam Shepard and Sissy Spacek.

Prices are $5.00 for bargain opening nights Thursday and Friday, May 5 and 6; $10.00 for the Saturday, May 7 performance, including the after-show gala reception; and $7.00 for all other performances. Discounts are available for groups of 10 or more, senior citizens and youths 18 and under. Seating is cabaret style. Tickets may be reserved by calling (203)765-432X.

-30-

The Suffield Players, Inc, Box 101, Suffield, Connecticut 06078

Home town release

FOR IMMEDIATE RELEASE
April 4, 19XX

NEWS MEDIA CONTACT:
George Chartier
(203)123-456X days
(203)123-246X eves
(DO NOT publish
these numbers)

GRANBY MAN PLAYS LAWYER
IN "CRIMES OF THE HEART"

SUFFIELD, CONN.—Granby resident Mark LaFlamme has landed a legal lead in the Suffield Players production of the Pulitzer Prize-winning play, "Crimes of the Heart." The show opens May 5 at Mapleton Hall, 1305 Mapleton Ave., Suffield.

LaFlamme is cast as the sympathetic attorney in the warm and zany Beth Henley play about three sisters suddenly reunited by a family crisis.

Making his debut with the Suffield Players in "Crimes of the Heart," LaFlamme joins a six-actor ensemble directed by Konrad Rogowski of Chicopee Falls, Mass., a veteran actor, playwright and director with the Suffield Players.

LaFlamme, a graduate of Ludlow High School, recently

—MORE —

The Suffield Players, Inc, Box 101, Suffield, Connecticut 06078

April 4 / Suffield Players / page 2 of 2

played the lead in Holyoke Community College's production of "How to Succeed in Business Without Really Trying," and has appeared in local productions with Agawam Repertory Theater and Enfield's St. Martha's Players. LaFlamme works at the Stop & Shop seafood bar in Enfield.

"Crimes of the Heart," winner of the 1981 Pulitzer Prize and the New York Drama Critics Circle Award as best American play, was made into an Oscar-winning 1986 film starring Tess Harper, Diane Keaton, Jessica Lang, Sam Shepard and Sissy Spacek.

The Suffield Players production will be presented Thursday, May 5, and runs Fridays and Saturdays, May 6-7, 13-14 and 20-21. Doors open 7 p.m., curtain 8 p.m. for all performances.

Seating is cabaret style. Tickets may be reserved by calling (203)765-432X.

-30-

— Home town release — 2nd version

FOR IMMEDIATE RELEASE
April 4, 19XX

NEWS MEDIA CONTACT:
George Chartier
(203)123-456X days
(203)123-246X eves
(DO NOT publish these numbers)

FARMINGTON ACTRESS STARS
IN "CRIMES OF THE HEART"

SUFFIELD, CONN.—Farmington resident Lee Little has landed a starring role in the Suffield Players production of the Pulitzer Prize-winning play, "Crimes of the Heart." The show opens May 5 at Mapleton Hall, 1305 Mapleton Ave., Suffield.

Little plays Meg McGrath, a failed actress and middle sibling in the warm and zany Beth Henley play about three sisters suddenly reunited by a family crisis.

Appearing in her fourth production with the Suffield Players in "Crimes of the Heart," Little joins a six-actor ensemble directed by Konrad Rogowski of Chicopee Falls, Mass., a veteran actor, playwright and director with the Suffield Players.

— MORE —

The Suffield Players, Inc., Box 101, Suffield, Connecticut 06078

April 4 / Suffield Players / page 2 of 2

Little, a graduate of Farmington High School and the University of New Mexico, teaches Spanish and French at Farmington Middle School and directs the school's annual "Salute to Broadway" talent show. Little most recently appeared in the Suffield Player's production of "Antigone's Revenge" in February in which she played the dual roles of the ghost of Antigone and her evil twin sister Desdemina.

"Crimes of the Heart," winner of the 1981 Pulitzer Prize and the New York Drama Critics Circle Award as best American play, was made into an Oscar-winning 1986 film starring Tess Harper, Diane Keaton, Jessica Lang, Sam Shepard and Sissy Spacek.

The Suffield Players production will be presented Thursday, May 5, and runs Fridays and Saturdays, May 6-7, 13-14 and 20-21. Doors open 7 p.m., curtain 8 p.m. for all performances.

Seating is cabaret style. Tickets may be reserved by calling (203)765-432X.

-30-

Special release for employee newsletter

FOR IMMEDIATE RELEASE
April 4, 19XX

NEWS MEDIA CONTACT:
George Chartier
(203)123-456X days
(203)123-246X eves
(DO NOT publish
these numbers)

TWO MASSACHUSETTS MUTUAL EMPLOYEES
STAGE DRAMATIC CRIME

Two Massachusetts Mutual Life Insurance Co. employees in the State Street, Springfield, Mass., office have dramatic, after-hours plans in May, and it will be a crime if anyone misses the action.

Konrad Rogowski, associate director of graphic services, will direct the Suffield Players production of "Crimes of the Heart," the Pulitzer Prize-winning play by Beth Henley.

Kelly Seip, a graphic services artist, will be featured in the local theater production opening Thursday, May 5 and running Fridays and Saturdays, May 6-7, 13-14 and 20-21 in Mapleton Hall, 1305 Mapleton Ave., Suffield, Conn.

— MORE —

The Suffield Players, Inc, Box 101, Suffield, Connecticut 06078

April 4 / Suffield Players / page 2 of 2

"Crimes of the Heart" is the third play Rogowski has directed for the Suffield Players and the first in which he does not appear on stage. Rogowski has appeared in 10 shows since joining the theater company in 19XX. He won awards as best actor and best director-honorable mention for his work in staging Lanford Wilson's play, "Talley's Folley," in a statewide Connecticut drama festival in 19XX. Newspaper reviewers applauded his portrayal of a troubled Pontius Pilate in the Suffield Players production of the rock opera "Jesus Christ Superstar" last November.

Meanwhile, Seip marks her lucky 13th production with "Crimes of the Heart." She recently appeared with a deadly knife in her back in the Players' "Evening of Murder and Mystery," and judges at the statewide Connecticut theater festival in 19XX picked her for the best actress and best costume designs awards for her work in the dramatic, two-character play "Gin Game."

Rogowski joined Massachusetts Mutual in 19XX; Seip, in 19XX.

Tickets may be reserved for the May production of "Crimes of the Heart," featuring the directing skills of these two Massachusetts Mutual troupers by calling (203)765-432X. Discounts are available for groups of 10 or more. Seating is cabaret style. Doors open 7 p.m., curtain at 8 p.m. for all shows.

— 30 —

— Reminder for special event —

FOR IMMEDIATE RELEASE
April 18, 19XX

NEWS MEDIA CONTACT:
George Chartier
(203)123-456X days
(203)123-246X eves
(DO NOT publish
these numbers)

MAY 7 AFTER-SHOW GALA

FEATURES SOUTHERN HOSPITALITY

SUFFIELD, CONN.—Southern hospitality and down-home cooking await theatergoers attending the Suffield Players production of the Pulitzer Prize-winning play "Crimes of the Heart" May 7.

An after-show gala at Mapleton Hall, 1305 Mapleton Ave., will offer the Saturday night audience a sumptuous buffet of finger food, champagne punch and conversation with the actors and director, all with a warm, Mississippi flavor in keeping with the theme of the play that is set in Hazlehurst, Miss.

"The first Saturday night party is a tradition with Suffield Players audiences," says production manager Margie Secora of Southwick, Mass. "The candlelit table heaped with

— MORE —

April 18 / Suffield Players / page 2 of 2

hors d'oeuvres adds a special touch to the evening. Everyone has a good time."

"Crimes of the Heart" is the warm and wacky story of three sisters united during a family crisis. Konrad Rogowski of Chicopee Falls, Mass., directs the six-member cast.

Tickets for the May 7 performance and after-show reception are $10.00 and may be reserved by calling (203)765-432X. Performances are May 5 and 6 ($5.00), May 13-14 and 20-21 ($7.00). Doors open 7 p.m., curtain 8 p.m.

-30-

The Suffield Players, Inc., Box 101, Suffield, Connecticut 06078

Feature story focusing on the director

FOR IMMEDIATE RELEASE
April 11, 19XX

NEWS MEDIA CONTACT:
George Chartier
(203)123-456X days
(203)123-246X eves
(DO NOT publish
these numbers)

NEWS FEATURE: CHICOPEE FALLS MAN DIRECTS
DRAMATIC CRIMES OF THE HEART

SUFFIELD, CONN.—Konrad Rogowski of Chicopee Falls, Mass., is counting the ways people carelessly—or intentionally—break others' hearts every day.

It's his job—at least for a few more weeks. Rogowski is directing the Suffield Players production of Beth Henley's Pulitzer Prize-winning play, "Crimes of the Heart." Opening night is Thursday, May 5, and with just a few weeks away, the anticipation is nearly heartbreaking.

Rogowski, who resides with his family on Wildemere Street, has won five awards for acting and directing in previous Suffield Players productions presented at the annual Associated Community Theaters of Connecticut festival. For his latest stage effort, he directs a six-member

— MORE —

April 11 / Suffield Players / page 2 of 4

cast of actors from Suffield, Enfield, Farmington, Granby, and from Springfield, Mass.

The warm and zany play "Crimes of the Heart" will be presented in Mapleton Hall, 1305 Mapleton Ave., for seven performances over three weekends: May 5-6-7, 13-14 and 20-21.

This is the third play Rogowski has directed for the Suffield Players, and the first in which he does not appear on stage. He has appeared in 10 shows since joining the theater group in 19XX. He won an award for best actor and an honorable mention for directing Landford Wilson's play "Talley's Folly" in a statewide drama festival in 19XX. Critics applauded his portrayal of a troubled Pontius Pilate in last November's production of the rock opera "Jesus Christ Superstar."

"It's very different, not being one of the actors in the play you're directing," says Rogowski. "This is the first time I find myself in charge but not able to get up and do the part, too. I have to sit in my chair and rely more on the actors to understand the emotions I want to convey. It's hard to keep my distance, but I have to allow the actors a certain amount of artistic freedom."

Rogowski turned his theatrical hobby into a dramatic avocation after acting at Westfield State College. He joined the Suffield Players cast as the dashing Jonathan Harker in the popular "Count Dracula" in 19XX, and then wrote and performed in his own sequel, "Orphans of Eternity," in 19XX.

As opening night approaches, Rogowski finds himself in two worlds: by day he is director of graphic services for

— MORE —

The Suffield Players, Inc., Box 101, Suffield, Connecticut 06078

April 11 / Suffield Players / page 3 of 4

Massachusetts Mutual Life Insurance Co. in Springfield, and by night he is a brooding man seated in a theater director's chair.

Rogowski is reluctant to give away too much of the plot of "Crimes of the Heart" for audiences who may not be familiar with the play or the 1986 Academy Award-winning movie of the same name. He is willing to say that the characters all harbor guilt — either for having broken someone's heart or contemplating doing so.

To give the audience watching the production a feeling that the four actresses and two actors are real, down-home Mississippians, Rogowski has hunted down a number of authentic items from Hazlehurst and nearby Jackson, Miss.

One of the banks has sent a calendar with its name imprinted; the local newspaper, the Copiah County Courier, shipped a local phone directory and copies of its paper with special headlines to use in the play. The Hazlehurst Chamber of Commerce sent a street map and a five-page history of Hazlehurst. The professional theater in Jackson is sending imprinted grocery sacks from the local market.

Rogowski took photos of a nearby house for the actors to study.

"This helps them reflect on the rest of the space they are performing in—the invisible walls on the stage and the places beyond the wings that no one sees but must imagine.

"I've also asked the performers to carry with them some personal object—shoes, a ring, a picture—that means something intimate, something they have an emotional

— MORE —

April 11 / Suffield Players / page 4 of 4

attachment to," says Rogowski. "That will help intensify the emotions on stage. I've done it in other plays I've acted in. It really works."

Memories are an important part of the play, as the three sisters search a scrapbook and their pasts for insight into why they behave as they do. Snapshots of the performers, taken from their own family scrapbooks, will be projected onto a screen at the beginning of the play, a technique Rogowski experienced last year during a dramatic song in the Players production of "Jacques Brel is Alive and Well and Living in Paris."

"We're dealing with small, human dramas here," the director says. "The paradox comes from the fact that funny things happen at unfunny times. Despite the barriers people create to prevent their own happiness, they survive in the end. The play is a celebration in that sense. There's lots of laughing, lots of joy mingled with tears," Rogowski says.

"Oh, I think the audience is going to have a great time."

* * *

Seating for "Crimes of the Heart" May 5-6-7, 13-14 and 20-21 in Mapleton Hall will be cabaret style. Because Suffield Players productions often sell out, reservations made before opening night are encouraged. Reservations: (203)765-432X. Prices: $5.00 for bargain opening nights Thursday and Friday, May 5 and 6; $10.00 for Saturday, May 7 performance, including the after-show gala reception. All other performances are $7.00.

—30—

Feature story focusing on props

FOR IMMEDIATE RELEASE
April 25, 19XX

NEWS MEDIA CONTACT:
George Chartier
(203)123-456X days
(203)123-246X eves
(DO NOT publish
these numbers)

AUTHENTIC PROPS ADD REALISM
TO "CRIMES OF THE HEART"

SUFFIELD, CONN.--The Suffield Players have friends in Mississippi who are only too happy to send up a package of grocery sacks, noodle scoopers and a complimentary calendar from the local bank.

The items were requested by Korad Rogowski of Chicopee Falls, Mass., to lend a down-home feeling to "Crimes of the Heart," the latest play he is directing for the Suffield Players.

"Crimes of the Heart," on stage at Mapleton Hall, 1305 Mapleton Ave. in Suffield and running May 5-6-7, 13-14 and 20-21, is the bittersweet story of three Mississippi sisters brought together by a family crisis. The script won playwright Beth Henley a Pulitzer Prize in 1981 and inspired the Academy Award-winning movie in 1986.

Rogowski wanted his six actors to convey a sense of really being from Hazlehurst, Miss., the town the playwright

- MORE -

The Suffield Players, Inc., Box 101, Suffield, Connecticut 06078

April 25 / Suffield Players / page 2 of 3

sets her story in, so the director gave Suffield Players publicist George Chartier a shopping list of props to locate down south.

Bill McCarty III, master electrician at New Stage Theatre in Jackson, Miss., was sympathetic to the Suffield drama company's ambitions, having been himself involved with a successful production of "Crimes of the Heart" a few years ago at New Stage. He immediately packed up a stack of paper sacks from Jitney Jungle, a popular grocery store chain, along with memo pads, rubber jar openers and color plastic noodle scoopers, all stamped with the Jitney Jungle store logo.

In his letter accompanying the theatrical CARE package, McCarty assured the Suffield Players that there is a Jitney Jungle supermarket "just down the street from the Botrell home in Hazlehurst," where a crucial event in the play takes place.

Actress Mary K. Makoski arrives home in the opening scene of "Crimes of the Heart" with a sack of groceries, and after a recent rehearsal Rogowski said "Just having her handle a bag with the name of a store that's not familiar to us in the Northeast but is really from the locale of the play–it helps the actress to believe her character comes from a real place."

Actress Lisa Parker clips an article from a newspaper in the first act of the play, and there's realism here, too. Shelly Jackson, who works at the Capiah County Courier, sent a half-dozen copies of the Hazlehurst Daily News and the Clarion Ledger, as did Jeff Edwards of the Jackson Daily News and the Clarion Ledger. Audiences attending the Suffield production will

- MORE -

Reminder release

FOR IMMEDIATE RELEASE
May 1, 19XX

NEWS MEDIA CONTACT:
George Chartier
(203)123-456X days
(203)123-246X eves
(DO NOT publish
these numbers)

EXTRA PERFORMANCE ADDED
TO FAST-SELLING PLAY

SUFFIELD, CONN.--In response to heavy ticket demand, the Suffield Players have added an eighth performance to the scheduled run of the Beth Henley comedy "Crimes of the Heart."

A matinee performance Sunday, May 15 at 2 p.m. in Mapleton Hall, 1305 Mapleton Ave., has been added to the scheduled run of the Pulitzer Prize-winning play that opens May 5 and runs three consecutive Fridays and Saturdays, May 6 and 7, 13-14 and 20-21.

Doors open 1 p.m. for the Sunday matinee. Doors open 7 p.m., curtain 8 p.m. for all other performances. Tickets:(203)765-432X.

"This is getting to be a regular thing," says Suffield Players ticket manager Marilyn Juneau in reaction to the need for the additional performance. An extra Sunday show was added to last March's run of "An Evening of Murder and Mystery."

"Our last show completely sold out a week before we opened. I guess that if you're going to have problems with ticket sales, these are the kind to have," Juneau says.

-30-

The Suffield Players, Inc, Box 101, Suffield, Connecticut 06078

April 25 / Suffield Players / page 3 of 3

have a chance to thumb through copies of these newspapers at intermission.

When the Suffield Players' publicist called the Hazlehurst Chamber of Commerce, Manager Julian Harris was ready. "Let's see, you'll need a phone directory, right? And a calendar with an advertisement from a local business, and some newspapers...."

Harris is no mind-reader, just experienced. Since "Crimes of the Heart" won the Pulitzer Prize and the New York Drama Critics Circle Award, drama companies across the nation have called Hazlehurst for help. Harris sent the Suffield Players a calendar from Copiah Bank, a street map, and a history of the Hazlehurst area that appears in the Suffield production's playbill.

Rogowski says the props from Mississippi don't look so different from their New England counterparts, "...but that's not the point.

"It's giving the actors a sense of time and place—a connection with that place where their minds are supposed to be. If the actors are transported and convinced from handling a Jitney Jungle sack and a Capiah Bank calendar that they are there in Hazlehurst, Mississippi, then you can bet a mint julep that the audience is going to believe it, too.

"That's one of the things theater does," Rogowski says.

"It transports us to other places and other experiences."

Tickets for "Crimes of the Heart," performed in Mapleton Hall, 1305 Mapleton Ave., Suffield, may be reserved by calling (203)765-432X. Seating is cabaret style and tickets are limited. Doors open 7 p.m., curtain 8 p.m. for all performances.

-30-

Feature focuses on performers

FOR IMMEDIATE RELEASE
May 9, 19XX

NEWS MEDIA CONTACT:
George Chartier
(203)123-456X days
(203)123-246X eves
(DO NOT publish
these numbers)

LUCKY 13th SHOW PRESENTS NO FEARS
FOR THREE SUFFIELD PLAYERS

SUFFIELD, CONN.—Triskadekaphobics they're not.

For those without a 12-pound dictionary, the tongue-twisting word means "those with a fear of the number 13." For Suffield Players Lisa Parker, Mary K. Makoski and Kelly Seip, who appear together this month in their 13th production with the community theater, the mood is anything but unlucky.

"Bother me? Heck, no," says veteran actress Seip of Springfield, Mass. "Lucky 13 means you're on to luck 26. Doing a show with Lisa and Mary 'K.' is like old-home week, like being back with the family."

"Seip is teamed with Parker of Enfield and Makoski of West Suffield in the warm and zany play "Crimes of the Heart," Beth Henley's Pulitzer Prize-winning tale of three

—MORE—

The Suffield Players, Inc, Box 101, Suffield, Connecticut 06078

May 9 / Suffield Players / page 2 of 2

Mississippi sisters reunited by a family crisis opened May 5 and will continue Friday through Sunday, May 13-14-15 and Friday and Saturday, May 20-21.

Despite the trio's long list of appearances with the Suffield Players, circumstance and casting have united them only twice previously on the Mapleton Hall stage—in "The Chalk Garden" in 19XX and "Tartuffe" in 19XX. Still, three performers in their 13th show should give some pause.

"Oh, have we reached 13 already?" says Parker with feigned wide-eyed innocence. "Why, I'll have to make some mint juleps to celebrate."

"Superstitious? Certainly not," Makoski sniffs. "But, could we check those numbers again? It doesn't seem like I've put on my makeup and pranced on stage that many times!"

In director Konrad Rogowski's interpretation of "Crimes of the Heart," Seip plays nosy next-door cousin Chick, opposite Makoski and Parker who appear as sisters Lenny McGrath and Babe.

Two shows last weekend sold out before opening night, according to Players ticket manager Marilyn Juneau. The remaining performances are nearly half-sold out, so reserving tickets as soon as possible is advised, she says.

Tickets may be reserved by calling (203)765-432X. All seats are $7.00 with discounts available for senior citizens, groups of 10 or more, and youths 18 and under. Doors open 7 p.m., curtain 8 p.m. for all performances but the Sunday matinee: Doors open 1 p.m., curtain 2 p.m. for the May 15 performance.

—30—

Season announcement

FOR IMMEDIATE RELEASE
August 1, 19XX

NEWS MEDIA CONTACT:
George Chartier
(203)123-456X days
(203)123-246X eves
(DO NOT publish these numbers)

19XX-XX SEASON FEATURES SCREAMS, GASPS, LAUGHS

SUFFIELD, CONN.—The Suffield Players 38th season will feature productions designed to provoke screams in the fall, gasps in winter, and laughs for springtime.

All shows will be performed in Mapleton Hall, 1305 Mapleton Ave., Suffield. Doors open 7 p.m., curtain 8 p.m.

The season will open Thursday, Oct. 18 with "I'll Be Back Before Midnight," a mystery thriller by Peter Colley featuring murderers and ghosts that go bump in the night. Just in time for Holloween, the thriller will be staged with special effects, such as simulated lightning and thunder aimed at the audience. The Players are rating the production "PG" and caution that the play may be too frightening for young children.

"I'll Be Back Before Midnight" runs Oct. 18-19-20, 26-27 and Nov. 2-3 and 9-10.

— MORE —

August 1 / Suffield Players / page 2 of 2

An eerie evening of three one-act plays, collectively called "A Twisted Trilogy," will be staged Feb. 14-15-16, 22-23 and March 1-2, 19XX. The three plays offer a different director and cast of actors as a showcase for the theater company's talents. The Players will select one of the three plays as the group's entry in the Associated Community Theaters of Connecticut drama festival scheduled for next spring.

The twisted trilogy of plays includes "The Nightingale and not the Lark," "The Audition," and the classic horror tale, "The Monkey's Paw."

The Players will conclude their 38th anniversary season with a 75th diamond jubilee production of "Personals." The musical comedy promises to explore the good, the bad and the ridiculous moments of modern dating through the personal ads. With a live band, "Personals" will be presented May 2-3-4, 10-11 and 17-18, 19XX.

Tickets will go on sale about three weeks before opening night for each production. Reservations can be made at that time by calling (203)765-432X.

—30—

Social

Suffield Players Show Modern Dating Is Like Halloween Night

The Suffield Players' spring musical "Personals" suggests that modern dating is like Halloween all year round: a scary experience that finds everyone hiding their real personalities behind masks, and everyone hoping to come away with a sweet surprise.

Opening May 2nd and running May 3rd, 4th, 10th, 11th, 17th, and 18th, the musical at Mapleton Hall in Suffield offers 15 scenes and songs that look at the good, the bad, and the ridiculous moments people endure while looking for Miss or Mr. Perfect.

Consider the way people write those personal ads for the newspapers, the first of the show's 15 songs suggests; listen up, all you creative writers who pretend in those ads to be macho millionaires, dreamy movie stars or brilliant brain surgeons:

"This has nothing to do with love.
This has more and more to do with diction.
Nothing to do with love.
This has mostly to do
With a quick turn
Of a cute phrase
And a knack for fiction."

"Personals" director Ted Levine of Springfield says "since going into rehearsal, we've been devouring personal ads in all the area newspapers, and we've all been struck by the perfect picture people have drawn of themselves." Perfection, he says, is not realistic. On the other hand, Levine says, in 15-30 words, it's only human to put your best foot forward. "Personals" is filled with funny moments when this best foot encounters a strangely different pair of shoes. The blind date can wind up being a weird clash of opposites, as another song in "Personals" offers:

"Her dress is kamali.
Her make-up's Kabuki.
Sort of Salvadore Dali
Meets young Pat Suzuki.
I'm out on a date in the Twilight Zone.
I'd rather dance alone."

In the Suffield Players' production, three women and three men play multiple roles in a series of sketches that examine video dating services, pick-up lines at the local bar, teenage fantasies, the struggle to let go of old relationships, overcoming painful break-ups, and the fear of commitment.

What saves the show from the gloom and doom themes of loneliness and mismatches is the wit in "Personals," Levine says. "People will come away from this show repeating lines and, I hope, laughing a little more at how unnecessarily serious we are when we're looking for a little romance.

"Still, I hope something else comes out of this production," Levine says. "I hope people will be more accepting of themselves and others and come to realize that, with all their weaknesses and quirks and emotional baggage that gets carried into new relationships from every other relationship, people are all the same in one way: they're scared and lonely and hungry for a little love, and they're willing to put themselves through some pretty wacky situations to find it."

As one person in "Personals" says while composing a newspaper ad,

"I know there's someone out there
Waiting somewhere in the night
Someone waiting for my fifteen words
To light up the black and white,
And I think this time I finally got it right!"

SUFFIELD PLAYERS Marge Patefield and Evelyn Holland (front), and Margie Secora, Lyle Pearsons, and Tim O'Brien (back) try to make the "Love Connection" in the Suffield Players' upcoming musical comedy, "Personals."

The Suffield Players caution that because "Personals" takes a humorous look at adult themes, parental discretion is advised.

Players' productions often sell out before performance dates, so reservations are encouraged. Tickets went on sale April 8th for all performances and may be reserved by calling 627-5749. Discounts are offered for groups, senior citizens, and students.

Seating is theater style for all performances.

Proceeds from the final performance of "Personals" will benefit the annual Eugene Biggio Memorial Drama Scholarship. The $500 scholarship is open to young people from elementary grades through high school who are taking courses, lessons or formal programs in drama, music or dance.

Lyrics by David Crane, Seth Friedman, Marta Kauffman

A feature story for a musical. This was reprinted word-for-word as submitted in a local home town weekly newspaper. Note the use of lyrics in the article to illustrate the emotional aspects of the musical

Specifics? You want specifics? Fine. Let's start off with a list of newspaper types:

◆ Shopping news

This is a weekly tabloid (half the dimensions of a regular, big city newspaper) with lots of advertisements from local businesses, listings of local interest that include school and senior citizen lunch menus for the week, and usually emphasizing good news about activities in town. The advertising often takes up three-quarters of the publication, but there's usually some editorial space, too. Photos show townspeople at the local fair or library bake sale, portrait pictures of young people accompanying announcements of being accepted into college, and lots of ceremonial ribbon cutting and check-giving pictures (known in the trade as "grip-and-grin" shots because the people are always stiffly facing the camera with frozen smiles, one pair of hands gripping a charity check and the other pair shaking hands just above or below the check).

Shopping newses live by the motto "all the news that fits, we print." They will print your news releases nearly verbatim and will run the most awful photos as long as the subject is local news. These newspapers will very likely publish a story about your show every week for six weeks straight as long as your releases offer new and interesting information each time. Most of your theater group's customers read the shopping news, so you should spend a lot of time and effort getting news to this paper early and often. Besides releases, these newspapers will accept good quality costume and set sketches. Sketches, because they're different from ordinary photos, capture a reader's interest.

◆ Small town daily

This usually has the same dimensions as a big city newspaper, but half the thickness. Lots of news here about local politics, sports, politics, civic events, and politics. If there is a fire or accident in town, you can be sure it will appear on the front page tomorrow. Small town dailies like to pose a Question Of The Day to a half-dozen people on the street and publish their responses with photos of these people squinting at the camera.

While the local shopping news will consider publishing every news release you send, the small town daily is a little more selective. It is trying to be more like a big city paper and less like a shopper. Its style usually winds up somewhere in-between.

This newspaper may use your feature story as is, but may also assign a reporter to rewrite the story with a few extra quotes from the publicist or the director. The small town daily may assign a photographer to snap pictures at rehearsal, but probably will accept good quality black and white photos from a publicist. If you're looking for a reporter to write a review of your show's opening night, this is the kind of newspaper to contact.

◆ Regional muckraker

This weekly tabloid lives for scandal and lionizes the local gadfly. Liberal political views abound, with a fondness for environmental and consumers rights issues. Big business is usually cast as the villain, and the plight of the underclass is given lots of ink. Avant-garde art and foreign films are regularly featured.

If you are promoting a play with a controversial subject or a new, daring approach to a traditional show, the regional muckraker will be interested. Send along an arts photo with dramatic shadows and people posed off-center, photographed at extreme angles; this paper loves that kind of thing. The muckraker couldn't care less about hometown news stories or pretty portrait photos, but you'll get the paper's attention if the show's director is willing to say eyebrow-raising, anti-establishment stuff.

If your group is doing a traditional version of *Oklahoma*, send this newspaper a brief listing for the calendar section and don't waste your time mailing the muckraker any other news releases.

◆ Local arts bulletin

Often published twice a month, these are springing up in medium-sized communities by people who are frustrated by the lack of space daily newspapers devote to the visual and performing arts. These bulletins may be tabloids or newsletters, but they depend heavily on the local arts community for financial support. You may want to advertise in a bulletin like this not only because the readers are more likely than the average person to attend arts events, but also because there's some prestige in putting in an appearance where your peers will see you and because it's good to support publications devoted to the arts.

Another version of this bulletin may be published by your local arts league or the mayor's council on the arts. In any case, by all means, send in your feature stories along with your best photos. Send a choice of photos. Bear in mind that the biweekly deadlines mean that you have to gauge your mailings more carefully. You can also expect to get only one major write-up.

Send your calendar listing *early*.

◆ Regional arts bulletin

This much the same needs and format as the local bulletin, but covers a broader population. It may be a statewide publication or a regional bulletin reporting arts news for several states.

◆ Big city newspaper

These days, most big city newspapers don't review amateur theater because there are too many groups and too few reporters. They usually don't want home town news releases announcing supporting roles, such as the news that Lillian Cox will play one of the suspects in Agatha Christie's *Ten Little Indians*. However, you might find the big city paper interested in some little moppet and her cute doggie cast in the starring roles of *Annie*, or a local carpenter playing the lead in *Jesus Christ Superstar*. Anything emphasizing a person in an interesting role, a startling coincidence, or an unusual twist on tradition will give you a chance at getting featured.

The big city newspaper might not accept your photos, preferring instead to send a staff photographer.

To get covered in the big city newspaper, your news releases must be well-written with a hint of cleverness.

The big city newspaper often needs a separate, brief release or fact sheet for its calendar section.

These are generalizations. To know for certain what kinds of news releases and how many releases each newspaper on your list will accept, you need to study two or three issues. If you're still not sure, phone the editor. Chapter 10 on **Media Relations** will tell you more about how to deal with reporters and editors. Please look it over before picking up the phone.

Journalism style

"Just the facts, ma'am."

That's what the publicity guidebooks say you should remember when writing your news release. "Avoid the flowery stuff. Use adjectives and adverbs sparingly. Don't hype —just type — the facts."

But, which facts? The facts you want to include in your release, besides the necessary who-what-where-when information, are facts that will interest potential audiences. Tell them what they can expect to see without sounding as if you're jumping up and down with excitement.

If you're not sure what elements of your show will draw audiences, look at the section about psychology in Chapter Two of this book.

Then, look at the way your newspaper publishes stories. Aside from the columnists who are writing their opinions on a subject, the usual journalist reports news in an unbiased style. This tone differs from advertising copy writing. The most common error most publicity writers make is not distinguishing between these two kinds of writing.

In your news releases, don't predict how audiences will react ("Audiences won't believe their eyes..."). Don't inflate or exaggerate ("A wonderful production of..."). Don't tease ("What's got 50 legs, 20 songs, romance and Paris?"). Don't insist or assume interest ("Shakespeare lovers won't want to miss..."). Don't address the reader directly with "you," "I," "we," or "they" ("You will see murder and mystery...").

Writing "the facts" doesn't mean being dull. You should watch for an opportunity to stick a "whammy" into your news release — preferably at the beginning.

A "whammy" is a surprise. It's a detail that causes a reader to say "How about that!" An untraditional approach to a production, a strange coincidence or contrast in casting, a situation that an audience or even the theater company never expected — all these have the potential for you to use as a whammy to draw attention to your show.

Fresh out of whammies?

Write about the theme of the show — what the playwright is saying about life: "Eugene O'Neill's *Moon For the Misbegotten* explores the difficult triumph of unselfish love over guilt and despair."

And don't assume that your audience is familiar with the show you're presenting. Even a classic like *Oliver!* needs some introduction: "...the musical based on Charles Dickens' rags-to-riches tale of an orphan boy's adventures in 19th century London."

When to mail news releases

Earlier in this chapter, you learned about how different kinds of news releases need to be mailed at peak times of public interest. Different newsrooms also have timing needs with which you should be familiar.

Like acting, timing in publicity is everything. If you mail the news release too late, it won't get through the newsroom in time to make the newsroom's deadline. Send it too early, and it will lie around and get buried in the editor's "to use later" desk tray — or, worse, it may get

A "whammy" is a surprise. It's a detail that causes a reader to say "How about that!"

published way too soon, with the result that the public will forget your news long before opening night.

Check your individual newspapers for exact deadlines and allow extra days for mail travel and people on the receiving end who may not open their mail right away. In general, you can depend on these guides:

✓ Mail a brief, one-page announcement for newspaper calendar columns five to six weeks in advance of opening night.

✓ Mail all other releases to daily newspapers about a week and a half before you want the news to be published.

✓ For weekly newspapers, mail news releases three weeks ahead.

✓ Most radio news desks need 10 days' notice for a public service announcement.

✓ TV community calendars need two to four weeks.

✓ Some school newspapers may need more notice.

✓ Quarterly publications need plenty more lead time, of course.

If in doubt about deadlines, call the news room and ask.

Summary

☞ Newspapers give the theater publicist more opportunities to announce news than do TV or radio.

☞ News stories are less expensive, provide more information, and carry more credibility than paid advertisements.

☞ News releases follow a standard format that editors and reporters expect publicists to follow.

☞ The formats of radio and TV news releases differ from newspaper releases.

☞ The theater publicist has many kinds of news releases to choose from, each with its own content and peak publication time.

☞ Different kinds of newspapers want different types of news releases. It pays to study samples and target news releases accordingly.

Dramatic Photos

Chapter 9

- Posing dramatic pictures
- Finding a photographer
- Creative uses for photos
- Writing captions

It's Wednesday afternoon in the newsroom of a local newspaper, and the editor in charge of the Arts & Leisure page is in despair.

The page will be running off the press in less than 24 hours. The events listing is complete and the editor has several brief stories of equal importance — any of which could be the major story on the page. Her problem is that she needs a photograph or some artwork to design the page around — "something that will catch the reader's eye and make the page sing," she mumbles to herself.

Her dilemma is your opportunity.

Including a good photograph with a news release more than doubles your chances of getting into the newspaper. If it's an outstanding photograph, it could be the centerpiece of the arts page.

Yesterday the editor ran a so-so story that probably didn't deserve the prominent placement on the arts page, but the picture was so dramatic that she knew readers would stop and look at the page. Today, however, she has only a few photos to choose from and they're all awful. She has opened a half-dozen envelopes, hunting for a dramatic photograph — heck, she'll settle for a halfway interesting picture at this point — but one by one she rejects what she sees.

Photo rights and wrongs

See if you can guess what's wrong with each photo:

Picture 1: Two men in blue jeans and plaid shirts are sitting across a card table, apparently discussing something. The scene is from a rehearsal for an upcoming production of *Twelve Angry Men*.

Picture 2: A group of seven women and men are in a line, grouped in twos and threes, dressed in a variety of street clothes except for one man with a cowboy hat. Their hands extend out in front of them. The handwritten description says the picture is from rehearsal for a production of *Oklahoma*.

Picture 3: Two women appear in a full-length pose shaking hands and exchanging a plaque. The woman receiving the plaque is accepting a prize for a play she directed which won first prize at a regional drama festival. The festival took place three weeks ago. The women are wearing black gowns and are posed against a red curtain.

Picture 4: A man and a woman face each other, wide-eyed with terror. He brandishes an empty jar which for some strange reason seems to frighten the woman. No names are attached to the picture, but the accompanying news release says the local high school is staging *The Bride of Frankenstein*.

What's wrong with these pictures? And how can you take a publicity picture that is so much better than these that the editor will choose it instantly over the others on her desk?

Mistake No. 1: No action, no costumes, no emotion. The photographer was right to decide not to show all 12 angry men in one picture. Editors normally prefer photos with no more than three or four people because faces are too small when too many are crowded into a picture frame. Faces are interesting in photographs because they can show a variety of emotions, and emotions are what make us human and fascinating.

Including a good photograph with a news release more than doubles your chances of getting into the newspaper.

Yet where is the emotion in the faces of these two guys? The play is not about 12 pleasant men. The photographer should have had the two actors lean into each other across the table, nose to nose, fingers arched threateningly, with the edges of the picture tightly cropped (framed) to communicate tension.

The actors could have been posed wearing contrasting suits — or someone with a suit and one in shirt sleeves — to suggest a confrontation of conservative and flamboyant personalities.

Another option is to have a third person in the middle of the two, trying to prevent them from slugging each other.

Stories — in the form of plays, movies, dance or prose — are about action and emotions, and the more powerful the emotions, the more interesting the story. Your publicity photos must communicate action and emotions.

By the way, if it's necessary to include a table in the composition of the picture, it's better to make things look authentic — or at least avoid looking out of place. In this case, if pictures are being taken early in rehearsal and the group is expecting to borrow a nice table but it hasn't yet arrived, I wouldn't use the card table. You risk suggesting to your public that they're going to see a cheap production. Instead, I would take the actors down to the local library or to the courthouse and pose the actors around a serious-looking meeting room table.

Mistake No. 2: Too many people doing too little and posing too vaguely. One cowboy hat does not say *Oklahoma*. Okay, maybe it does, but who wants to go to the production pictured here?

It is important to send newspapers interesting publicity photos three to four weeks before your event (remember that it may take a week or more after mailing for the picture to appear in the newspaper) because the photos plant a seed of interest in a reader's mind. Then, when the reader sees another photo or article, or sees a poster or a road sign, your show is familiar. Human beings are visual creatures. We grasp tremendous amounts of information quickly from a single glance at a photograph in the newspaper.

So, while it is hard to arrange for all the costumes and props and scenery for a show to be available to take publicity photos six or seven weeks before opening night, I hope you see why it is necessary to find a few pieces. You cannot ask the public — your potential audience — to look at a photograph of actors dressed in casual rehearsal clothes and imagine that these will be transformed by opening night into star-spangled costumes. You must stir their imaginations with a few, select props and costume accessories.

In our *Oklahoma* example, the creative publicist might suggest that the costumer borrow several hats from the local costume shop, as this is where the group will be renting their headgear in a month anyway. To simulate fringe, the costumer might take strips of plain cloth, cut them up and tack these to the shirts. For black and white photos, the color of the material won't matter much (but see Mistake No. 3 for the one time color does matter very much).

Other props: A coil of clothesline implies a lariat. Cap pistols from the toy store are easy to get. A neckerchief worn cowboy style or around the head, prairie woman fashion, goes a long way to suggest classic images of the West. An antique store down the road almost certainly has a wagon wheel you can pose actors next to.

A little imagination and a handful of easily found props can go a long way to give a photograph a theatrical look.

Now, if this is a well-known musical, a photo illustrating a beloved song can quickly bring the song to a viewer's mind and prompt an immediate decision to order tickets. Think quickly: how can you photograph two actors cuddled together, gazing up fondly at the roof of a surrey with fringe on the top? Remember, the photograph doesn't have to show the entire carriage, just the fringe from the title of the song.

Finally, see the end of this chapter for information on how to prepare a *caption*. Descriptions of photos must be typed and attached in a specific way to photographs mailed to the news media.

Mistake No. 3: Oh, please! This is known in the trade as a "grip-and-grin shot." Desperate, unimaginative editors will print this picture, but only desperate, unimaginative readers will look at it for more than two seconds. It is a waste of time taking these pictures which only succeed in looking like everyone else's. Same is bland. Same is invisible. Do you want your group to be invisible?

There are better ways of using photography to illustrate news of an award-winning production. Show a scene from the play. Show the director gesturing instructions to two actors in an action scene. How about a startling trick photograph in which the director, dressed in light-colored clothes, hugs her plaque while standing against a black background with disembodied hands applauding around her? (The hands belong to actors dressed in black from head to foot so that only the hands are exposed.)

If you were an editor and you had three grip-and-grin photos from three civic groups, would you use any of these if you also had a creatively posed photo?

People, we're in theater. Let's get dramatic!

Now, about the color of the gowns and the curtain in our disastrous grip-and-grin photograph: Unless your newspaper is running color pictures, the color photo submitted by the unwitting publicist will be printed in black and white. This photo would not be printed in black and white because *red photographs as black* in a black and white format, and we know what happens to the black gowns when they appear against a red-turned-to-black background, don't we? Right. The gowns vanish and so do the chances of this photo being used by the newspaper.

Avoid this problem. Watch your colors when taking pictures, and, when sending pictures to newspapers, use black and white film every time, all the time.

Oh, by the way. As you may have guessed from reading the last chapter, this photo has still one other thing wrong with it: it's three weeks late. The story is old and nearly useless to most journalists.

Ready for the last one?

Mistake No. 4: By now you should be way ahead of me. Why isn't this guy in a distinctive costume, such as

Your publicity photos must communicate action and emotions.

a white lab coat? He could have borrowed one from any science teacher in any high school or college. Why isn't this woman in a monster fright wig and makeup? If a wig wasn't available before dress rehearsal, cotton candy could have been used to dress up the hair for the photo — it would look freaky and would easily wash out afterwards.

Why couldn't Dr. Frankenstein be holding a genuine beaker? The same science teacher with the lab coat could lend a couple of pieces of lab glass for the photo and, probably, for the play.

In fact, in a production of my stage version of *Dr. Jekyll & Mr. Hyde*, a university chemistry professor gave me four boxes of old, surplus beakers, bottles, test tubes and burner valves. A glass blower on the campus made me a condenser (a coiled tube of glass that every mad scientist uses to connect bubbling beakers). The photos using these free props were stunning. You can do it too.

Helpful hint: if you photograph clear containers with liquid, as in our example with Dr. Frankenstein and the jar, don't use a clear liquid that can't be seen in the photo. Use tea or other dark drink. For this example, how about tea doctored with a dissolving Alka-Seltzer® tablet?

Since this is a dramatic pose, how about heightening the drama with an interesting camera angle? Instead of photographing the actors at shoulder-level, the camera can be lowered to waist-level and aimed upward; or the photographer can stand on a table and shoot down at the actors as they look up. Again, the picture can be taken from over the shoulder of one of the actors. Vary the traditional camera view to discover a dramatic, new way of looking at things.

Guides for dramatic photos

By now, you get the idea: a dramatic photograph that will make a newspaper editor cheer and make you, the publicist, a success, should follow these guidelines:

▲ Use black and white film using high-contrast subjects and backgrounds. Avoid black-red, orange-pink, yellow-white, blue-green and similar combinations that will photograph as the same shade on black and white film.

▲ Limit the number of people in your pictures to maximize close-up facial expressions.

▲ Crop your actors tightly within the photograph frame. Show actors from the waist up unless you have good reason to show them full length.

▲ Use a few props and the suggestion of costumes.

▲ Pose actors so that body language and facial expressions convey action and strong emotion.

▲ Avoid standard poses. No "grip-and-grins." Try an imaginative, even a trick photograph.

▲ Shoot from dramatic angles rather than straight on.

▲ Avoid group poses where everyone has the same tone clothes. All light or all dark clothes blend into an indistinguishable blob of disembodied heads.

▲ Always attach a caption to your photos with all pertinent information, including indentifications of people in the photos.

Locating a photographer

Anyone can take bad photos, but those won't bring in audiences even if the newspaper prints them. Find a good photographer and pay a fair price for the service. You should recoup the cost in bigger audiences.

Here's a cost-saving way to hire a good photographer: Ask the owner of the camera shop in town to take pictures for your group. Offer to reimburse the photographer the cost of the materials only, in exchange for a free advertisement in the playbill (but get permission from the playbill supervisor).

Or strike this attractive deal with a photographer struggling to bring in business to the studio: In exchange for taking all publicity photos for your group and only charging your group for the cost of materials, the photographer may retain exclusive rights to sell reprints of the photos to the cast and crew as souvenirs. Give the photographer space in the theater lobby to set up a display of studio photographs complete with brochures, business cards and a sign that says the she or he is the official photographer for your show and is available for hire.

What? There's no photo store in town? Take out a want ad to find a local photography hobbyist, place a notice in the playbill, check with advertising agencies for names of free-lancers, locate a high school or college photography club, or offer the local newspaper's staff photographer a financial incentive or trade in services to moonlight for your production.

When you think about it, there are lots of photographers out there. Find a good one and make a deal no one could refuse. You can't afford not to have a good shutterbug on your publicity team.

When you locate a photographer, check out the quality of work before hiring. Review sample photos to determine if the photographer is any good. Once satisfied, review your publicity needs and agree on a price for services. Get the fee in writing.

Expect to be billed for these photography costs: photographer's time, materials (film, paper and chemicals), and transportation costs.

What about the negatives?

Normally, the photographer gets to keep the negatives and charge your group for reprints any time in the future that additional prints are requested. However, this may prove inconvenient and even tragic for your group if the photographer moves away and, years later, negatives are needed and can't be found. It's worth negotiating with the photographer to give or sell your group the negatives after a production closes.

Preserve your pictures

Like all other historic material, photos and negatives must be stored in a dry, cool place. Attics and cellars are not good places, usually. Negatives should be properly labeled and stored in plastic sleeves, perhaps in a three-ring binder. Ask your photographer to be sure that the set of pictures you'll store in your historic file are washed clean of corrosive chemicals that could prematurely age your pictures.

Your photographer, the owner of a professional camera shop, or the curator of a well-run museum can give you additional advice on how to safely store negatives and prints. Write up a list of precautions and instructions for people collecting and

Pay a fair price for a good photographer. You'll recoup the cost in bigger audiences.

storing pictures in the future. Fifty and even a hundred years from now the people in charge of your theater group will bless you.

Save money with contacts.

No, not people-contacts; *contact sheets*. After photos are taken, it'll take a few days to develop the film and print a contact sheet. A contact sheet displays the positive images on the film in strips of miniature pictures that are the size of the film. A single 8-by-10-inch contact sheet can show as many as 36 frames of film. From the contact sheet, select the best poses and print the pictures in quantity. Ask your photographer to lend you a *loupe* —a hand-held magnifier —to check the focus and other details of pictures on the contact sheet.

Using contact sheets saves money. Rather than ask for every frame of every roll of film to be enlarged and printed right away, you pick the poses you want to pay for. These are the ones that get printed.

Publicity needs

You can use photographs in several ways to promote your show:

Pictures taken early on in rehearsal can be used to send to newspapers for publicity, packed in news kits for reporters and reviewers, placed in the playbill, and even used to illustrate posters and fliers. Photos taken at final dress rehearsal or once the show is up and running can be used for later publicity, including publication of annual souvenir books, fund-raising literature, and retrospective displays. As I mentioned in the last section, cast and crew members may wish to purchase souvenir photographs.

Screening and halftones

Photographs that are used in playbills, posters, or other printed matter must be screened first to ensure quality reproduction. When photos are screened, they are converted to a pattern of dots, called a *halftone*. If you'll look closely at any photograph in a newspaper, you'll see this dot pattern.

Any printer, including most quick-copy shops, can screen photographs for you. You may also check with your local newspaper to see if it provides this service. Expect to pay $10 to $15 for an 8-by-10-inch black and white halftone. You can save money by screening several small pictures onto a single sheet.

You don't need to screen photographs that you mail to the news media. Newspapers and magazines screen all pictures they use. Chapter 11 on **Working with Printers** explains more about preparing materials for printing. Color photographs must be specially prepared for full-color reproduction.

Color or black and white?

Black and white film is still the standard for publicity photographs sent to newspapers. If newspapers want to run a color photograph, as many newspapers have the capability to do these days, an editor will send a photographer. Still, it doesn't hurt to include a color snapshot along with your black and white print when you mail photos to the newspaper. Do this only if you have a spectacularly colorful subject, however. Include a note to the editor with the mailing asking that the newspaper consider running a color photo of your show. Invite the editor to send a photographer.

If you need both color and black and white pictures, and both prints and slides, consider this trick: Begin by taking pictures with color print film. When the prints are developed, lay them on a copy stand (a special table fitted with lights, designed for copying photographs) and photograph them using a camera loaded with slide film and fitted with a copy stand lens. When the color slide film is used up, reload the camera with black and white print film and photograph the color prints again. Under most circumstances, you'll get acceptable black and white prints this way. See also the section later in this chapter on the pros and cons of print and slide film.

Beyond newspaper publicity

Besides sending photos to the newspaper, you can use photographs in other ways to promote your show:

— Send photos with a news release to TV stations to give assignment editors an idea of what your show looks like. Don't send photos to radio stations; radio doesn't care what you look like.

— Display pictures in the theater lobby but be careful not to give away any of the current play's surprises. Include backstage production shots. It's always nice to have framed photos of past productions on display to encourage people during intermission to reminisce. Publicity displays cry out for color photos. If you can't afford to display a wall or bulletin board full of color photographs, try this compromise: Amid a display of several large black-and-white photos, place one or two color pictures. The contrast will be dramatic.

— Get permission from officials to set up a display in the lobbies of local banks, shopping malls, town hall and the local library. If these places don't have display space you can use, bring your own: mount photos, captions and a poster (with clear information on production dates and how to get tickets) on a bulletin board, and set this up on an easel. Staple a card on the back of the bulletin board with your name and phone number. Mark your calendar to remember to pick up the display as soon as the show is over.

— Include "head shots" (described in the next section of this chapter) in your playbill beside the brief biographies. Include an action photograph of your last show in the current playbill to remind your audiences of the last production.

— To illustrate a brochure announcing the next season, use photos from the previous season's productions. This does two things: It reminds audiences of how good the last season was, and shows new subscribers what a great season they missed!

— Take a series of photos to record the process of completing a challenging set construction, costume design or makeup job. Use these pictures to illustrate lectures to local school and civic groups and at your regional theater conference.

— One of the best ways to thank volunteers is to give them a souvenir photograph of the show.

— Show slides at the cast party and at your theater group's annual meeting. Let people come up with funny comments about what's going on in the picture.

Safely store negatives and prints. Write up a list of instructions for people in charge of collecting and storing pictures in the future.

Dramatic Photos 9.7

— Prepare a promotion book for people selling ads in the playbill: include photos of recent productions along with recent playbills and a hand-out fact sheet about the current production.

— On special anniversary years, use the photos along with other memorabilia to mount a display in the town hall, the local historical museum, or other public building.

— For plays with flamboyant costumes, ask your local quick-copy printer to help you enlarge photos to life size. Cut away the backgrounds and mount the figures on foam-core or other stiff cardboard. Place these in prominent places for unusual displays.

Four kinds of poses

Whether planning for newspaper publicity or other promotional uses, you can expect to photograph four major kinds of poses: *head shots, action poses, design photos* and *backstage pictures.*

Head Shots

Head shots are head-and shoulder-portraits (unless you're a boxer, of course, in which case we're speaking about a more violent kind of, um, development—!).

If you use head shots in the playbill beside biographies, it's customary that only photos of the actors and director appear. Ignore this tradition at your peril. Once you decide to add a head shot of the stage manager, general manager, choreographer or band conductor, it's a slippery slope toward making your playbill look like a high school yearbook! However, for newspaper publicity purposes, such as home town stories and feature articles, you might include head shots of the choreographer, set designer, costumer or other creative personnel.

To mail to newspapers, head shots need not be larger than a 4-by-5-inch print. These fit conveniently in regular envelopes, a real savings over the cost of larger prints that would require larger envelopes and higher postage.

Head shots are also useful to display in the lobby of your theater. Chapter 14 on **Signs and Displays** offers tips on how to display head shots in the lobby.

For lobby display and playbill purposes, it's traditional to photograph head shots of actors without makeup or costume accessories. Audiences who see what the actors look like in real life appreciate the craft of acting all the more.

Professional theater photographer Bob Thomas from Leominster, Mass., offers this valuable tip for taking head shots: "Have your set construction people make up a flat: Paint it dull black or gray, or cover the flat with a felt or velveteen material and smooth out every wrinkle. Use this as your background, and use the same background color for each show. Over time, your head shots will have a consistency that will make your lobby displays look professional.

"Show actors the contact sheets and let them pick their own shots. This improves your relationship with them." To that advice I have to add this caveat: Be prepared to reassure the insecure actor who can't stand any of the photos.

DRAMATIC PHOTOS: Showcase emotions to tell your audience what it can look forward to experiencing at the theater. No special backdrop needed — only bold lighting and powerful poses. [Photographers: Thomas A. Hoebbel, top left and right; Norman Roy, right and bottom right; George Chartier, bottom left.]

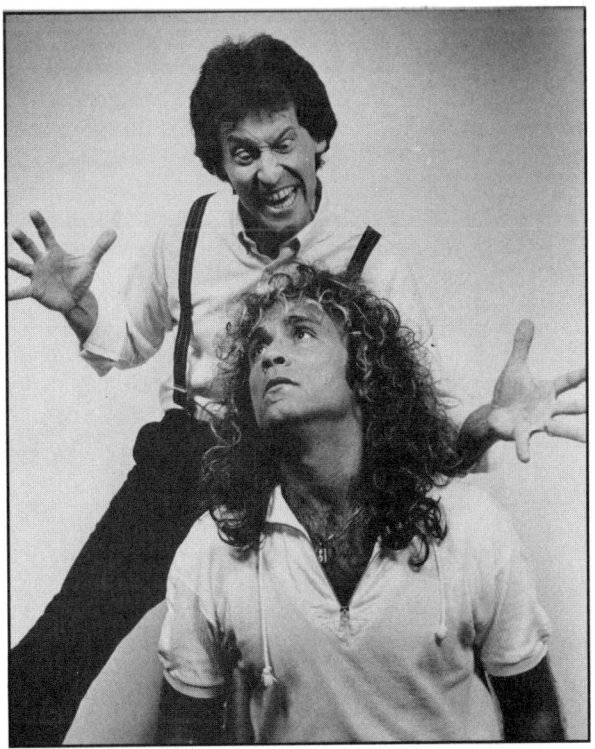

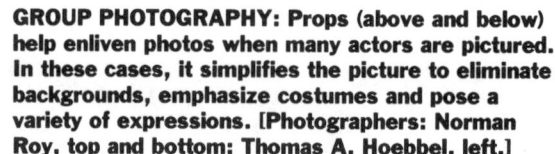

GROUP PHOTOGRAPHY: Props (above and below) help enliven photos when many actors are pictured. In these cases, it simplifies the picture to eliminate backgrounds, emphasize costumes and pose a variety of expressions. [Photographers: Norman Roy, top and bottom; Thomas A. Hoebbel, left.]

9.10 Full House

POINT OF VIEW: The dramatic mood of a photo can be intensified by altering the normal perspective of the viewer. Stand on a chair (below) or a ladder (right), or scoot down on your knees (below right) to magnify a new perspective. [Photographers: Robert Thomas, right and below right; Norman Roy, below.]

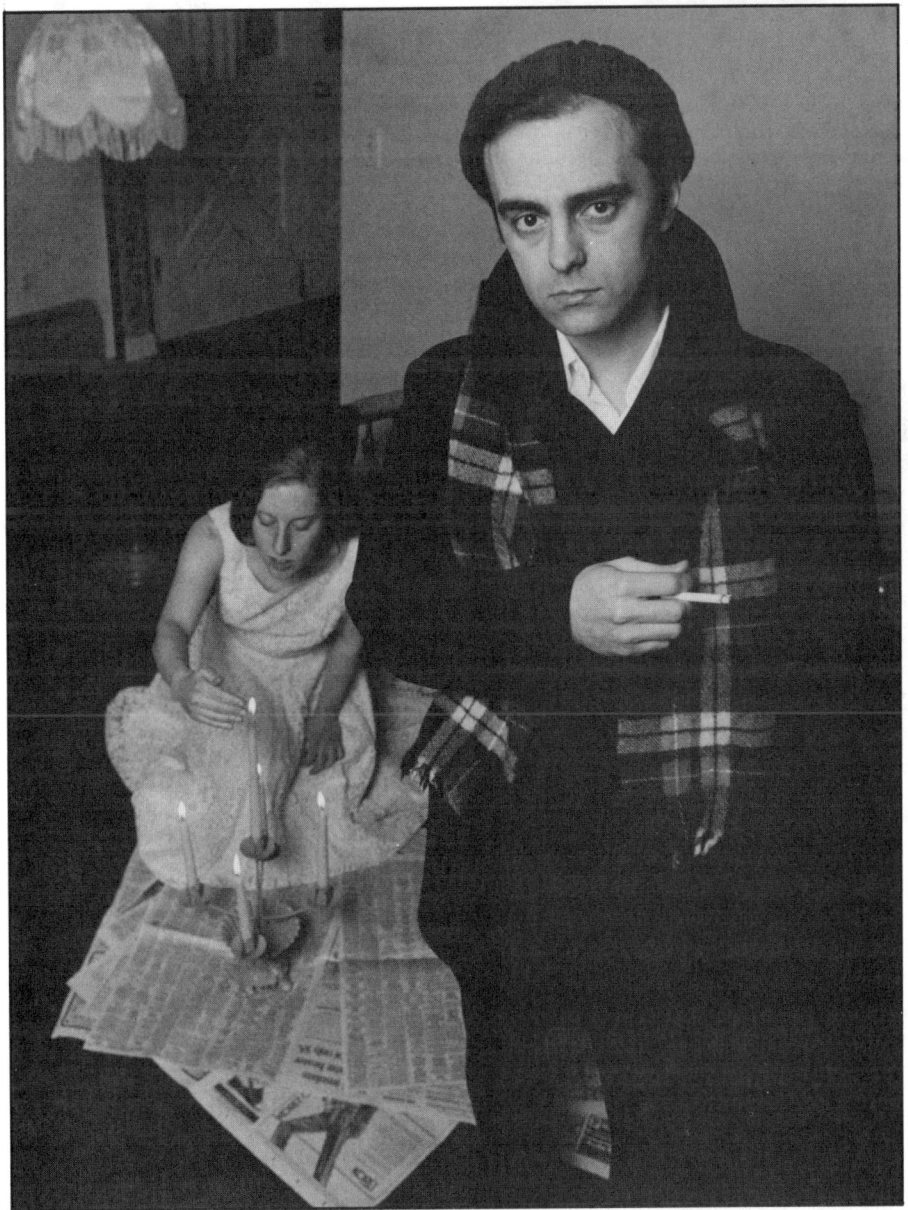

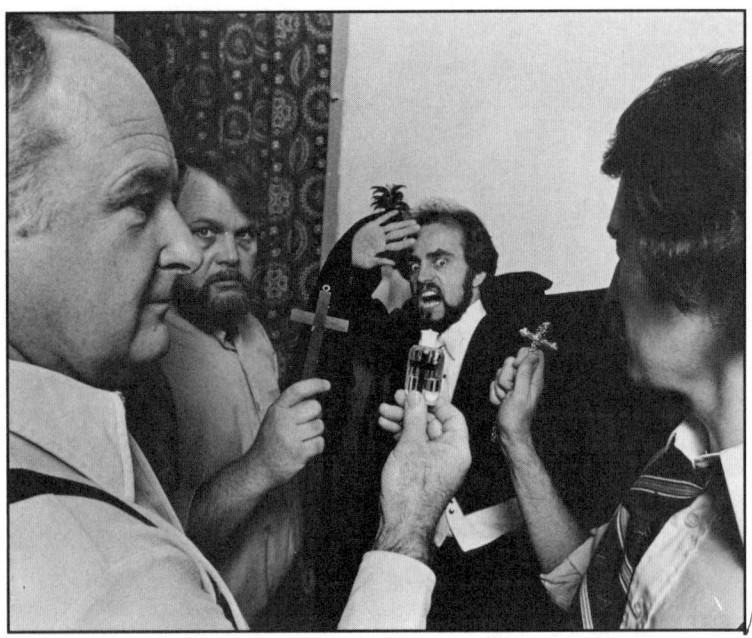

MOOD AND MISCHIEF: A busy photo with many actors (above) can be simplified by eliminating all but the essential elements. The result (right) is a more powerful photo. A trick double exposure (below) appropriately promotes a stage version of *Dr. Jekyl & Mr. Hyde*. [Norman Roy photos.]

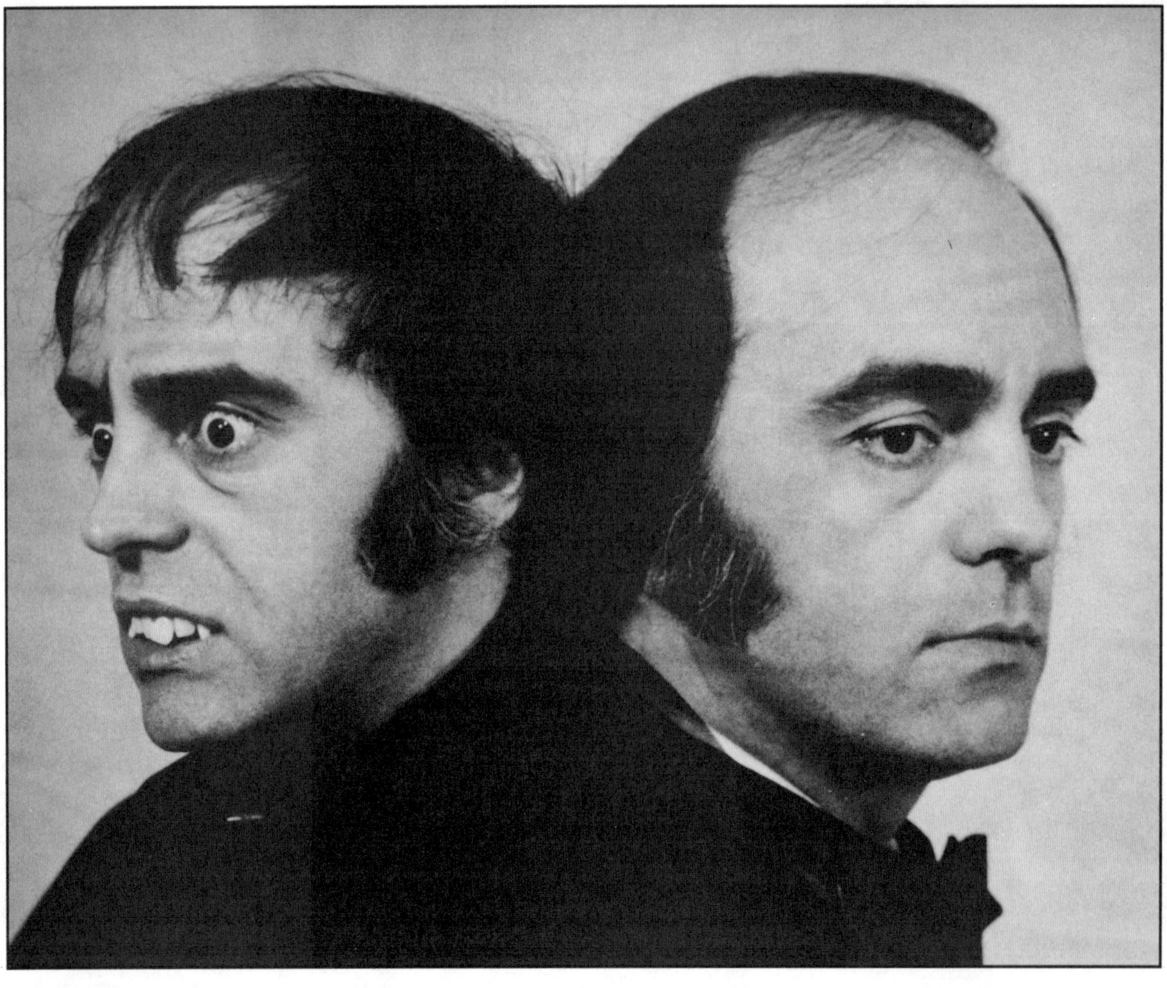

9.12 Full House

See the section called *Lights! Camera! Hold It!* later in this chapter for more tips from Bob Thomas.

Action Poses

This chapter began with examples of action poses that newspapers don't want and how to correct these common errors. The emphasis is on the word a-c-t-i-o-n. Show some action — or *reaction* — in these pictures.

Action poses for news releases should be printed on either 5-by-7 or 8-by-10-inch paper. Since newspapers almost never publish photos larger than 5 by 7 inches, it seems to me a great waste of money to print 8-by-10-inch photos for editors. As with head shots, you'll save on the smaller sized envelopes, too. The exception is the occasional knock-out, eye-popping, WOW photograph that you know will impress an editor. Go ahead and splurge on big prints if you're lucky enough to get a photo like that.

If you plan displays in store windows or lobbies of banks or libraries you'll need large action photos.

Besides taking publicity photos early in the rehearsal schedule, you should take both black-and-white and color pictures of the best scenes from your play either at dress rehearsal or immediately after the first or second performance. You can use these photos in brochures and displays for years to come.

After weeks of rehearsal, it's a shame not to capture the successful completion of a team effort on film. These action photos, taken near opening night, are an important historical record of your theater group. They require some effort to produce because one of two situations occur: If your photos are being taken while rehearsal is going on, people may be moving quickly and the photographer must react quickly to capture these moments. The other choice for photographing action is to ask actors to go back after a performance and run through all their costume changes and set changes so that the photographer may take formal poses. I have found success in both methods of recording the play's action.

Certainly, there are many reasons to shoot the cast after opening night. No, wait; let me rephrase that. What I mean is this: There are advantages to photographing the cast after the first performance. First of all, it's often the case that the sets and costumes are not finished until moments before the opening night curtain rises (and, often enough, not even then!). Secondly, actors move too quickly during key moments in the show to be captured on film in any other way but by posing these scenes. Thirdly, posing actors allows a photographer time needed to climb ladders or flop flat on the stage and shoot up to create dramatic pictures. Finally, special pictures, such as the entire cast assembled on stage along with the crew and management staff, won't happen unless arranged especially for the camera.

Yet, I find an energy and spontaneity in the photos taken while the actors are performing during final dress rehearsal that is often lacking in posed pictures. If you can afford the time, effort and expense, I recommend taking a few pictures during rehearsal and then supplementing them with posed pictures.

Whether your action pictures are taken on the run or posed, the publicist needs to sit through a

Action photos, taken near opening night, are an important historical record of your theater group.

rehearsal and take notes on possible shots. These shots should be discussed with the director to ensure that the key moments — as envisioned by the director, who is the creator of the production after all — are correctly captured on film. Many times during these discussions with the director I have found that I've missed some superb little moments in a play that say everything about what the play is about. The reason I'll miss these moments is because I haven't sat through every rehearsal and thought the play through anywhere near as deeply as the director who is immersed in the production.

On the other hand (oh, there is always that other hand!), beware the director who may be a genius with getting actors to speak their lines but has no eye for the visual. The publicist must step in on such occasions to decide what scenes will look best on film and will be most useful for publicity.

As I mentioned earlier, taking a photo of the entire company on the set of a show is a profitable idea: Nearly everyone in the picture will want to order at least one souvenir print and will be willing to pay a reasonable sum. Taking one good group shot is a lot less expensive than taking a score of individual pictures of the actors and crew teams.

For goodness sake, however, find a way to make full-cast pictures more lively than your run-of-the-mill class photo. Example: For a group shot of the musical *Jesus Christ Superstar*, the Suffield Players in Suffield, Conn., posed people in groups on several levels so that they were all visible on the multilevel stage. Everyone's arms extended either straight up in the air or outward as if acknowledging applause. A fog machine was set to run on high to create an eerie background, and then lights were aimed to shine through the fog like majestic search beams. The picture was shot from floor level, looking up to the actors.

I've said it before and I'll repeat it here: We're in theater, folks. Let's get dramatic!

See the section on *Posed Photo Sessions* for more tips on taking action photos.

Design Photos

Your costume, set, lighting and properties designs should be showcases for your creative staff. Preserve their creations on film. Take both full-view and close-up photographs. You can use these in displays, to illustrate points during fund-raising and friend-raising lectures to local groups like the Chamber of Commerce, and to boost your theater group's fame in local, regional and even national craft and design magazines. These publications are always looking for a well-illustrated how-to article. They often pay, too.

Backstage Pictures

Your technical crew, designers and administrative staff are important people. Sadly, too often only the actors get their pictures taken. Have a camera loaded and ready to capture these moments for displays, lectures and posterity:

▲ the costume designer pinning an actor during a fitting.

▲ the lighting designer holding up and looking through several gels, or a lighting crew member adjusting a lamp from atop a ladder.

▲ set construction — before, during, and final steps.

▲ set design: the bare stage before and the fully dressed set.

▲ the properties person assembling a clever creation, such as dipping wood or polystyrene chunks in paint to create a heap of prop chocolates for a party scene.

▲ the choreographer putting dancers through the paces.

▲ the rehearsal pianist at the keyboard, surrounded by singers working out a new tune.

▲ the sign painters lifting off a stencil.

▲ the publicity crew assembling a bulletin board display.

▲ the director in a quite moment of reflection.

▲ the sound crew with earphones, hunched over their tape players.

▲ the musicians tuning up.

▲ the photographer lining up actors for a group shot.

▲ the lone house manager doing a final check before doors open, standing amid a sea of empty seats.

While we're on the subject, pleasepleaseplease — ! — don't forget to take pictures of the pizza parties and the picnics where you'll find people hugging and laughing. Include these moments of pure joy that don't show anyone working when you prepare a brochure or poster or playbill advertisement to recruit new actors, staff and crew. Everyone wants to join an organization that portrays its people having fun and not just working all the time.

Posed photo sessions

Ask the stage manager to arrange for all the actors to be on hand at an agreed time and location to be photographed for publicity. Print up a small flier (you can fit several on a standard sheet of paper) with the date, time and location, and hand these to the actors as a reminder.

For photos taken early in the rehearsal schedule, discuss the play with the director ahead of time and agree on about eight poses. Make a list of suggested props and costume accessories based on your discussion with the director and ask the stage manager to hand the list to the persons in the show in charge of props and costumes, along with directions to have these items ready on the day of the photo session. A couple of long mirrors should be on the list so that actors can check their costumes and makeup. Ask the director to have a makeup artist on hand with supplies if the show features special character makeup.

A few days ahead, call the stage manager to see if the props and makeup artist are ready. Call the photographer and confirm plans.

When the photographer arrives, offer a warm welcome and introduce the director, stage manager and cast.

A time saver: Before photographing action poses, take the head shots. While individual head shots are being taken, other actors can be getting into costume. During photo sessions, I try not to leave actors standing around with nothing to do.

If a photographer with limited experience is taking the pictures, consider these tips:

Take pictures of the pizza parties and picnics to use in brochures to recruit new people. Everyone wants to join an organization having fun and not just working.

Discuss the play with the director ahead of time and agree on the poses. Make a list of props and costume accessories

- ✓ Use an un-ironed cloth or other plain background so that your actors stand out.
- ✓ Stand actors at least 18 inches away from the background so they don't cast shadows (especially with the camera flash).
- ✓ Triangulate your lighting (see details later in this chapter) to properly light your subject and eliminate ugly shadows.
- ✓ Take several frames of the same pose in case actors flinch or close their eyes.
- ✓ Watch out for shadows cast onto faces by hats, hands or the bodies of other actors.
- ✓ Lessen annoying reflections of shiny objects with a coating of hair spray.

Regardless of who's photographing, remember the actor's chant, "Rings and watches": If the play's characters shouldn't be wearing these, remind the actors to pocket the items.

Before taking any action pictures, you or the director should review the plot of the play with the photographer (if you hadn't already done so before the day of the photo session). If the photographer is familiar with the show, ask what poses come to mind. Let the photographer re-pose actors after you or the director have set up a scene. Even if you don't like all the photographer's suggestions, let him or her snap a few extra poses. This avoids hurt feelings and — who knows? —the poses might surprise you! Remember, however, not to take up too much of the actors' time with a lot of experimenting.

Shoot everything that moves?

When photographing scenes from your show close to opening night, you don't need every scene captured on film — just a few of the best. It's important to get a variety of scenes. I like to be sure that at least one close-up and one full-length shot of every major actor is included in the list of photos I prepare ahead of time with the director. I also try to get a wide view of each major stage set. Ask the lighting crew if the lights can be run at a level or two higher than normal so you get plenty of light on stage.

Lights! camera! hold it!

Professional photographer Bob Thomas takes pictures for many theater groups and has developed a system that works. The directions that follow are for taking still, posed pictures. Imagine that you're either taking early publicity shots or shots right after opening night. In the latter case, the audience has left and the stage manager has asked the actors to come back on stage — first for a group shot of the entire cast, and then for specific scenes.

Here's Bob Thomas:

"I definitely prefer to pose actors. It only takes about 20 minutes if the costume and scene changes are simple.

"I set up two flash strobes with reflectors in the audience. To set off my strobes, I use a radio remote control on my camera. A flash attached to the camera is not that great. Faces tend to bleach or the on-camera flash will create weird shadows behind the actors. The strobe lights avoid these problems and override the orange tone that the tungsten stage lights produce with color film.*

Taking a light reading

"I focus the lights on the stage to get the maximum coverage. Then I stand on the stage where the actors will be placed. Using the remote control unit, I fire off the flashes and with a hand-held light meter, I take several readings from left to right along the front of the stage. Then I take light readings from the front of the stage to the back, until I know what f-stop (exposure) each area will have.

"The flash meter is pre-set with a shutter speed of 1/60 of a second, and an ASA (film speed) of 125. As the flashes fire, the meter records the exact light output and calculates the correct f-stop. I try to shoot at f-8; this ensures a good depth of field, or deep focus, which is essential for large groups. A good depth of field means that the last row of people is in as good focus as the first row.

"I always do the [full] cast shot first. That way, if there is a large chorus some of them can leave and you can concentrate on the [remaining] smaller groups.

"As you move from area to area on the stage, take new readings and move lights as necessary [to achieve an f-8 exposure]. I try to work in one basic area to save time, using wide-angle and close-up lenses to compose my shots.

"Don't limit yourself to one shot per scene. Try different angles. When doing the full cast photo, always take three or four frames, bracketing [adjusting] the exposure at least once.

Head and shoulder portraits

"For portraits, I use the same flash strobes on stands that I use for the cast photos, except that I use white photo umbrellas instead of reflectors. These soften and spread out the light.

"I use three strobes. The first is the main light, or key light. This is set about 45 degrees to the subject. The second light is the fill light. This is set closer to the camera and further away from the subject than the main light. The third light is the hair or back light, set high and behind the subject, lighting the head and shoulders.

"The subject is sitting on a stool in front of the backdrop. Using the light meter, I take separate readings for each strobe, adjusting the position of each one until I obtain a certain ratio [minus 1, 1, and plus 1] among the lights. For example:

"If the main light reads f-8, then set the fill light at one stop less (f-5.6 or f-4), and set the hair light one stop more (f-11).

"Once again the flash meter is pre-set to a shutter speed of 1/60th of a second— the normal synchronized shutter speed setting for the camera when using a flash.

"Use a tripod. This keeps the camera steady and provides consistency in framing from subject to subject.

With photography, there is no substitute for training, experience and equipment. Your publicity depends on it.

---

*For more tips on dealing with tungsten lights, see the section later in this chapter on choosing between print and slide film.

"When using a 2 ¼ camera I use a 150mm lens. With a 35mm camera I use an 85mm or 100mm lens. This avoids distortion that 50mm lenses can cause when shooting faces. Use Kodak VPS III 120 film or Gold 100 for color, and T-Max 100 for black and white."

Proper lighting by triangulation

If you don't have fancy camera equipment like Bob, and a professional photographer is not available, there are a few ways you can produce acceptable pictures using a good camera and some simple equipment.

Remember, however, that there is no substitute for training, experience and equipment. If you don't have any you should find someone who does. Your publicity depends on it.

If you're taking pictures early in rehearsal for publicity, you'll need to set up your own lights because no theater lights will be hung and strung yet.

Here is an inexpensive method of lighting your actors for pictures: Go to your local hardware store and buy two simple scoop lamps and a small spotlight lamp. These lamps should take ordinary 100-watt light bulbs. They usually have a single center socket and a clamp at the rear. Clamp your lights to ladders or poles. Position your lights in a triangle as follows:

Light #1, called the main light, shines on the side of the face away from the camera. Set it at a 45 degree angle about six feet from the subject. Position the main light high so that it catches the subject's eyes at 11 or 1 o'clock.

Light #2, the fill light, is close to the camera lens on the opposite side from the main light. Position the fill light farther away than the main light so that the fill light illuminates the scene but doesn't eliminate interesting shadows on the subject created by the main light.

Light #3, the accent or back light, is the spotlight. Place this high behind the subject to shine downwards toward the camera but not into the lens. The accent light brushes the hair to emphasize texture.

You may want to experiment with a fourth light, called a background light, set on a short stand hidden behind the subject and shining away from the subject and the camera. This light helps separate the subject from the background.

Once the lights are set up, use a light meter to measure the brightest light in the scene. Hold the meter, or your camera with its built-in meter, at the side of the face that will be closest to the camera when the picture is taken. With a hand-held meter, take the reading and choose the proper f-stop (how large the aperture will open to expose the film) to match the shutter speed of 60 (1/60th of a second). With a camera using a built-in light meter, set the shutter speed on your camera to 60 (1/60th of a second) and then take the light reading; adjust your aperture according to the in-camera meter reading.

A word to the wise: Try this out early before you need to take pictures for your group. It takes a little practice to get the light angles correct.

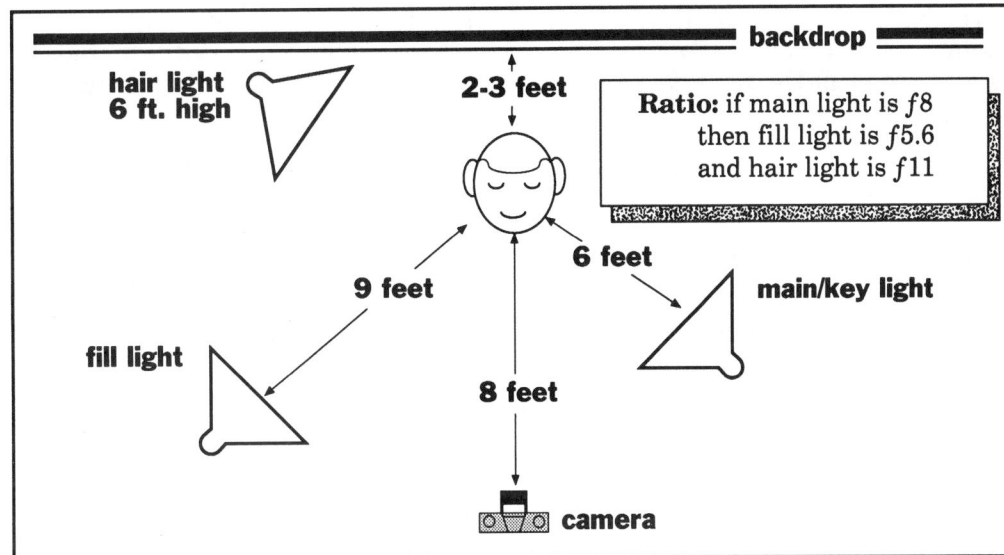

portrait lighting by triangulation

Prints or slides? slow or fast?

Color slides have certain advantages over color prints. Color prints fade quickly while slides will retain their rich colors for decades if properly stored. Color slides can be stored easily in trays or 20 to a sheet in plastic pages that go into a standard three-ring binder. At cast parties, sales calls and special events, projecting slides on a big screen creates an exciting, cinematic atmosphere.

On the other hand, most of your publicity needs demand prints, not slides.

Daylight color film — either print or slide film — will have a strong orange tone when exposed to theater lights. This is because theater lamps use a tungsten filament that has a warm orange glow that daylight film is particularly sensitive to. To correct this problem, you either have to supplement the theater lights with camera strobe or flash lights, lights on poles that use ordinary incandescent light bulbs, special film that is tungsten balanced, or a tungsten-corrective filter on your camera lens. *If you're using black and white film, you don't need to worry about tungsten color balance.*

I don't recommend using a lens filter because it slows down the speed of your daylight film. That is, you need to compensate with a drop of a full f-stop on your camera when you add a tungsten filter. It's better to buy the color balanced film. Look for the letter "T" for "tungsten" after the film number.

A word about film speed. The "faster" the film is, or the higher its ASA (or ISO) number, the more likely the film is able to absorb light quickly — an advantage in low-light situations. On the other hand, the slower the film is, or the lower the ASA, the clearer and sharper will be the image in print or slide. Outdoor daylight film has a low ASA of 25, 64 or 100. Faster indoor film is rated around ASA 400.

Kodak makes a 160T color print film available through many good camera stores. If you live too far from a good camera shop, you can order this film from big camera stores that advertise in the back of photography magazines available on your newsstand or at the library.

However, the problem with ASA 160T is that you can't use this to take action pictures during a dress rehearsal; it's too slow in the darkened theater, even with stage lights up full. When I take color pictures while actors are performing, I use an ASA 640T color film manufactured by 3-M Company and available from a supplier in California called Freestyle. Order from Freestyle toll-free at 1-800-292-6137 (in California, call 1-800-545-1011) or write to the company at 5120 Sunset Blvd., Los Angeles, CA 90027. To ask for information without ordering, call 213-660-3460.

Even at ASA 640, you may not find this film fast enough to capture scenes in a darkened theater. What I do is "push" the film. This means I double the film speed by setting my camera to ASA 1280. My camera's built-in light meter then thinks I have ASA 1280 film and gives me appropriate readings. When I take the film to the camera store or mail it for processing, I attach instructions to "push-process this roll of film once (640 x 2 = 1280)" and the film is properly developed. The result is slightly grainy pictures, but I find that for most theater groups' needs the quality of push-processed pictures are quite acceptable.

One moment, please:

At the end of the photo session, thank the actors, the stage manager, the director, crew members and the photographer. Agree on a date and location to review the contact sheet with the director. Later on, when looking over pictures with the director, keep in mind the lessons at the beginning of this chapter that describe what makes a good picture. If a picture violates these rules, think twice and three times before mailing it out to newspapers — even if the director likes the picture. You're the expert on publicity.

How to prepare captions

Photographs mailed to newspapers must be accompanied by a caption. A *caption* is a three-to-five-line description of who is in the photo, what is going on, what group is involved, and where and when the public may learn more. Write the caption so it stands independent of a news release. It's effective to give a caption a title in capital letters:

```
RADIO VOICE: Mark Quinn of
Middlesex will take on a range
of comic and  dramatic roles in
the Sutter Players' live radio
show, "1940s Radio Hour" opening
May 10 at Sutter Grange Hall on
Grange Road in Mansfield.
Tickets: 627-6767.
- Photo by Dusty Shutter
```

Type the caption on the bottom half of a full sheet of stationary, and tape the top of the photo to the top half of the page in this way: Put the tape on the rear of the photo like a hinge, so the image side of the photo won't be damaged when the tape is torn away. The sheet with the caption is taped to the picture so they won't get separated in the newsroom. Include a MEDIA CONTACT note and a release date on the caption sheet, just like a news release.

Finally, on a crack and peel label, type the name of your group, the name of the show, production dates

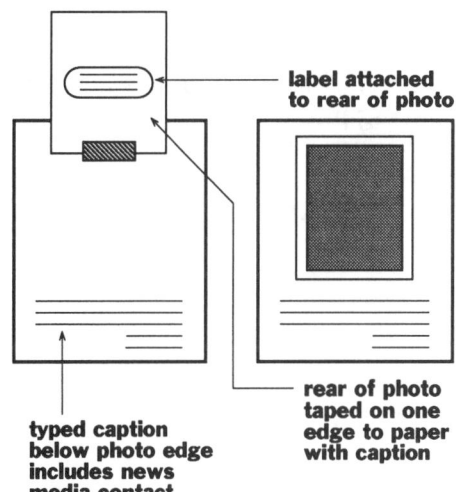

Mail photos in an envelope with a cardboard insert to lessen the chance of the envelope being folded and the photo becoming damaged. Write "PHOTOS — DO NOT BEND" on the envelope (write on your envelope before inserting pictures).

Saving money on mailings

If your news media mailing list is large, your expenses for photographic prints may become a budget-buster. You can control costs in two ways: Limit the number of pictures you mail, or save money through a volume discount.

If you want or need to make many duplicates of photographs to send to an extensive media list, check your telephone directory's yellow pages for a big-city photo processing lab that specializes in large volume, discount printing.

Not every news release needs a photograph, and no newspaper will publish a photograph with every story it prints. Stagger your photo

All photographs mailed to newspapers must be accompanied by a caption.

(including the year), the names of the persons pictured, and a photo credit line the (name of the photographer). *Stick this to the back of the photo* just in case the caption and photo get separated.

Never write on the back of a photo — the pressure of the pen or pencil could show through and damage the picture. Don't use paper clips, either; they'll also mar photos. Don't use glue or rubber cement because these will damage photos over time.

Newsweekly:	Globe	Herald	Tribune	Journal
News release #4 (Tickets on sale)		A	B	C
News release #5 (Feature story)	A		D	
News release #6 (Hometown story)	E	F	G	H
News release #7 (Reminder photo)	B	C		

distribution. If you have four weekly newspapers in your region that will take news about your theater group, work out a photo schedule.

In the chart on page 9.21, the letters A, B, C, etc., represent different photographs (E, F, G and H are head shots). The four news releases (#4, 5, 6 and 7) are described in detail in Chapter 7. This chart shows how, by staggering photo mailings and being selective, you can cut your mailings by more than 25 percent and still cover the territory.

Summary

- ☞ Sending photographs to your newspaper doubles your chances of getting your story published. Photos for newspapers should always be black and white.

- ☞ Close-ups or waist-to-head shots are more dramatic than full-body poses.

- ☞ Most likely to be printed in the newspaper: photos with contrasting expressions, photos shot at unusual angles, and photos showing physical conflict or tension.

- ☞ Find a good photographer and be prepared to pay well for the service. Good photos are rare and worth the cost in resulting better publicity.

- ☞ Take publicity photos six weeks before opening night to allow time for developing, printing and mailing.

- ☞ Include a caption with every photo you send.

- ☞ Save money by staggering your photo mailings.

Media Relations

Chapter 10

- Newsroom organization
- When the media ignores you
- News kits
- Reviews vs. previews
- Dealing with radio and TV
- The news conference

Publicists live with dread: The dread of getting something wrong in a news release or on a poster. The dread of missing a deadline. The dread of opening up a newspaper day after day and never finding any of your news published, which brings with it the dread of no one showing up for your production.

There is also the dread of being misquoted when a reporter calls for an interview, the dread of a bad review, and the dread of just not knowing how to talk to a journalist when things aren't going well.

This chapter will help ease the dread, although it will never completely go away. A healthy fear of the news media is important to keep publicists from getting cocky and taking journalists for granted.

Journalists are very directed people. They are always looking for a story. Experienced journalists have keen powers of observation and sharp memories. They are busy, busy people, too, and easily become cynical about public relations people who want to use the news media to hustle news about their clients. The reason journalists are like this is partially because the job makes them this way, but also because people with these traits are drawn to the profession.

It is possible to develop a pleasant working relationship with journalists, but a professional publicist should also keep in mind the business relationship when dealing with them. They have a noble and important job to do: keeping the public informed. A publicist's job is similar, although more narrow and biased. The more a publicist understands and sympathizes with a journalist's job, the better the relationship and the more the two professionals can do for each other.

Newsroom organization

When you mail a news release to a radio, television or newspaper newsroom, your words may pass through many hands. At the newspaper, your release may travel from reporter to arts editor to managing editor, typesetter, paste-up artist, and printing press camera operator.

In the radio newsroom, your PSA may go to the news director, while an offer to give away free tickets will be directed to the marketing manager. The host of a radio talk show will receive your news about your show opening.

In the news department of a small television station, your news release goes to the news director. At a large station, the news director has an assistant, called an assignment editor, who keeps a calendar of possible news stories and assigns TV crews a list of stories to cover each day.

Find out who your contact is for every newsroom on your mailing list. Address your releases to them by name and title, and update your lists once a year.

If the media ignores you...

If you find after awhile that your releases and photos are regularly ignored by newspapers, then by all means call the editor and ask for advice on what you can do to improve your chances of getting your material considered for publication.

If possible, visit the editor with samples when seeking advice. This will give you an opportunity to shake hands and establish a rapport with editors and reviewers. If you've never visited a busy newsroom, do yourself and the editor a favor and make an

If your releases are regularly ignored by newspapers, call the editor and ask for advice

appointment to visit briefly. It's an education! Many newspapers offer formal tours. If you plan on joining a tour, phone ahead to arrange a brief meeting with the arts and entertainment editor.

However, avoid frequent visits to the newsroom that may result in making you a pest. Editors are busy people. Save your visits for an initial "hello," a meeting when you find you're not getting any coverage, and the occasional emergency delivery when you need to ask for a favor in person.

Journalists will probably tell you that their greatest complaint is that they receive publicity material too late for them to use, and that the material isn't in the proper form (Chapter 8 on **News Releases**). They'll also lament that there isn't room for your material all the time because news space is limited.

If you hear these complaints but you still believe that you're submitting good material correctly, be understanding but persistent: Ask again how the material you've brought along would be more *useful* to the journalist and more *appropriate* for publication or broadcast. Journalists will always find room for an interesting story.

Journalists live and die by deadlines, so when you call, always ask if the journalist is on a deadline. Try to contact journalists very early before deadline or a little while after deadline. If you're contacting a newspaper that appears on newsstands first thing in the morning, you're likely to find a sympathetic ear at the newspaper from 11 a.m. until 3 or 4 p.m., before the evening deadline looms. Journalists writing for a newspaper that publishes in the afternoon are working on deadline from early morning until around 11 a.m. Anytime after that is best to pick up the phone.

Do you really want to make a journalist feel good? When you call and introduce yourself, start off the conversation with a sincere compliment. Mention an article from the previous day or two that struck you as well-written. The reporter or editor will be pleased because 99 percent of the comments journalists hear about their articles are complaints. Be prepared to hear the journalist faint with a thud when you say "Nice job!"

Just don't polish the apple too long. Move on to the purpose of your call. Time is money — yours and especially theirs.

News kits

A news kit contains all your publicity information on a show: news releases, photos, a minature poster, a season brochure, fact sheets on the show and on your group, directions to the theater, and a coupon for a free non-alcoholic drink at the refreshment bar. The kit is usually a folder with the name of the group and the show on the cover and two pockets on the inside to hold materials.

How you present your kit is important. You may want to select colors or patterns for your folder that tie in with your show or with your theater group. You can carry the color theme right through to your envelope to help your mailing stand out among the dozen or more look-alike manila envelopes most editors receive every day. Office supply stores and stationery departments sell large mailing envelopes in bright colors.

With color envelopes you need to use white address labels, however. Computerized post office character-readers have trouble making out lettering against a color background.

Always have one or more kits in the box office, and instruct the box office manager to keep them on hand in case a reporter shows up unannounced and needs information on the show.

Dealing with reviewers

If you want a newspaper to write a review of your show, call the newspaper about four weeks before opening night. Ask for the editor in charge of the arts and entertainment pages.

When you get through to the person working at this desk, identify yourself as the publicist for your theater group, briefly explain that your group is producing a show that opens on such-and-such a date, and ask if the newspaper could send a reviewer for opening night. Offer to send the editor or the reviewer a news kit.

Your chances of getting a fair review are improved when the reviewer reads your news kit. This is because your kit, and especially your feature stories, will familiarize the reporter with the underlying themes of the play, the director's vision, and your group's efforts to present the play in an interesting and entertaining manner. A news kit won't guarantee a good review, but if the material inside is well written, it gives your show a fighting chance.

Here are more tips for dealing with reviewers:

▲ After securing a preliminary agreement from the newspaper to send a reviewer, mail the news kit immediately and, about a week later, phone the reviewer and ask (1) if the kit arrived, (2) if the reviewer has had a chance to look at it, and (3) if there are questions about the show.

▲ Let the reviewer know you'll set aside a pair of tickets at the box office in his or her name, and ask if the reviewer has a seating preference. Offer to seat the reviewer in the middle of the audience — not in front or on the aisle — so the reviewer can take notes without feeling conspicuous. Be aware that occasionally a journalist will take advantage of the offer of complimentary tickets and ask for more than the standard two. In fact, I've heard of one journalist who regularly gets four or more so that she can bring her whole family. Discuss this possibility with your theater group's business manager and be prepared to either allow extra free tickets to maintain good will, or to tactfully decline the request. I don't think it's proper for a journalist to ask for free tickets at all, but I realize that a theater may have to compromise if the publicist fears offending a reviewer.

▲ The night before the reviewer is to arrive at the theater, call up again to verify that the reviewer is coming and has read the news kit. In case of a last-minute cancellation, ask the reviewer or editor to send a substitute and request that the substitute receive the news kit immediately to study. Be prepared to hand-deliver a new kit if the newspaper has misplaced the first one.

▲ Never put a reviewer on the spot after the show by asking "How did you like it?" Instead, say "Thanks for coming" in a warm, sincere manner, and then just hope for the best.

Your chances of getting a fair review are improved when the reviewer reads your news kit.

▲ If you don't like the published review, it's better to say nothing. You won't get a retraction printed, and your angry letter to the editor will just make enemies at the newspaper. Learn from the experience and try next time to provide the reviewer with material that will better educate the writer about the show. Or, just don't invite the reviewer back. Whatever happens, resist the temptation to complain.

▲ If you like the review, it is not necessary to thank the reviewer merely for doing his or her job. Never, ever offer a journalist a gift. (Free tickets and the free drink at the theater is merely to cover the reporter's business expenses.) However, if you believe the reviewer has written a particularly *perceptive* or *balanced* review that clearly shows that the reviewer put a lot of time and *effort* into the writing, you may send a brief, polite, reserved note stating this. Note this key difference: It is okay to congratulate a journalist for being professional, but it is the kiss of death to offer thanks for allegedly favoring your group.

Reviews: to be or not to be...

I am always wary of reviews. Reviewers from small newspapers may be inexperienced in reviewing or theater work. The potential runs high at small newspapers that you'll encounter a reviewer with a cruel streak or a blind spot for certain genres.

The first thing to ask yourself is whether you *need* to be reviewed.

Grade school and secondary school theater is almost never reviewed because the shows usually have a brief one-weekend run, and by the time the review is published, its key purpose — to help the public decide whether to attend — is gone. Besides, these young people are too inexperienced to warrant a review.

On the other hand, college theater, presenting students who are following a dramatic arts curriculum, is often required to be critiqued. The difference between college and community theater is that college theater involves people being professionally trained, while community theater almost always comprises untrained people performing theater for low-cost fun.

Community theater, then, runs the greatest risk of being unfairly panned. At a large newspaper, you run the risk of encountering a critic who has seen lots of professional Equity shows and may measure your theater group's amateur performance by this yardstick. A good defense against this is to read published reviews to find out whether your big-city critic believes it's wrong to "spare the yardstick and spoil the amateur." Stay away from a critic that likes to show off how much he or she knows about the theater.

Once more with feeling: Read published reviews before deciding if you want that writer talking about your show in public. No review is preferable to an unfair one.

Reviews are necessary in big cities where the public wants to know what they're in for before buying an expensive ticket. Big city theaters want to be reviewed (sometimes) because word of mouth doesn't travel quickly enough to fill large theaters night after night for long runs. For most amateur productions that run just two weekends, however, I regard a review as a waste of promotional effort and an unnecessary risk.

Now that I've scared you nearly out of your wits, let me say that reviews are valuable, and if you have confidence in your theater company's production and in the integrity of the reviewer, invite a reviewer by all means. You can enlarge the published review on a photocopy machine and display it in your lobby, and reprint the best words of praise in your playbills and fund-raising literature.

When the review is published, make copies for everyone in the show or prepare an enlarged one to be posted by the cast and crew's coffee pot. But *before* you distribute copies or post the review — good or bad — *show the review to the director*. The director is in charge of the show and should be the one to officially break the news — good or bad — to the company.

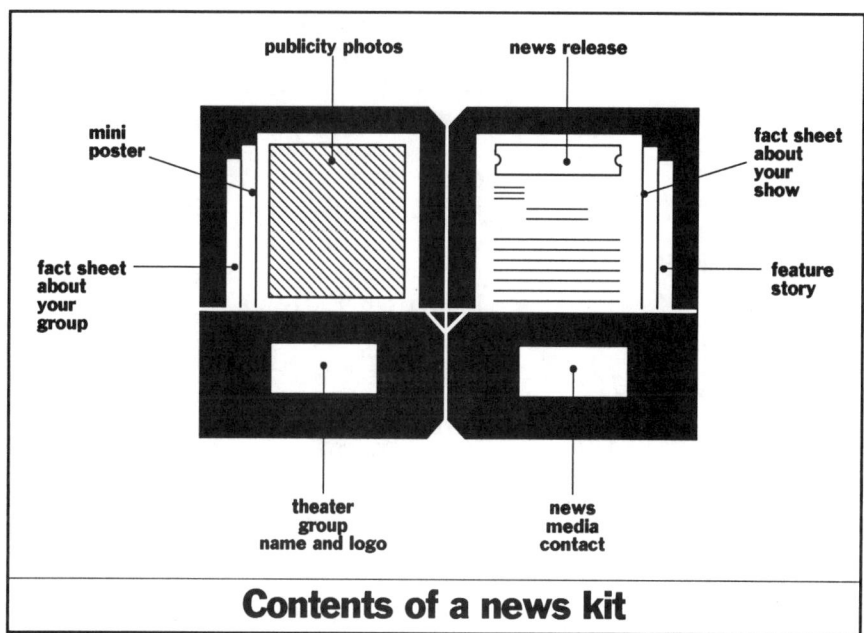

Contents of a news kit

Previews vs. reviews

I advocate working with the news media to create a *preview story* rather than a review. It serves the public better because the news is out sooner. In small and mid-sized towns, an opening night review won't get published until after the first weekend, and by that time half the potential audience has seen the show and won't benefit from the review. In a two-week run, an unfair review will kill the second weekend and there won't be time for word of mouth to correct the damage.

A preview story in a daily newspaper usually appears a day or two before opening night. A journalist is invited by the publicist to stop in at rehearsal about a week before opening night. The journalist can observe a few scenes, collect some colorful details about the busy comings and goings of the crew, and interview the director and some of the actors.

Since the production is still in rehearsal, a responsible journalist will never report that the show is not worth seeing, no matter how bad things look. The preview story almost always tells readers how hard everyone is working and how everyone is looking forward to opening night. The preview story also is likely to focus more on the director's philosophy and the playwright's ideas rather than on the quality of the acting.

Preparing for the interview

If there's no time to send information ahead, have a news kit waiting for the journalist who comes to rehearsal to write a preview story. Offer a photocopy or text from the playbill if the finished playbill hasn't been printed yet. Discuss the probable publication date of the story to be sure the journalist understands the public's need to see the preview before opening night.

You should know about an ironclad rule in journalism: *The journalist will not show you a copy of the story before publication.* Don't ask to see the story. If you have concerns about the journalist's approach, gently bring up

Stay away from a critic that likes to show off how much he or she knows about the theater.

The preview story almost always tells readers how hard everyone is working and how everyone is looking forward to opening night.

your concern with the journalist after the interview. A less direct approach is to ask what angle or direction the journalist sees the story heading, or what the journalist sees as the focus of the story. Don't argue with the journalist, of course; if you have a disagreement, casually ask if the journalist has considered this or that idea. Keep the conversation amicable.

You should coordinate the journalist's visit with the director's schedule. Be sure the cast and crew all know that the journalist is coming. Equity actors require notice of still and video shoots, but even non-professional actors and directors are self-conscious about being watched by outsiders while they work. I learned this the hard way once when a camera crew I'd arranged to come to rehearsal arrived without my having warned the actors. One actor was so upset at the prospect of facing a camera crew and possibly blowing his lines that he stormed off the stage and quit the show. I thought he — or the director — was going to kill me!

Try to have some costumes and props ready because a photographer may very well accompany the journalist.

Review speaking points with the director to be sure the director's thoughts are organized; a week before opening night, the director has a lot of details to think about.

Arrange for a quiet corner at the rear of the rehearsal hall for the director and the journalist to talk without interruption. Stay nearby while the interview takes place so that you may keep others away and still be handy should the director need you to answer a question. *Don't hover* over the director and the journalist, however. Your job was to put these two people together. Now let them do their jobs.

What to say in the interview

To get the best results out of an interview, you should prepare your actors and director.

Whoever is being interviewed, they'd better know a few things about the history of the play, including any awards it won, where and when it was first staged and who starred in the first production. If the play was made into a movie, questions will certainly come up about this. Biographical information about the playwright is almost always a source of conversation.

You may prepare fact sheets to help inform your theater people, but be sure they understand that it simply looks terrible to read off the sheets during the interview. They should learn the stuff ahead of time, just like they learn their lines for the stage. That's what the pros do, because the pros understand that selling the show isn't just the publicist's job. Anyone likely to be interviewed by a journalist better look and sound sharp.

The interviewer will ask all the typical questions posed to actors: How do you remember all those lines? How did you get into acting (or directing)? Do you want to turn professional one day? Watch out for these questions! They steal precious interview time and lead the interview away from the task at hand, which is to promote the current show. Advise anyone scheduled for an interview to steer the conversation back on track as quickly and politely as possible when these questions come up. They should talk about the play. Talk about the play. *Talk About The Play.*

The following sections on doing interviews on radio and TV offer more tips on how to sound and look good.

Live interviews on radio

Many radio stations have some type of interview format — a talk show or a morning DJ who interviews guests in the studio. These programs are always looking for interesting people, but before you make a phone call to offer to go on the air, you should think things out.

If you're promoting a musical, the guest you supply to the radio program will almost certainly be asked to sing a few lines. It will appear rude for the actor to refuse, so the actor must be prepared to sing acappella. If the actor has a strong voice and the song is an upbeat, quick tune with few pauses, it should sound okay. Review your play's royalty contract for restrictions on broadcasting any portion of a production, including live singing on radio or TV.

The actor should know how to sing into a stationary microphone. The proper way is to breathe *above* the microphone, not into it, so the p's and b's don't *ppppop* and *bbbblow* annoyingly. Singers should back off when belting out a big note so listeners aren't suddenly jolted. The actor should be prepared to sing sitting down if the only microphone available in the radio studio is the table-top kind.

Finally, the actor should bring a copy of the lyrics along. Live radio is no time to forget lines.

Two or three actors who can sing harmony sound even better.

An actor in a straight play may be asked to deliver a few lines from the show. In this case, a monologue can be very effective. The actor should rehearse how to briefly explain for listeners where the monologue fits into the play. The monologue should be at least 20 seconds but no more than 40. The actor should take a dramatic pause after the introduction before launching into the monologue. Avoid character voices with ethnic accents unless the actor can do the accents authentically, and skip such monologues if the accents are thick and likely to be difficult to understand outside the context of the play.

Giving away tickets

If you are selling tickets, you should negotiate with your show's general manager to be allowed to give away some tickets on the radio. "Papering the house" is a traditional, reliable way of getting people talking about your show.

Radio DJ's are happy to give away tickets on the air because free tickets allow the radio station a chance to reward listeners. You should never have to pay the station to give away tickets to your show.

The tickets should be given in pairs. You shouldn't need to give away more than a half-dozen pair of tickets to get word of mouth going about the show.

If you have arranged for someone in the show to be interviewed on the air, this is the perfect opportunity to give away tickets. Otherwise, call the marketing manager to arrange for tickets to be given away during specified times and days. Ask the marketing manager's advice about when the radio station has found tickets move most quickly. Normally, two days before opening night is ideal. If the tickets are given away any earlier, listeners tend to forget about the show; any later, and people don't have time to plan to attend.

Prepare a brief announcement about the show for the DJ, including a one-sentence description of the show's theme.

Selling the show isn't just the publicist's job. Anyone likely to be interviewed by a journalist better look and sound sharp.

Gift Certificate

Congratulations — you've won a free evening of live theater! This certificate is good for two free admissions to the Suffield Players opening nights production of

"PERSONALS"

the zany musical that looks at the good,
the bad and the ridiculous moments of modern dating!

OPENING NIGHTS:
Thursday, May 2 & Friday, May 3

Mapleton Hall, Suffield, Connecticut
Doors open: 7 p.m. – Curtain: 8 p.m.

To reserve your seats, call (203) 627-5749 at least 24 hours before either opening night. When you arrive at the box office, exchange this certificate for complimentary admission tickets, and get ready for a musical, wacky evening of LIVE THEATER in Suffield!

This certificate is good only for opening nights May 2 or 3 and cannot be exchanged for other performances. This certificate must be presented at the box office on the evenings of the opening performances. Because Suffield Players productions are popular, your complimentary admissions cannot be guaranteed unless you phone in your reservations.

Mapleton Hall: 1305 Mapleton Ave., Suffield, off Route 159, 1 mile south of Riverside Park

Cautionary note: "Personals" takes a humorous look at adult sexual themes.

COMMUNITY THEATER: *Entertainment That's Alive and Dramatic!*

Prepare a packet of information about the show to accompany each pair of tickets. The packet should contain a map to the theater, a flier about the show, and box office information in case the winner wants to order more tickets. Specify in the instructions that the tickets are non-negotiable; that is, they can't be turned in for cash. Explain in the instructions any rules for exchanging tickets. For example, ticket exchanges must be made before opening night or the theater cannot guarantee that seats will be available.

Stamp the tickets "complimentary" to be sure they can't be sold. Ask the radio station to write down the names, addresses and phone numbers of the winners so you can add them to your mailing list (and to verify that tickets were given away).

Working with commercial TV

Contact TV news departments sparingly — once or twice a year at the most unless you have an unusually cooperative local station and no competition in the community. It's easy to wear out your welcome with your TV news station unless you take care to understand what TV is looking for and how it operates.

Do not bombard TV with the same number of news releases you send to newspapers and do not expect constant coverage. In a major city, TV stations receive hundreds of requests a day from organizations seeking publicity. The overworked TV news room seeks only the most visual, dramatic, unusual, simple-to-understand stories that affect the broadest number of people in the community. Compared to the two dozen local stories a major town newspaper may cover in a day, a local TV station may be able to report on four or five stories on the evening news.

TV talk shows usually fall into one of two formats: "happy news" or "issues and answers." The happy news talk show interviews local artists, community volunteers, store managers with a unique product, the coordinator of next week's craft fair or antique auto parade, the student who won the recent tri-county spelling bee, and anyone putting on a show in town — upbeat, non-controversial topics.

If you book your director or actors on a happy news show, follow the advice on preparing for the on-air interview that appears earlier in this chapter; most of the advice applies. In addition, because this is TV, consider having your actors arrive at the studio in costume and makeup, but discuss this with the TV show's producer ahead of time.

Also discuss with the producer what scene the actors could present. The scene — a song, a physical scene, a romantic moment or a tense confrontation (always pick something highly emotional) should be short — about one and a half minutes to two minutes is best. The camera crew will need to know the general blocking of the actors to prepare camera shots. Actors will likely be equipped with clip-on lapel microphones during the sit-down segment of the interview, but these get in the way when they stand to do their scene. You might suggest to the producer that the actors can perform more freely if they can switch to an overhead "boom" microphone during their scene.

The issues and answers talk-show format is primarily interested in self-help stories, health news, and the controversial topic of the day. If your play has a message about AIDS, euthanasia, rape, or racial bigotry, you might have a chance. If your play is tied into a seasonal event — a murder-mystery for Halloween, a play about a political campaign around Election Day — TV could be interested. With the news media, but especially with TV, timing is everything.

Contact TV when your show has interesting, colorful costumes; unusual makeup (a monster play); dramatic action (sword duels, fisticuffs, a realistic and possibly gory death scene such as in *Julius Caesar*); dancing and singing; extremely unusual special effects (the creation scene in Frankenstein); or a well-known personality (a town selectman has a role in the show). Remember, TV is primarily visual — and coincidentally, its visual elements are often what lure your audiences to your show!

Invite TV to videotape an action rehearsal a few days before your show opens, and make sure costumes and scenery are ready. Prepare key people — a lead performer and the director perhaps — by asking them to think ahead about what they want to say about the play. Warn them that they'll have only a few fleeting seconds, so they should know what to say. They should say something that conveys the *mood* of the show: "The murder even scares me!" or "I leave every rehearsal humming the songs — they're so lovely: La-la-lumm, da dumm..." or "The hardest part of rehearsing is just getting through the scenes without laughing; we'll be in control by opening night — but just barely!" or "As a boy I dreamed of meeting Peter Pan; who'd have thought that when I grew up I'd become the boy... who never grew up?!"

As George Burns says, "It's easy to ad-lib when you rehearse."

How do you invite TV? Call the station and ask for the name and office address of the news director (at a small station) or the assignment editor (at a large station that has more than one camera crew). Send a news release to that person a week before you would like a camera crew to come out to the theater to tape rehearsal scenes. Add a stick-on note to the news release informing the TV journalist about the visual possibilities that could interest viewers.

Then, two or three days before you want TV to arrive, call your TV news room contact persons. Introduce yourself and identify the group you represent. Ask (1) whether the journalist has received your release, (2) if they think a preview of some action/costumes/special effects would interest TV viewers, and (3) if they think they can schedule a camera crew to swing by the theater during the next rehearsal.

Be careful when you make your call: Phone late morning or early afternoon. Decision-makers are making decisions around 10 a.m., so it's best to call after

TV news seeks only the most visual, dramatic, unusual, simple-to-understand stories.

11 a.m. and before 3 p.m., when the late-afternoon rush to assemble the evening news begins.

When talking to the harried assignment editor or news director, *speak slowly, articulately*, and in *short sentences*. Expect that she or he has misplaced or even never seen your news release and be prepared to explain *succinctly* what you have in mind. TV people are among the busiest people I know, so you have to get their attention and get to the point of your phone call without any unnecessary preamble.

If you get turned down, ask why and learn from the experience. No matter how abruptly you may be treated, thank the TV news person for listening. Resolve to try again.

Community access cable TV

Many possibilities exist for promoting your show with cable TV, such as creating and airing your own documentary. For details, look at the discussion on "TV or MTV" in Chapter 18, **School Promotion**.

The news conference

Let me be brief about what to do if you're considering calling a news conference: Don't. News conferences are reserved for earth-shattering, cataclysmic, industry-shaking, apocalyptic announcements. Anything less, and reporters will not show up. I can't think of a single instance when a community theater should call a news conference. Not one.

If you choose to ignore this advice and really, really, really think you've got a stop-the-presses reason to call a news conference, phone your favorite journalist first and ask for a professional opinion. Then tell your show's director to forget about the idea.

Summary

- ☞ Journalists are approachable. If you have a problem, call the newsroom and discuss your concerns.

- ☞ Get to know the journalists you'll be working with regularly. Address correspondence to them by name.

- ☞ Provide news kits to educate journalists.

- ☞ Weigh the pros and cons before inviting a reviewer. A preview story is always safer.

- ☞ Prepare the director, cast and crew for interviews.

- ☞ Consider radio's many options, including interviews and giving tickets away on the air.

- ☞ Understand that television news is competitive and unlikely to be interested in your show unless you stress the visual elements.

- ☞ Don't call a news conference.

Working With Printers

Chapter 11

- Selecting a printer
- Saving money at the print shop
- Glossary of printer's terms

Your printer doesn't know it, but he's part of your publicity team.

For the active publicist producing many kinds of promotional materials, the printer is a major business partner. If your printer fails, you fail. When he does a nice job printing your posters, fliers and playbills, you look great.

So, I humbly suggest that you select your partner carefully or you will live to regret it. Opening a carton the day before your show opens, to find a thousand or more badly printed playbills inside, is an unforgettable and avoidable experience.

What Print Shops Offer

You should pick your printer based not only on price, but on how helpful and knowledgeable the printer is. To avoid having to settle for the first available printer, do not wait for a crisis to begin your search for your business partner. Schedule a few visits to area shops to learn what they offer.

Modern print shops offer plenty. They will copy your original artwork full-size, reduce or enlarge it, produce a negative image, make a reversed or mirror image, color parts or all of a black and white original, and staple, fold, bind and seal.

The majority of modern print shops offer two basic kinds of printing: electrophotography and offset lithography. Each has advantages.

The electrophotographic, or electrostatic process is used in those wondrous photocopy machines located in every business office. Photocopy machines use static electricity and heat to fix powdered zinc or selenium onto the surface of paper. Isn't science wonderful? Many modern photocopy machines (do not make the common mistake of using the trademarked company name *Xerox* in the generic sense to describe all copy machines) produce such accurate copies that the United States Bureau of Engraving and Printing has had to redesign our currency with hard-to-copy threads woven into paper money to thwart counterfeiters.

A new generation of photocopy machines now allows you to easily produce multicolored copies of a black and white original simply by changing removable cartridges of color toner. Yes, science is wonderful!

A more complex form of color photocopying can make remarkably good full-color copies of drawings, paintings, photographs and even slides. For bulletin boards promoting a theater group's shows, I've brought color slides from rehearsal and enlarged them to 8-by-10-inch color copies at half the cost and a fraction of the time your photo store asks to produce an enlargement from the photo negative.

When you only need a few copies, color photocopying is less expensive than printing with ink. Color copying lets you produce realistic, full-color samples of a proposed project. The technology is great for making signs, awards, and other limited-edition promotional items.

New, computerized technology offered by the top photocopy machines can take an 11-by-17 inch original, enlarge it 400 percent in one shot, and print the 42-by-66-inch enlargement in 16 easy-to-assemble sheets. This technology came in handy during production of *Personals*, a musical about modern dating. The set designer asked me to find a way to cover several eight-foot stage flats with larger-than-life personal ads. I pasted together columns of want ads from the local newspaper (carefully painting out the reply box numbers to avoid legal problems), and took the ads to a printer where they were enlarged and copied several times. This stack of "wallpaper" was stapled to the flats to produce a great backdrop for a funny show.

With this technology you can produce life-size cutout copies of your starring actors that will make dandy promotional displays, or serve as stand-ins when the actors miss rehearsals. (Joking. I'm joking.)

Print shops that offer nothing more than quick photocopy services like these are usually fine if your printing needs don't include large quantities of copies. If you need more than 300 copies of something, however, you should compare the cost of photocopying to printing with ink.

The next level up from photocopy centers is the print shop that has one to four small printing presses. These presses use a paper or metal plate that has been photoengraved with the image of your original artwork. A coating of ink from a well is applied to the engraved plate; the plate's freshly inked pattern "sets off" its image onto a roller with a rubber-surfaced fabric, called a blanket; and the blanket transfers the pattern onto a sheet of paper. That's where the term *offset printing* comes from. Science again!

Like most photocopy machines, small offset presses found in quick-copy shops are usually limited to printing onto sheets of paper no wider than 11 or 12 inches. Many of these smaller machines aren't made to handle paper with a shiny or glossy surface, but they're fine for most standard printing assignments: letter and legal-sized fliers, and 11-by-17-inch posters.

From small shops you progress to large companies with presses than print two colors at the same time and print thousands of broadsides on web presses (a *web* is a large roll of paper).

The cost of color

One expense often overlooked in designing posters and other promotional materials is the cost of color ink. Most small offset presses print one color at a time and then, after the paper dries, the sheets are run through the press again with a new plate and a change of ink. To change colors on an offset press, the printer must wash off the old ink from the press rollers and the ink fountain. This prevents ink colors from mixing.

Since black ink is standard for the majority of printing projects, your printer will bill you a "press washup" charge for each additional color you request. Different colors in a multicolor job appear in different areas on your artwork, so a new printing plate is needed for each occasion that a new color ink is run through the press. You will be charged for all printing plates.

A flier printed on both sides of the paper, with two colors on each side, will need four plates — two for each side. Keep this in mind when considering ways to cut costs.

The number of copies you get from an offset printing press is inexact because ink presses can occasionally pick up more than one sheet of paper at a time, or the ink may spread unevenly on a few copies. A good printer will run more copies than you ordered to make up for the possibility of imperfect copies. When you pick up your completed order, you can check the quality and quantity of the finished product in this way: Compare samples pulled from the top, middle and bottom of the stack. To quickly estimate if you have enough copies, count out 25 copies and place this stack against the remainder; compare and multiply with your eyes the number of stacks of 25 needed to match the larger, uncounted stack.

It's rare that a printer will "short" your order, but you don't want to get to the last night of your show and find that you have 50 fewer playbills than you planned.

Like all other situations that managers encounter, you can avoid many problems by anticipating anything that could possibly go wrong. You won't think of everything, but you can cut down on the likelihood of many crises with a little foresight and checking.

Selecting a printer

Whether you're printing a letter-sized flier or a three-color poster, you need to be careful in picking your printer, because anyone with a press can set up a business and call himself a printer. Most printers are helpful and knowledgeable, but the rogue and incompetent exist in every profession.

Moreover, not every printer can handle every assignment well. Most printers can copy a letter-size flier. With more complicated projects, however, you'll want to look carefully for a printer who knows how to run large paper through a press and how to position the printing plates so that your colors come out consistently bright, even, and aligned on every copy.

When you visit a printer for the first time, ask to see a variety of samples. Look for items that resemble a project you have in mind to determine how skillfully the printer will handle yours. Ask for a price list for standard printing jobs and ask for help to understand how to estimate the cost of a project.

To learn a lot in a short time, stop in at the busy noon hour to watch customers picking up their orders. Do they look pleased as they examine their orders? Are they complaining about orders not being ready when promised? Does the printer have trouble locating an order? How well does the printer treat customers? When the printer hands over a finished product, does he take an extra moment to look over the copies one last time to be sure they're acceptable? A good printer takes pride in the quality of every job that leaves his shop.

What printers need to know:

When you go to your printer with an assignment, you should bring along everything needed to complete the job. The original artwork should be clean. Projects requiring multiple colors need separate artwork for each color printing plate.

Before working up finished art, I like to bring a detailed sketch to a printer to discuss in what form the final artwork needs to be prepared. This is particularly true for multipaged and multicolored projects.

Whether you are having a preliminary discussion, asking for a cost estimate, or presenting a finished artwork for printing, you should bring your printing needs

If you need more than 300 copies of something, you should compare the cost of photocopying to printing with ink.

When discussing a project with a printer, you should bring your printing needs written down on a "spec sheet."

written down on a "spec sheet." The "specs" or specific needs your printer will want to know include:

▲ The size paper on which your project will be printed. Sticking to standard sizes saves money.

▲ The kind of paper you want to use. Paper varies by *weight*, *thickness* and *finish*. Regular copy machine paper is rated "20-pound" stock and has a smooth, finish; fine stationary can come in 60# weight with an embossed finish that feels like linen, tweed or pebble. Thick, stiff paper comes in index stock or cover stock, which is good for posters. If your artwork contains large areas of heavy black ink, you'll want to choose a thicker paper for less see-through. The paper's surface can be finished with a dull or glossy chemical coat on one or both sides. As you've probably guessed, prices for various kinds of paper varies widely.

▲ Paper color. Fine print is hard to read on dark-colored paper.

▲ Ink. How many colors? Black counts as one color. A flier printed in red and black ink on yellow paper is a two-color job.

▲ Sides. Do you want printing to appear on one or both sides of the paper? Which colors on which sides?

▲ Copies. How many do you want?

▲ Halftones, trapping, bleeding (See the glossary at the end of this chapter.)

▲ Binding. Do you want pages stapled? How many per item and where do the staples go?

▲ Folding. If in thirds, do you want an accordion or regular fold? Provide the printer with a sample to make your wishes clear.

▲ Delivery date. When do you want the order ready to pick up?

See Chapter 7 on **Budgeting and Money Management** for an example of a spec sheet.

Saving money

Printing costs can make up a third of publicity expenses, so it pays to watch for ways to save money at the drawing board and at the print shop.

Full-color posters printed on 24-by-36-inch, heavy cardboard is out of the question for most community theater groups working with a limited budget. A powerful poster usually doesn't need a lot of color — just the right colors in the right places. Pamphlets and playbills needn't always be printed on glossy paper. There are lots of classy papers your printer can show you that cost half what you'll pay for glossy paper.

Keep in mind these options when designing on a tight budget:

1. Limit the size

If you keep your poster to 11-by-17 inches, you'll find that most quick printers have several kinds of stiff paper, called *cover stock*, available in this size, and most printing presses can handle this size. Larger posters cost more money and you'll find yourself going to larger, more expensive printing companies than you need to. Besides, libraries, schools, and stores with limited bulletin board and window space will be more willing to let you display a poster if it doesn't take up too much room. Choosing odd-sized fliers leads you to print on large paper and to pay for paper that is trimmed and thrown away.

2. Limit ink colors

Consider using only black ink for your promotional materials (and see suggestion #5). Printers use black ink all the time, and every extra color ink you add means the printer must take time to wash the black ink off the press, run the paper through with the new color, and afterwards wash that color ink off the press. A second color ink in a short-run (less than 500 copies) printing job can easily double printing costs. On the other hand, take your design to one, two or three local printers and compare charges to add one or more colors — you might find a bargain. Remember, printers consider black a color. A poster with black ink and green ink is a *two-color* poster. Printers don't have all colors on hand, so give your printer enough notice to order ahead.

3. Enhance by hand

This works for limited numbers. You can print a poster in black ink and then apply color markers, glitter or other enhancements by hand to small areas on the posters. Invite a crew to a poster party to do this, put on a video to keep the troops entertained, and you can have charming posters at low cost. With playbill covers or fliers, you may find an appropriate crack and peel colored sticker from your stationery store that a team of volunteers could apply by hand. This is time- and energy-intensive however. It may pay to print a second color if you require more than 150 copies.

4. Avoid "bleeding"

If printing runs off the edge of the paper, such as a design with an all-red background and no white border, the design is said to *bleed*. Bleeding off one or more edges is an attractive design element, but it costs extra. To get the effect of bleeding, a printer uses oversized paper to print your design with a white border, then cuts the white edges away. A ½ inch border is standard. The printer will charge you for the time it takes to trim the edges. If you have access to a large paper trimmer at work or at school, you could save bleed-trimming charges by cutting the paper yourself.

5. Consider color paper

Black ink on color paper gives the impression of two colors for the price of one. Speak with your printer ahead of time in case color paper has to be ordered.

6. Avoid halftones

To reproduce a photograph in print, the printer must convert the image into a pattern of dots, called a *halftone*. Printers charge $10.00 to $15.00 for each 8 ½-by-11-inch sheet of halftones. If you're planning to assemble a photocollage or to publish numerous photos in a flier or playbill, consider how the cost of halftones can quicky inflate your budget. Use halftones frugally or avoid them altogether. Instead, use line art (See the glossary at the end of this chapter).

7. Avoid coated paper and varnishes

Glossy posters are nice, but like extra color inks, paper that has a glossy surface or a poster that needs a layer of varnish to protect the ink can double the printing cost.

To reduce the cost of printing, limit the ink, choose less expensive paper, and eliminate halftones.

Consider printing your posters on paper instead of cardboard, especially if your posters are likely to be hung indoors. Explore with your printer the wide variety of uncoated paper available — papers with textured surfaces, for example. When trying to reduce the cost of printing, the three easiest ways are limiting the ink, choosing less expensive paper, and eliminating the cost of halftone conversions.

8. Limit the number of copies

Assume everyone in the company, including the cast, crew and board of directors will take one poster as a souvenir, and these will never go up in the drug store window, the library door or the bank bulletin board. Calculate carefully how many posters you'll really need, and note over several shows if either too many posters are left over or, just as bad, if you run out too quickly and wish you'd printed more. Don't leave stacks of posters unattended. Bring posters to the theater and ask people to sign for them; note the number taken and where in town they'll be placed. Don't be overly stingy, but avoid being too generous.

Allow cast and crew one souvenir playbill each but ask the house manager to instruct ushers to be cautious after this. If you see theater personnel grabbing heaps of "extra playbills" for friends and your budget is too tight to permit this unchecked, lock playbills in the office between shows. Ushers can be trained to understand that these materials are in short supply, and then to politely ask "how many do you need?" After each show, playbills left behind by the audience can be collected and inspected for re-use if some are still in fine shape.

Over the course of a few shows you will learn to predict better how many playbills you need to print.

9. Give the printer enough time

A printer has every right to hit you with a hefty "rush charge" if you come in at noon and want 300 posters printed by 5 p.m. the same day or 1,500 20-page playbills by tomorrow. Avoid rush charges and threats on your life by checking with your printer to learn how much time various jobs require.

10. Use several proofreaders

There is an especially painful and deserved place in hell for artists and writers who trust their own eyes, and you'll know this the first time fifteen people call you and say the phone number for the box office is wrong after posters are up all over town! Believe me, this nightmare is more likely to happen than you can imagine. Fortunately, there's an easy way to avoid the cost of printing something twice: Before taking the mechanical to the printer, ask several people in your theater group to carefully read everything to be sure the details and spelling are all correct. Ask someone who is not in your group to examine your mechanical, too; theater people may overlook crucial information that an outsider will recognize is missing.

11. Get advance advice

Show your preliminary design to the printer and discuss the order a week or more before it's due to be dropped off for printing. A good printer will suggest how you can redesign your poster or flier to avoid costly things like bleeding edges, odd-sized paper and expensive inks. Of course, if your printer is willing to trade the cost of printing for an advertisement in your playbill, or if a major business is willing to underwrite the printing cost, this is the best way to save on posters!

A glossary of printer's terms

ART - All illustrated materials — photos, drawings, etc. —used in preparing a job for printing.

BLEED - If a printed image extends to the edge of the paper, with no border, this is called "bleeding." It implies that the ink runs, or bleeds, off the paper. If you want one or more edges to bleed, the image must be printed on larger paper and then trimmed to size. Bleeding can make artwork look dramatic, but you'll pay for the larger paper and trimming.

BLOW-UP - Any image that is enlarged is a *blow-up*.

BOARDS - Thick, flat cardboard onto which is pasted original artwork and type. You compose your *mechanicals* on boards, and hand the boards to the printer.

BODY TYPE - Lettering used for the main part or text of a printed piece, excluding section titles, headings, headlines and other display type.

BOLD FACE - **Lettering that is heavier than the text type.**

BROCHURE - A pamphlet bound in booklet form (see FLIER).

CAMERA-READY - The form in which your original artwork must be for the printer to reproduce on the press. A camera-ready original, or *mechanical*, has all the text pasted down, and all drawings and halftones reduced and pasted in place. If you hand a printer a mechanical with instructions to reduce a separate piece of artwork and past it onto the board, your mechanical isn't camera-ready.

CAPS - Capital letters.

COLOR SEPARATION - In photography, the process of separating full-color originals into primary printing colors. In lithographic printing, the manual separation of colors for individual printing plates. You can save money at the printers by asking your artist to prepare color separations, such as using separate overlays for each color.

COPY - Original written material before it is typeset.

CROP - To eliminate portions of an illustration or photograph, indicated on the original with *crop marks*.

CUTLINE - A line of type identifying a picture. Also called a *caption*. To crop photographs, mark in the margins with an eraseable grease pencil.

DIE CUT - To cut out special shapes from printed sheets, much as a cookie cutter is used on dough. You will pay lots extra for die cuts.

DISPLAY TYPE - Lettering made larger than the text, used to attract attention. Headlines are one kind of display type.

DUMMY - A preliminary layout showing the positions of headlines, text, and art as they should appear in the final production. A dummy paste-up is a layout with copies of the material pasted in place. The dummy is never meant to be reproduced, only used as a guide.

EMBOSSING - An image raised above the surface of the paper. If the embossed image is not printed over but left the same color as the paper, it is called *blind embossing*.

There is an especially deserved place in hell for people who proofread their own work. Seek others to check your work.

A photo screened to produce a HALFTONE.

FACE - A style of type or lettering. Each typeface can be typeset in regular, bold or italic form.

FLIER - A printed announcement on a single sheet of paper. Sometimes picky people will say that if a flier is folded, it's called a pamphlet. Printers call a pamphlet with several bound pages a brochure.

FLUSH LEFT or FLUSH RIGHT - Type set to align along the left or right. Type set both flush left and flush right is called "justified."

FOLIO - A page number.

FONT - In typesetting, lettering that is one size and style.

FORMAT - The page size, margins, type size and style, printing instructions, etc., of a printed piece.

GALLEY PROOF - Long strips of paper with typeset text that have not been cut and pasted into pages.

GANG - Printing more than one item on a sheet (see UP).

GRIPPERS - Metal fingers on a printing press that clamp onto sheets of paper to control the flow as they pass through the press. The gripper edge is the unprintable leading edge of paper that the grippers clamp onto. You should allow a half-inch gripper edge on all mechanicals that you bring to the printer.

HALFTONE - The reproduction of a photograph (or continuous tone) through a screen that converts the photo into a pattern of dots. Newspapers automatically convert publicity photos to halftones, but if you are including photos in your playbill, poster or newsletters, your printer will charge you to make halftones.

HICKIES - Imperfections or spots in the printing caused by dirt on the press, a dry roller, etc.

HIGH CONTRAST - Photographs where the tonal difference in areas is great, such as deep black areas and bright white areas butted up against each other. A high contrast photo reproduces better than a photo with lots of hard-to-see grays and little or no black and white areas.

ITALIC - *A style of typed lettering that slopes forward, as opposed to normal, upright type. Used to emphasize words.*

JUSTIFY - To space out letters and words so that they align with both the left and right margins. Like this. The opposite is *unjustified*, or *ragged*.

LAYOUT - The drawing or sketch of a piece proposed for printing. After a preliminary layout, an artist prepares a more detailed dummy and then pastes up a mechanical, ready for the printer to reproduce on the press.

LEAD or LEADING - Rhymes with "bread." In typesetting, the amount of space allowed between lines of type.

LINE ART - A drawing (not a photograph) suitable for reproduction without screening.

LOGO or LOGOTYPE - The name or symbol of a company made into a special design, used as a trademark in promotion.

LOWER CASE - Smaller letters in type, as opposed to capital letters. Capital letters are upper case.

MECHANICAL - The paste-up of artwork. A mechanical may have blank spaces where the printer will need to paste in halftones and artwork.

OFFSET - A printing process that uses an intermediate cylinder to transfer the image from the engraved plate to the paper. Short for *offset lithography*.

OPACITY - The property of paper that minimizes the amount of printing that shows through the opposite side of the page or the next sheet.

ORPHAN - A word or syllable isolated at the top of a column or page. Good typesetting avoids ophans (see WIDOW).

OVERLAY - A transparent covering over a mechanical where the artist marks color breaks, instructions or corrections. In color separation, stacking the overlays will create a composite picture.

OVERPRINTING - Printing over an area that already has printing.

OVERRUN - Printing in excess of the specified quantity.

PAMPHLET - See FLIER.

PASTE-UP - The original art and text arranged and affixed to a base board or paper, ready for the printer to reproduce. Also called a *mechanical*. Paste-ups don't always use paste; professionals use wax so that the pieces of the paste-up can be repositioned without tearing.

PICA - Printer's measurement for lines. Six picas equal approximately one inch.

POINT - Printer's measurement, principally used in designating type sizes. There are about 72 points in an inch.

REAM - 500 sheets of paper.

REGISTRATION - Two or more images printed in exact alignment. You should put registration marks (usually a circle with crosshairs) in the unprinted margins of your overlays and on the base mechanical.

SCALING - Calculating how much to reduce or enlarge an image to fit properly into a space on your layout.

SCORE - To impress or indent paper so that it folds easier.

SERIF - In some type faces, the short, decorative cross-lines that terminate the main strokes of letters. Type faces lacking serifs are called *sans serif*.

STOCK - Paper to be used for printing. See your printer to discuss the artistic and economic merits of various paper stock.

TEXT - The main part of a printed piece, minus the headlines and other display type.

TRAPPING - The ability to print one color to completely fill a space surrounded by a previously printed color, without the two colors showing overlap. Trapping requires color plates to be printed in close registration.

TRIM MARKS - Marks placed on the mechanical to indicate the edges of the page. For the printing press, you need a half-inch gripper edge beyond one pair of trim marks.

TYPO - An error, such as a misspelling, in typing or typesetting.

-UP - "Two-up," "three-up," etc., refers to printing more than one item on a larger sheet of paper to take advantage of full press capacity. If you wanted to print audience surveys measuring 5-¼ by 8 ½

E E
Serif Type **Sans Serif Type**

Working With Printers 11.9

inches, you could print these two-up on a letter-sized sheet of paper (8 ½ by 11 inches).

WASH-UP - Cleaning the rollers and ink fountain on a printing press before changing ink colors.

WEB PRESS - A press that prints from rolls of paper. Newspapers use web presses.

WIDOW - A syllable or single word at the end of a paragraph on a line by itself. Good typesetting avoids widows (see ORPHAN).

Summary

- ☛ Select your printer carefully. Not all printers are appropriate for all jobs. Visit printers before you need them to observe what they offer and how they treat customers.

- ☛ Meet early with your printer to plan a job. Discuss various alternatives in design and paper stock to save costs. Have all format information ready.

- ☛ Become familiar with the design and printing process. Learn what takes up a printer's time and find ways to prepare materials to avoid unnecessary costs.

- ☛ Be sure all material is proofread by several people before bringing mechanicals to the printer.

- ☛ Give your printer enough time to produce quality work.

Posters

Chapter 12

- What makes a good poster
- Working with your designer
- Timetable for poster production

A well-designed theater poster goes beyond its function as an advertisement for an event. It becomes a work of art.

The posters that Henri de Toulouse-Lautrec painted of Parisian dance halls are considered priceless masterpieces for their bright, bold, simple style. Study these and try to emulate their genius.

Notice that I said their *genius*, not their *style*. The style of a poster is a combination of the artist's talent and the subject of the poster.

Great posters may cost no more than mediocre posters. Expensive posters are not always effective. Remember this next time an administrator or artist tells you "we have to have six colors and print the poster on heavy cardboard with a coat of varnish."

Nonsense. Posters with just two colors on white paper can be brilliant and effective. Breaking the bank isn't going to improve a design much.

Look at the now-classic posters for *Les Miserables, Phantom of the Opera, A Chorus Line,* and *Cats*. These are stupendous, flashy, big-budget musicals, yet their posters are dramatic and memorable in their simplicity.

While there are exceptions (*Joseph and the Amazing Technicolor Dreamcoat* can hardly be promoted with a black and white poster... or can it? Hmmm!), nearly any play or musical can be translated into a poster with a limited palette and a reasonable budget. In amateur or professional theater, controlling poster costs is always important.

Why good posters work

Posters are especially effective in attracting an otherwise uninterested audience. For people who are not interested in your event, for those who don't read newspapers or who tune out radio advertising—even for those who don't care what your production is because they are not regular theater-goers —the poster can serve as a powerful, convincing recruiter.

A well-designed poster appeals to the unconscious mind's emotions before the conscious, analytical part of the brain has a chance to reject the subject.

Wait! Stop! Go back and re-read that last sentence! Now you know the secret to dramatic poster design!

Three pairs of lips forming different expressions — what could be simpler to promote a comedy about three women? The lips were printed bright red [Artist: Chester Makoski].

A well-designed poster appeals to the unconscious mind's emotions before the conscious, analytical part of the brain has a chance to reject the subject.

Arrest and impress

Think of your target, this preoccupied, less-than-enthusiastic potential theater-goer walking along the street. She's got bills on her mind. She's wondering about her husband, the kids, and what's for supper. She's thinking about getting away for some tennis this weekend, about a problem at work, about crime in her neighborhood, about her love life—anything but the play by the Middlesex Thespians opening next week.

Then, out of the corner of her eye, in the middle of five or six notices posted in a shop window, your customer sees your poster and it arrests her attention. It stops her in her tracks, plows through her thoughts and hits an emotional, psychological button in her crowded, busy brain.

She's so intrigued by the poster, even at a distance, that she crosses the street to get a closer look.

Congratulations! You've got her attention, but now you must hope that the poster is sufficiently startling to hold her there a moment. The poster must delay her long enough to get her mind thinking about what she's feeling. Then the poster must compel her to read the fine print that tells where and when the play is being staged.

▲ Does the poster clearly reveal what the play is about?

▲ Does the poster suggest what chief emotion someone should expect to experience in seeing the show?

▲ Is the information organized, and is the image powerful enough to make the viewer want to remember it later?

▲ Will the emotions and the ideas stirred up by the poster linger long enough to remind our customer to call a friend later that day and make plans to see the production?

Frequency and partnership with other promotion

Posters work best as part of a mix of promotional tools. The combination of messages from several directions builds up a familiarity in the mind of the uninterested customer. A rule in advertising is that someone usually has to hear a message three times before it sinks in.

Here's how this works: Someone sees a poster on Monday, hears a radio announcement Tuesday, sees another poster Wednesday. By the time the article about the play appears in the newspaper on Thursday, the news about the play is familiar. People take interest in things that are familiar. For this reason, use the poster illustration in all print pieces promoting the production. The repetition will make the image familiar to the public.

To help your promotional message become familiar to your customers, it's important that your poster design, while being different enough to stand out from the competition, must still present images that the public will recognize.

The power of symbolism

Posters deal with symbols. The simplest symbols communicate hundreds of ideas that take thousands of words to describe. Think of the flood of emotions that rush through your brain when you see these symbols: *a swastika, a clenched fist, an eye shedding a tear, a hand touching a*

ARMY ISSUE: The stencil typeface, familiar for its use on military crates, is combined with helmets to evoke the impersonalization of war (below). The textured background suggests a gritty subject [Artist: Donna Ilardo].

VARIATIONS ON A THEME: Three treatments of a familiar theme, vampires (above), show that even an old idea can be rejuvenated [Artist: Chester Makoski].

COMEDY is communicated with a design (below) that's recognizable even from a distance. Ticket information and credits are organized and subordinate to the art [Artist: Elizabeth Dowling].

Color, size, the number and placement of elements, and the use of symbols to tap unconscious emotional memories—these are the tools of the skilled poster artist.

breast, a gravestone, the Eiffel Tower, a star-filled sky, a hand-grenade, a high-heeled shoe.

Using any of these symbols in a poster is like pressing a button wired to the human brain, commanding it to search its millions of neurological memory files. Studies show that the most enduring memories are those attached to emotions. Now consider how the sight of a single symbol can cause someone to recall deeply emotional experiences faster than any computer ever will, and you begin to see why it's so important to choose the right symbol in a poster. You want to trigger an emotional memory.

Psychologists Sigmund Freud and Carl Jung pioneered the study of interpreting symbols to understand the brain's unconscious activity during dreams. They found that, just as all human brains develop and physically function much the same way, there are symbols that appear in dreams which have nearly universal meanings.

For example, analysts say that dreaming of a closet may symbolize secrets or signify the womb. Garden gates suggest a paradise where our hopes and dreams await fulfillment. Springtime images recall childhood; winter, old age. Bells can be the conscience ringing out a warning. Think of the different feelings and images in your mind as you contemplate a white lily, a red rose, and a yellow daisy.

Color, size, the number and placement of elements, and the use of symbols to tap unconscious emotional memories—these are the tools of the skilled poster artist.

Understanding how to use this deep, involved knowledge to create meaningful art is a rare and beautiful gift. Not everyone has this ability.

This is why poster design should not be left to the first person who comes along in your theater group who says "I like to draw."

In a moment, I'll tell you where to find a good artist. But first, here are a few more tips to help you recognize an effective poster:

More tips on good posters

Many badly designed posters unwittingly suggest chaos because there are too many disorganized parts. The title of the play is here, the ticket information there, three or four graphic symbols are some place else, the name of the group and the director stuck another place — chaos!

To organize your poster, make your graphic image dominate. The printed words, which appeal to the intellect, should be subordinate to the symbolic elements that appeal to the emotions. Even the play's title should be subordinate to the art. You want people to react to the artistic design of the poster from across the street. When they are lured close enough, they can read all the stuff about ticket prices, dates, and who wrote the lyrics.

Remember this rule of subordinating everything to the symbol, and your posters will have power! Think of the poster for *Les Miserables*: the drawing of the waif takes up the top three-quarters of the poster, the name of the play is directly below, and all other writing is very small. You can put this poster in a window and it will be recognized 100 feet away because the graphic symbol is simple and dominant!

The symbol itself does not have to be enormous to dominate. The other key to creating a dominant element in

RIGHT TYPE: Classic use of lettering (below) is modeled after poster of the Civil War era — a perfect choice for a period play [Artists: Jim Bump and Katie Van Vorse].

COMMUNICATING THROUGH SYMBOLS: A skull in flames with a double image of a face (left) suggests hellish torment [Artist: George Chartier]. Ancient Greek statues come to life with mixed emotions (below) in a stark poster for the Greek tragedy *Medea* [Artist: Karl Prewo]. A heart, elegant letters and a visual pun sum up the many moods of Jacques Brel's music [Artist: George Chartier].

Posters 12.5

your design is to use blank space effectively. The Broadway poster for *Phantom of the Opera* shows the white mask and a long-stemmed rose tucked all the way down in the lower left corner of the poster. The title of the play is pushed way up to the top of the poster, and the rest of the written information is jammed into a small horizontal area below the mask and rose. The information is all there, but it doesn't get in the way!

Finding, cultivating a good artist

It's worth the time and effort it may take to locate a good artist. For ideas on where to find artists, try the suggestions for recruiting publicity people that I list in Chapter 6 on **The Publicity Team**. In addition, watch for talented people displaying their work at high school and college art shows.

You want a student studying graphic design. The artist should have some appreciation for the theater and be knowledgeable about typography (the use of different styles of lettering) and printing. Ask teachers for recommendations. Carefully study an artist's portfolio. Look at what the artist can do with one or two colors. Especially watch for the artist whose designs are uncomplicated by excessive detail, who uses large areas of solid color, and who knows how to place subjects creatively off-center within the picture frame.

Once you find one, it's important to avoid loading down the artist with too much work. In the theater company I worked with for more than ten years, I broke the pattern of using the same artist for every show. The poor guy wasn't getting any rest and I worried that his creative juices would be strained. Also, I observed that his posters varied in quality depending on the amount of enthusiasm he had for a show.

I found other people in my theater group who jumped at my invitation to try their hand at designing a poster. Soon, I was able to call up several artists in May or June and say, "Are you interested in designing the poster for one of the three plays next season?" I asked the artists to think about their assignments over the summer, meet with the directors, and have preliminary designs completed by Labor Day.

When audiences entered the theater on opening night of the first show in October, there were approved, near-finished designs for all three posters for the season on display in the lobby. Now the audience knew instantly what the new season promised—not just with a listing in the playbill, but with large, dramatic posters tapping away at their unconscious dreams!

So, spread around the opportunities. Don't burn out your artists. Gather a stable of artists, just like an advertising agency, and let them choose among themselves which play they'll illustrate. This makes for happy artists, variety in design, and fresh opportunities for talented new people to join your theater group.

Remember, however, that even with volunteer artists, the publicist has the decision-making authority over whether a design is acceptable for the theater's commercial use. This does not preclude the publicist from consulting others in the company, as the following story illustrates:

Communication avoids errors

I made the nearly disastrous mistake not long ago of giving a script to a very good artist and not specifically instructing him to speak with the director of the play.

The artist, who works out of his home on such projects and rarely shows up at the theater until opening night, went straight to his drawing board and produced what I thought was a clever, acceptable design. I'm an artist myself, so relying on my instincts and experience, I approved the design and asked the artist to prepare the final version for the printer. The artwork was due at the printer's shop in about a week and a half.

At around 1 a.m. the next night, I found myself suddenly sitting up in bed, wide awake, my heart racing with dread as I realized that the director hadn't seen the poster. The only person who had dealt with the artist was me. What if the director didn't like the poster? After all, this was his play. He had as much say in the design as the artist and the publicist!*

On the phone the next morning I apologized to the artist and the director for this blunder, and I arranged for the artist, the director and me to look over the design together. The director rejected the poster. It was a fine design, he said, but it didn't communicate his interpretation of the play.

The artist, a gentleman and a professional, listened to the director's thoughts about the play. He went back to his drawing board and in just one week produced an entirely different design. The new design, with the input of the director, turned out more interesting and psychologically more powerful that the original.

Back at home, I sent the artist a thank-you note. Then I picked up a note pad and wrote 500 times *"I will make sure the artist talks with the director."*

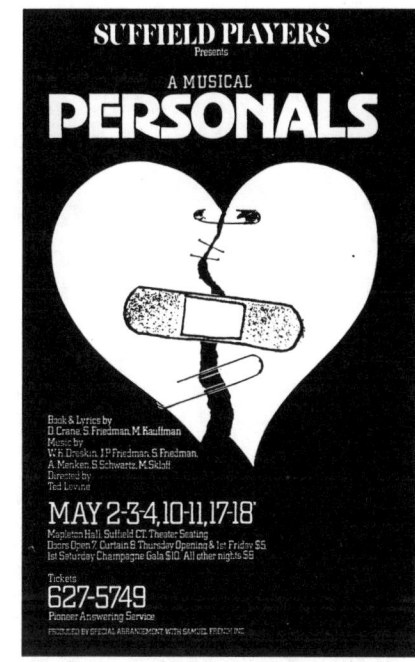

**Before and after:
Artist Chester Makoski redesigned the poster for the musical *Personals* after discussing the play with its director. One poster suggests warmth and wholeness, the other communicates the great fear of dating — a broken heart.**

From concept to printed art

Here is your timetable and guide to producing a poster; it also appears in the **Master Battle Plan** (Appendix A):

1 At least ten weeks before opening night, give the artist the assignment. This consists of getting the artist to agree to produce a piece of work on time and within budget. The artist needs to read the play and must meet with the director to discuss the director's concept of the play. The artist needs to receive the assignment more than two months before opening

---

* For a season of plays, the artistic director (rather than the individual show director) usually works with the designer to create a series of posters that has a consistant style.

Most scripts inform you on the first page how to credit the author in your posters, playbill and other printed promotional materials.

night because it will take time to conceive, modify, prepare, print and distribute posters.

2 The publicist should give the artist a typewritten sheet of paper listing all the wording for the poster. The publicist should obtain this information from the general manager and get approval of the fact sheet before handing it to the artist. The basic information includes:

- the name of the play
- production dates
- names of playwrights
- the theater's name and location
- name of the director, lyricists, composers
- how to obtain and pay for tickets
- royalty credit line
- curtain times

The royalty credit line identifies the agency granting permission to produce the play. It's the agency to whom your theater group pays royalty fees which are passed on in part to the playwright.

Most scripts inform you on the first page how to credit the author in your posters, playbill and other printed promotional materials. Many scripts even come with specific rules describing how large the playwright's name must be in relation to the name of the play. Look for this information and be sure that the artist has these instructions.

At this time, get some idea from the general manager what shape the theater group's finances are in, so you can suggest to the artist how much leeway is available in designing the poster. Chapter 11 on **Working With Printers** tells you how to save money at the print shop.

If you don't know what size the posters should be, you should discuss this with the artist and perhaps get advice from your printer. As you might guess, the price of a poster varies with its size. To prepare a proper design, the artist will need to know the dimensions of the poster.

3 Determine with the production manager how many posters will be needed. Assume that everyone connected with the production will want a souvenir poster. Plan to save a half-dozen for the artist and the theater group's history file. It's not too early to start thinking about where posters should be displayed and who will put them up. Consider printing extra posters to sell in the theater at intermission.

Establishing a "poster league" can make the job of distributing posters easy. Ask your theater company president or the production manager for names of volunteers. Consider contacting older, retired members of your group that have not been active in awhile and ask them if they can give two hours of their time in a few weeks to put up posters in town. Another possibility is to trade services with a group: ask the local scout troop to help put up posters in exchange for the loan of theater equipment for the scout's annual banquet.

4 About eight weeks before opening night, the publicist should check on the artist's design. Review the wording for accuracy. At this meeting the artist should present the design to the director and general manager for approval. I recommend including the general manager because this is the person who approves the bills. The general manager may know more than you do about how much a poster could cost to print.

Also, the general manager will serve as a second check, along with you, to prevent approval of a poster design that might be too racy, confusing or unacceptable for some other reason. When it comes to a split vote, it's usually best to strongly consider the director's judgement, since it's the director's play. You're the publicist, however, and you're supposed to know best what will attract the public to the show.

5 Immediately show the design to one or more local printers that you regularly deal with. Discuss the specifics of the printing job—the kind of paper and ink, etc. Ask the printers to quote you a price and give you a deadline for delivery of the artwork. Once you've selected a printer, reserve time on the printer's schedule and confirm the date you'll deliver the artwork.

6 Six weeks before opening night, the artist should have final, original art ready to go to the printer. Proofread this artwork. Proofread it again. Have the director, the president, your mother and a neighbor proofread the information. Triple check the show dates, location, and box office phone number—the most likely items to have errors.

I once had five people look at a poster design. After the poster was printed, we realized that the area code for the box office phone was off by one digit. Please don't trust your eyes or even everyone else's in your theater group. Show the poster to someone who is only mildly interested in the theater. This person will catch obvious errors that everyone in your group will miss.

7 Bring the artwork to the printer. Ask the printer to look carefully at the way everything is laid out and to tell you then and there if it looks like there will be any problem reproducing the poster. There's always a chance that you'll need to return the artwork to the artist for adjustments.

You should have selected paper and ink during your previous visit. Hand the printer a "spec sheet" that confirms such information as the number of posters needed, when you'll need them, the kind of paper, color ink, etc.

Include your name and daytime phone number on the sheet and ask the printer to call you if any problems arise. You should allow the printer anywhere from five to ten working days to produce your posters.

Finally, confirm the price of the printing job and arrangements for payment. Never pay in advance.

8 Inform the general manager what price the printer quoted and what payment arrangements the printer wants. Call the printer a day ahead to confirm that the job is running on time. The posters should be printed one day before they're due for you to pick up because they need 24 hours to dry.

9 About four weeks before opening night, your posters should be ready. Publicists know that timing is important for the release of information. Announcing news prematurely gives the news too much chance to become old. Announcing too late doesn't give customers time to react. For most amateur theaters, single tickets go on sale three or four weeks before opening night.

When you pick up your posters at the printer's shop, pull out several samples from different places in the stack—a quarter of the way down, half-way down, and the bottom of the stack. Compare these samples to be sure quality is consistent. Quickly estimate the number of posters the printer has delivered to be sure you're not short.

If all is well, arrange to pay the printer promptly. Immediately pull the best samples and save these for the artist, for the history file, the director and other VIP's. Remember to return the original artwork to the artist.

10 Within seven days of picking up the posters, or no later than about three weeks before opening night, get your posters displayed. Call together your volunteers. Have a hit list of key places in town where posters should go. Next to each location on your hit list, write down the name of the volunteer responsible for bringing a poster there. Give each volunteer a copy of the list of places she and he have pledged to go. Ask the volunteers for suggestions of other sites and add these to your list. Ask volunteers to note an "expiration date" on the back of the posters if they're putting them up in windows. Get the volunteers to promise to take down the posters within 48 hours after the final show. Invite the volunteers to the cast party. Invite the artist to the cast party.

Summary

☛ The most effective posters have a simple design using a limited palette of colors. Words should be subordinate to the art.

☛ Posters should be designed by an insightful artist who understands how the choice of appropriate symbols in the design can affect the viewer on an emotional level.

☛ Assign an artist to design a poster at least two months before opening night. Be sure the artist has all necessary information, and that the artist and director discuss the play together.

☛ Select a printer who appears knowledgeable and helpful.

☛ Make a "hit list" of key places in town to place posters.

Leaflets, Brochures and Other Handouts

Chapter 13

- Purposes and uses
- Content and design
- Methods of distribution

Modern promotion would be lost without free fliers, pamphlets and brochures. Then again, people who hate junk mail probably wish modern promotion would get lost.

Nevertheless, even when we reach the day when information arriving on home computers will replace most of our paper mail, publicists will still find opportunities to distribute information by hand. Airport and hotel travelers will still stop at booths to select leaflets about tourist attractions. Businesses will still hire young people to stand on street corners and hand out leaflets and pamphlets advertising sales. People attending festivals will continue to look for free literature about things to do on the weekend that will let them escape the pressures and drudgery of daily life.

Like news releases and posters, handouts are among the tools the publicist can use to create a diverse mix of promotion. They are used primarily for three purposes: fund raising, audience development and volunteer recruitment.

Defining handouts

▲ A *flier* is a single sheet of paper folded and usually mailed.

▲ A *handbill* is unfolded and passed out by hand.

▲ A *leaflet* or *pamphlet* can be either a flier or a handbill. Leaflets and pamphlets are generic terms for any single-sheet handouts.

▲ A *brochure* is a booklet of several pages, usually stapled. It has also come to mean a large sheet of paper folded several times to appear like a booklet.

I wrote down these definitions for my sake as well as yours. They confuse me all the time!

Paper handouts take other forms: Bookmarks imprinted with information about your organization. Wallet cards with a calendar printed on the other side. Posters, if they're given away as promotional gifts, can be considered handouts. Technically, playbills are handouts, too. In fact, any informational papergoods that you give away can be called a handout, but this open definition is leading us into lexical quicksand.

This chapter is concerned mostly with traditional handouts: leaflets and brochures. Here are the basic ones publicists work with; they are often created and distributed in cooperation with another manager involved with fund raising or audience development:

The show announcement

For every show your theater company produces, you'll need an announcement to send to people on your mailing list. Many theaters make it a policy to send patrons a notice a week or more before tickets go on sale to the general public, so that they can have a chance to buy tickets early.

The show announcement may be a large flier or a printed postcard. You can produce your own postcards cheaply by printing a black ink reproduction of your poster on stiff paper called index stock. Talk to your friendly neighborhood printer for details.

If you can work a deal with your local bank, a *bank notice stuffer* is a surprisingly effective way of announcing your show—but it

SUFFIELD PLAYERS Presents

"HAYFEVER" by Noel Coward

Mapleton Hall, Suffield CT

OCT. 23, 24, 25, 31
NOV. 1, 7, 8, 14, 15

Refreshments Available
Doors Open 7 p.m., Curtain 8 p.m.
Thursday Opening & First Friday $5.00
First Saturday Champagne Gala $10.00
All Other Nights $7.00
Cabaret Seating

For Tickets:
(203)627-5749
Pioneer Answering Service

Produced by Special Arrangement with Samuel French, Inc.

A THEATRE PROGRAM PRESENTATION

THE BEACH PLAYS — LIFEGUARDS & STONESKIPPERS

Written & Directed by Robert R. Lehan

Nov. 19 - 22
8:30 PM
LAB THEATER
CAMPUS CENTER

Westfield State College

Students $1.00 • General Admission $5.00

THE SHAPE OF NEWS: Three effective ways of announcing show information: A bank stuffer (above left) can be included with a bank's monthly transaction statements to customers; a postcard (above) can be sent through the mail; and a calling card (below) makes a handy pocket reminder all year long.

STAGEWORKS OF LEOMINSTER

presents

"STUCK IN A TREEHOUSE"	Jan. 10 & 11, 1992
"PERSONALS"	Feb. 7, 8, 13, 14, 15, 1992
"THE CRUCIBLE"	April 3, 4, 10, 11, 1992

Mail: 232 Pleasant Street • Leominster, MA 01453
Ticket Phone: 508-840-3339

SELLING YOUR SEASON: Each show of a season is described with distinctive artwork in this detailed but organized flier (right) while Lewiston/Auburn's Community Little Theater (Maine) teases before revealing its season by warning that the brochure "contains theateractive material."

1992 ... OUR 25TH ANNIVERSARY SEASON!

THEATREWORKS new milford

Arsenic & Old Lace
The classic story of two charming and innocent ladies who populate their cellar with remains of socially and religiously "acceptable" roomers. By Joseph Kesselring.
February 14 - March 14

Twain Rides Again
Directed, performed and written by Michael-John Cavallaro, this will be an expanded encore presentation of 1991's hit.
March 20 - April 4

Cat's Paw
A gripping thriller about terrorism; but it does not come at the subject in a way everyone would expect. What if a terrorist came along who was brilliant, articulate and who was right? By William Mastrosimone.
July 24 - August 15

Society Page
An evening of two original one-act comedies, Society Page and Keep the Knife Dull, written by local playwright Sean O'Connor.
May 1 - May 9

ASSASSINS
Stephen Sondheim's dark musical comedy about the people who have killed or tried to kill US Presidents. History lesson, carny show and bad dream all swirled into one, Assassins is a spangled celebration of America, a land where anybody can grow up to shoot the President.
September 18 - October 17

COBB
The story of the greatest baseball player of all time, Ty Cobb, as told by Ty Cobb. Through Cobb's four incarnations we learn the story behind one of baseball's biggest, most controversial, legends. A new play by Lee Blessing.
June 5 - June 20

The Lion in Winter
King Henry has 3 sons: Richard, Geoffrey and John. He wants to keep the kingdom together after his death, but all three sons covet the crown, and revolution is likely. The King favors the youngest, the Queen favors the eldest, and the middle son hopes to play both ends against each other and come out the victor. A comedy-drama by James Goldman.
November 20 - December 19

◆ **RESERVATIONS: (203) 350-6863**

Don't miss any of this year's exciting shows — subscribe! A limited number of season subscriptions are available at the box office. For $55 you get all seven shows — a 20% savings off the cost of individual tickets.
Performances are Fridays and Saturdays at 8:00 p.m. All Tickets $10.00.

- A note on reservations — All reservations are on a first-come first-served basis. Reservations will be held until 5 minutes before curtain, after which they are released. If you find you cannot come, it is very important that you call the theatre and cancel the reservation.
- Senior Citizens — There is a free open rehearsal for senior citizens the night before all openings.
- Group Rates — Group rates are available for any party over 20. House sales, a great idea for fund raisers, are also available. Please call for more information.
- Donations — Do you like what you see here? If so, become a part of it by donating whatever you can — time, money, props, furniture, costumes. Any and every contribution will be greatly appreciated.
- Theatreworks is located on Brookside Avenue (off Route 202, next to Morey's IGA Supermarket) in New Milford. Our mailing address is: Theatreworks, P.O. Box 165, New Milford, CT 06776.

All information subject to change.

Theatreworks New Milford • P.O. Box 165 • 5 Brookside Avenue • New Milford, Connecticut 06776

WARNING
DO NOT OPEN

This brochure contains theateractive material. In the event of contamination, you may develop symptoms of being thoroughly entertained. Your only chance to survive is to . . . .

A handy way to promote a play or a season...

means planning ahead several weeks before opening night. A bank notice stuffer is a flier announcing your show. It matches the size of the envelope that a bank uses to mail monthly customer account transaction reports—the listing of activities in your checking and savings accounts. Banks often include an advertisement or bulletin about bank services with these monthly account reports, so a bank that supports local arts organizations might not mind stuffing an announcement about your show in the same envelope with the monthly account mailings.

Similarly, ask your local grocer if employees at the cash register can drop mini handbills (stuffers) into sacks along with groceries.

Think of the thousands of people you can reach this way without paying a penny for postage! Your investment will be the cost of printing the announcement, unless your local bank or grocer is willing to pick up the tab on this, too. The printing cost can be substantially reduced if the announcement is designed to measure the same size as the envelope. Print announcements three-up on 8 ½-by-11-inch sheets of color paper and have the printer cut them apart. For every 100 sheets printed, you get three stuffers.

The season announcement

This may be a flier or a brochure. You'll send one of these to people on your mailing list if your group produces more than one show a year. Of course, if your theater group's management doesn't plan very far ahead, you can't send a season announcement. Before the end of the last show of your theater season, your group should have the next season planned, complete with dates and location(s). At the last production of the season, you should have your season announcement ready and on display for audiences to take with them.

Your season announcement should include a brief description of each production. Don't simply list the playwright and director. Indicate whether the production is a comedy, drama, satire, murder-mystery, or musical. Mention what themes the production explores or what the basic situation is in the show:

> 1776 is the lively retelling of the story of America's decision to declare its independence. Filled with witty and moving songs, stirring speeches and a parade of famous characters from the original thirteen colonies—including John Adams, Benjamin Franklin and Thomas Jefferson—this musical inspires pure joy and genuine patriotism.

To get extra mileage out of your publicity efforts, consider inserting into your season announcement a separate handbill stressing the first show of the season.

Fund-raising handout

This can come in two forms—the annual handout mailed to subscribers and patrons that is used for major fund raising; and a supplemental handout that is on display all year long in the theater lobby and possibly inserted in the playbill. Fund raising is a sophisticated, complex art all its own apart from publicity. Work with your group's fund-raising staff to develop effective materials.

Volunteer membership solicitation

This is a valuable handout that community theaters should use constantly. Non-profit groups have used this handout for years to get people to volunteer their time on committees.

This handout lets people know that they can become an active member of your theater company by volunteering as an usher, snack bar helper, publicity assistant, stage hand, or a helper with costume-making, set construction and design, sound and lighting design and operation, and any other job they can imagine.

Make the idea of joining a theater company sound exciting and creative. Remind people in your handout that joining your group is a guaranteed way to make warm, interesting friendships. Stress that volunteers need not feel that they must bring a special talent or skill to the group, because your group offers on-the-job training.

I'm not sure how librarians feel about this, but I always thought it would be interesting to place a membership flier or brochure in the pages of theater books. People who would take out a library book about the theater are probably good candidates to join your theater company.

Souvenir anniversary booklet

This is a nice gift for patrons who have made one or more substantial contributions or have given money to your theater group regularly over many years. When your theater company celebrates a major anniversary, publish and distribute a booklet listing all the shows your group has produced over the years, along with the dates. List any awards won, the names of artistic directors or theater company presidents, and other historical information about your group. Include lots of good quality photographs. Every once in awhile it's nice to reward patrons for their generosity with a special surprise gift like this.

General information

In all your handouts, consider including a map and street address to help newcomers find your theater. Obviously, you should include a phone number and a mailing address so people can contact your theater company. Also, clearly note if your theater is accessible to persons with disabilities that impair their mobility. Note if your theater is air conditioned. State what forms of payment for tickets are accepted.

It's effective to quote praise for your productions from newspaper reviews. If your group isn't regularly reviewed, survey your audience after performances and reprint words of praise from their comment cards.

Designing and printing

See Chapter 6 on **The Publicity Team** to learn where to locate a good volunteer artist to design your handouts. Chapter 11 on **Working With Printers** will show you how to save money.

To get ideas on designing handouts, collect samples from other organizations. Emulate the best materials distributed by groups more advanced than you. Community theater should study handouts produced by equity theaters. Don't limit yourself to

...is with a bookmark like this one. Here is side two (artists: Rachel Kuper and Cathy Schorra).

These Seats Could Be Yours...

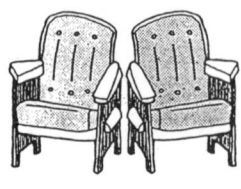

For The Entire 1991-1992 Season!

Subscription series tickets are on sale until early fall. But any seats not renewed by May 24 will be released and assigned to new subscribers on a first come first served basis. *These are the best seats in the house, and they will go fast!* So send your order form right away to the Jorgensen Auditorium Box Office, The University of Connecticut, 2132 Hillside Road, U-104, Storrs, CT 06269-3104.

If you have recently sent in your order, we thank you! An acknowledgement card will be sent to you shortly.

The Royal Family requests the honor of your presence at The Suffield Players' production of Princess and the Pea May 10, 1985 at Mapleton Hall. Opening Night Festivities include a kingly punch and courtly tidbits.

ONE OR MORE SHOWS can be promoted with special handouts and mailings. A postcard (above) makes a handy reminder to subscribe, a formal invitation (left) makes patrons feel special, and a folded leaflet (below) promotes a major production with details too numerous for a brief news release.

☆ ☆ ☆ ☆ ☆ 35th Anniversary Season
SUFFIELD PLAYERS
presents

MUSIC!
LIGHTS!
ACTION!

☆ JESUS CHRIST
☆ ☆ ☆ SUPERSTAR !

★★★ The Theatrical Event of the Season! ★★★
The Most Talked About Show in Years!

Jesus in rolled-up shirtsleeves and a plaid blazer slung over his shoulder? The apostles in gray pinstripe suits? Roman guards replaced by modern police in riot gear?

What's going on here?

It's the splashy, flashy rock opera *Jesus Christ Superstar*, coming to Suffield in November, presented in a never-seen-before setting created by director Lyle W. Pearsons to open the Suffield Players' gala 35th anniversary season. (You expected anything less?)

This is the pop opera that stunned audiences on both sides of the Atlantic a decade ago, the modern translation of the Gospel of Matthew that sent guitars wailing and audiences cheering.

Now the Suffield Players will present *Jesus Christ Superstar,* but with a new vision that goes beyond time and space. The Suffield Players production of the greatest story ever told will be played out on a grand scale with a contemporary message about modern heroes.

Superstar is about ageless forces that venerate and then destroy, that twist dreams into war and messengers into martyrs.

You'll see special effects blazing out of scores of colored lights and lines of television screens on stage. There'll be music synthesizers in the band to serve up an inspiring orchestral sound. You'll witness a political nightmare in Pontius Pilate's court, a haunting jury of chameleon faces, a palm-branch march to Jerusalem transformed into a political tickertape parade - *and so much more!*

Two years in the planning, *Jesus Christ Superstar* will present a cast of 45 performers - the largest cast of any Suffield Players production *in 35 years!*

Directed by Lyle W. Pearsons, award-winning director/actor/playwright *(Count Dracula, The Second Coming, and Tartuffe),* with music directed by Ted Levine who has wowed audiences with his smash Players productions *(Jacques Brel* and *High School).*

★ ★ ★ *Coming in November* ★ ★ ★
*Never before like this -
with flash and drama, music
and moments to cherish!*
JESUS CHRIST SUPERSTAR!

★ ★ ★ Reserve Your Seat Today For This Spectacular ★ ★ ★
Suffield Players Event! Call (203)627-7824 *after Sept.12*

☆ ☆ ☆ ☆ ☆ ☆ ☆ *Don't miss this latest production by the award-winning*
SUFFIELD PLAYERS

JESUS CHRIST SUPERSTAR

A ROCK OPERA
by Andrew Lloyd Webber and Tim Rice
Authors of Cats and Evita
Directed by Lyle W. Pearsons

NOV. 6,7,8 & 13,14

Suffield High School,
Mountain Road, Suffield, Connecticut
Fridays & Saturdays - Curtain 8 p.m.,
Doors Open 7:15 p.m.
Sunday Matinee November 8 - Curtain 2 p.m.,
Doors Open 1:15 p.m.
$10 General Admission, Group Rates Available

(203) 627-7824 Tickets on sale after Sept. 12
Pioneer Answering Service
☆

PROMOTING YOUR ACTIVITIES: A newsletter (left) can inform patrons about upcoming shows, special events, theater improvements, and the need for props and volunteers. Special pamphlets (below) can recruit new members with the promise of "on-the-job training."

Include a map and street address to help newcomers find your theater. Clearly note if your theater is accessible to persons with disabilities that impair their mobility.

theater, either. I've adopted (notice: I said *adopted*, not *copied*) ideas from brochures and fliers distributed by symphony orchestras, museums, schools, charities, banks and insurance companies. Good design is good design, wherever it comes from.

Whatever you produce, make sure it communicates good quality. By this I don't mean that your handouts should look expensive, only tastefully designed. The ink and the paper, the layout and the writing, the photographs and illustrations—all should suggest that your theater company takes pride in projecting a professional image. Above all, be sure that all copy is well written and free of errors.

Distributing handouts

Mail handouts to patrons. Put them in the civic news bins in your local supermarkets, the library, the Chamber of Commerce, town hall, tourist bureaus, the YMCA and YWCA, banks, on the counters of costume shops—any place where people who might be the kind to join your group mill around.

Ask local realtors to hand out your fliers when they give material to new home owners. Is there a Welcome Wagon in town? Offer to help in exchange for the organization agreeing to help you by distributing your fliers.

On the Saturday before opening night, stand on a busy street corner downtown and pass out handbills. If your town has an annual Know Your Town fair, build a festive-looking booth and hand out information here to everyone you see.

Does it have to be said? *Dress up* when calling on places to leave promotional material. Wear a badge with the group logo. Speak slowly and politely.

Above all, get out the word! Fund raising, audience development and volunteer recruitment is a never-ending job that is critical to the survival of your organization.

Summary

☛ Handouts are used for three vital promotional purposes: Fund raising, audience development and volunteer recruitment.

☛ Whatever you produce, make sure it communicates good quality. Be sure the people distributing your publicity also communicate quality in their dress and manners.

☛ Use handouts constantly to let everyone know about your organization. Promotion is a never-ending job that is critical to the survival of your organization.

Signs And Displays

Chapter 14

- Creating effective indoor displays
- Designing and producing outdoor signs

Publicity displays in the lobby of most community theaters are produced at the very last minute—and they almost always look that way.

At dress rehearsal, the publicist enters the theater with copies of recent newspaper articles, sets up the playbills, and then sits down to watch the show. *Everything is under control,* thinks the publicist, counting off the items that come to mind: news releases, posters, playbills, invitations, advertising. Check. Double check. Good.

Then the harried house manager rushes up and says "the lobby looks kind of, you know, naked. Do you have some posters and photos or something we can, you know, sort of stick up on a wall or something to dress things up? Whatever you got," the manager says disarmingly, "but I need it now."

Sirens and warning bells go off in the publicist's mind. The last time the house manager tried to "sort of stick up" a publicity display, a few items were placed at such weird angles and spread out so sparsely that audience members milling around at intermission tried to be helpful and straighten things out.

"Next time," the publicist thinks, rising from the seat and heading to the car to look for some spare materials, "I've got to find a bulletin board and put together a display at home ahead of time. Then I could bring it in, put it on an easel, and watch dress rehearsal in peace."

Displays with a message

The theater where you're presenting your play is a great place to promote the show, the group, and future productions. You have a captive audience strolling around before and after the show and all during intermission.

While your audience is in the theater, you should give them things to look at that will prompt thought and discussion.

Display items fall into three categories: past, present, and future. Items from past shows remind audiences of shows they enjoyed, and inform newcomers about your theater company's past accomplishments. They can also inflict a little regret and anxiety, suggesting to audiences, "You'd better subscribe and not miss any more great shows like these!"

Items from the current show give audiences insight into the history of the play, the themes it explores, the artistic efforts of your group, and the creative possibilities awaiting people who join your group.

Posters and other materials promoting future shows help stir up audience interest and ticket sales. People haven't left the theater and already you're preparing them for the next production!

Delicate items should be put behind protective glass and stored safely between shows.

Here are a few display ideas:

▲ Posters from past shows can line a long corridor or fill the wall behind the snack bar. Buy or build frames with simple backings that make changing posters easy. Create a uniform look by making the frames all the same size and proportioned to hold your largest posters. Add a black backing to make smaller

During intermission, use a slide projector in the lobby to show pictures from past shows.

posters look finished. Consider aligning these in chronological order.

▲ Place framed 8 x 10" black and white portraits of the cast members in the lobby with their real names neatly printed beneath each photo. Put Velcro tabs on the back of the pictures and mount them on a cloth-covered board to make rearrangements easy. Do the same for the next idea...

▲ Create a gallery of framed color photos (at least 8 x 10"—larger pictures are better) of scenes from past shows. At the end of the line include a few black and white pictures (to distinguish them from the past shows) of the current production.

▲ Display the set designer's miniature stage model, along with sketches of scene changes, swatches of fabric from hand-sewn drapery and furniture coverings. Include director's and designer's notes on design plans and photos of crew members constructing the set.

▲ For a costumed play, dress a mannikin (you may be able to borrow one from a friendly department store, use a tailor's dummy and attach a foam head used for wigs, or cut out a flat mannikin from a plank of wood). Divide the mannikin in half the long way. On one side, dress the dummy in the paper or muslin pattern material, complete with pins and pencil lines; on the other, recreate a completed costume. Post a board behind the mannikin with the designer's costume sketches or copies of the drawings and photographs from the books your designer used as sources for the costume.

▲ For a play with special lighting effects, display the light plot and circuit diagram, a few pages from the script with cues written in, and a chart describing the different kinds of lights and gels.

▲ For an original play, display early drafts of the script with words crossed out and marginal notes.

▲ For a history play, display library books opened to appropriate pages; maps and charts; models of battle scenes; and period items collected from antique shops or loaned by museums that help audiences understand what life was like at the time.

▲ Display posters—even if they are still artists' conceptions—to promote future shows.

▲ During intermission, use a slide projector in the lobby to show pictures from past shows. Use an automatic advance to prevent people from saying "Oh, go back! Let me see that one again!" Alternately I've run the remote control from inside my trouser pocket while standing casually nearby. Everyone thought the projector was running automatically and no one asked me stop or go back.

▲ If you get a favorable review, take it to a quick-copy business and get it enlarged to poster size—say, at least 20" wide. Mount this on cardboard or foam-core and display it somewhere in the lobby where people congregating to look at it won't block traffic.

▲ Display a series of reviews in a similar manner. Be sure the name of the newspaper and the date of the article appear. Add a stripe of color for a border on these black and white displays.

▲ If your group contributes to other organizations in town, promote this with a display. Show photos of young people who have received scholarships from your group.

▲ Post a list of volunteer activities available when people join your group. Include snapshots of smiling people working at different tasks. Indicate in the display that your group offers "on-the-job training." Provide pencils and cards on which people can write their names and phone numbers, and a container to drop the cards in.

▲ Place a guest book or fill-in cards near the door with a sign offering to place people on a mailing list for news of future shows. Use the cards to survey your audience with a few brief check-off questions. Display fliers about your current or coming season.

▲ To boost fund raising, post a diagram of your theater, showing drawings of photos of people busy at various duties. Indicate in large, bright numbers the annual cost of cleaning the theater, building sets, running lights, supplying makeup, creating costumes, facilities and equipment renting, printing playbills and posters, and meeting other theater expenses. Place membership application forms nearby.

Other large displays

Bank lobbies, libraries, town hall and store windows are places in town where you might create additional displays.

For a romantic play in February, go to one of your faithful merchants who advertise in your playbill, and offer to create a window display of Valentine's Day merchandise from the store if the merchant will allow you to display a few pictures and a poster from your show over to one side. Florists and candy stores are ideal candidates.

Work with your local library to create a display of books related to your current play. Post your bulletin board behind a display of books on a table. If you're afraid of pilfering, cut a sheet of stiff polyurethane to cover the bulletin board and staple it in place around the edges.

Place bulletin boards away from direct sunlight to protect photos and other objects from fading. Also, away from direct sunlight, a plastic cover won't glare back at viewers.

Back your bulletin board with a single color of construction paper. Black is best because everything shows up against it. Ask your photographer to print 8 x 10" photos with a small white border to set them off from the background, or mount the photos on color or white paper. Below the photos place a card with a neatly lettered caption.

Keep your bulletin board display s-i-m-p-l-e. Don't try to create a chaotic collage that looks like it was assembled by rubbish artist Kurt Schwitters or Pablo Picasso during his cubism period. Don't place 15 items at individual, weird angles or overlap things in bizarre ways that scream "Look, this was arranged by an ARTISTE!" Arrange the elements like the pips on playing cards, in a pleasing, symmetric grid. Add a neatly lettered card that says "Tickets on sale now: 444-2333." Liven up the formal arrangement with cut-out foil stars, hearts, question marks (for mysteries), musical notes, ballet slippers, bats or other accents that tie in with the show's theme—but keep it simple.

Staple a shallow box to the bulletin board and fill it with leaflets for people to take with them.

Attach a card with your name and phone number to the back of the bulletin board to confirm ownership. Do the same to the easel the board rests on if that belongs to you, too.

If you put a display in a bank and the bank is an advertiser in the playbill or a contributor to your annual fund, place a prominent, neatly lettered sign with the display stating this (don't mention the amount of the gift). Of course, you should get the bank manager's permission to set up a display.

You should also present displays at theater and art festivals, and town fairs. For outdoor displays, cover your bulletin board with a sheet of polyurethane for protection from wind and rain. Attach a few balloons or flags to the corners to attract attention. Anchor the board to the easel and anchor the easel to the ground with tent stakes. Attach wide ribbons in candy stripe fashion to the cords leading to the stakes to make them more visible and to prevent people from tripping.

Mini displays

This is the netherworld between displays and signs. Here are three related items. Perhaps you can think of more:

▲ Tent cards and other table cards: These are folded notices printed on stiff paper, usually having two or more panels, that are placed on tables for people to read. Table cards usually appear in restaurants and cafeterias. They're not intended for people to take with them, but only to look at. Check them frequently and replace then promptly.

▲ Hanging decorations: These are like table cards but suspended from the ceiling or light fixtures, hanging a little above eye level over dining tables in restaurants and cafeterias.

▲ Paper placemats or tray liners in local dining establishments.

Outdoor signs

This has happened more than once to me: I see a poster in a shop window and then an article in the newspaper. I phone for tickets and ask for directions. When I locate the right street, I find myself driving up and down the street (usually a long one) looking for the theater. On the third or fourth pass, I spot a small sign above a doorway that identifies the building (which looks much like other buildings on the street) as the adopted home of the theater group.

This is not good. If there is any doubt in your mind that the building in which your theater group will perform is not clearly identifiable as a theater, please put up a sign.

CREATIVE DISPLAYS: A series of color photographs depicting the use of makeup to age the actors (above) was displayed in the theater lobby to educate and entice the audience.

Cut-out signs (above right) catch the eye with unconventional shapes, larger-than-life figures and bold, sparse lettering.

The sign for *Count Dracula* was designed as an indoor display.

Check regulations at your town hall governing signs.

A sign not only helps out-of-town visitors locate your building on the night of the show; it serves as a free, 24-hour advertisement for passersby. If a sign is up in front of the theater just two weeks before opening night, that's two weeks of promotion directed toward everyone who walks, bikes, skates, rides and drives by. Signs should be part of your bag of promotional tools.

Signs may appear in several places: in front of the theater building, at the ends of the street (if it's a small street tucked into a maze of streets), on the town green, and on the main road through town — perhaps at the city limits or at the intersection with the side road leading to the theater.

Contact your local billboard company. It may be interested in supporting activities and might put up a large reproduction of your poster with no rental charge. You might be asked to pay a production charge, however.

In front of the theater building itself, a traditional theater marquee is the best kind of sign to put up, but zoning laws and historic building provisions may prohibit this. Check regulations at your town hall governing signs. Be sure temporary signs are taken down promptly at the end of each production. Towns don't appreciate outdated advertising clutter.

Sign options

▲ A CLOTH BANNER: Sailcloth or parachute silk with painted or silk-screened lettering, temporarily hung over the theater entrance, across portico pillars, or between posts planted on the lawn. Vertical banners may be hung between portico pillars and anchored at the top and bottom. Banners may need half-moon slits cut into the fabric to allow the wind to safely pass through. Add grommets to attach ropes.

▲ PENNANTS AND FLAGS: Displayed from poles in front of the theater, these work great on windy days but hang limp and unreadable in calm or rainy weather.

▲ A-FRAME SANDWICH BOARDS: Two signboards hinged at the top, separated at the bottom to form an "A" when viewed from the side. Sometimes wooden or metal legs are attached. This is an easy sign to build and transport. To prevent strong winds from picking up your sandwich board, attach hinged cross-supports near the base and hang sandbags on these, or anchor the sign with tent stakes and rope pulled taut across the supports.

▲ V-FRAME SANDWICH BOARDS: Similar to the A-frame design, but hinged on the sides. This sign is viewable from more angles than the A-frame but it's less stable; anchor it well. Like the A-frame, it's better to attach legs to this sign so that the bottom of the signboard doesn't rot from sitting in the grass or resting on soil.

▲ SWING SIGN: A single signboard hung by hooks from an A- frame. The sign is portable, so anchor it.

▲ STILT TOWER SIGNS: A freestanding two-, three-, or four-sided structure consisting of a panel of wood on each side to hold signs, raised to eye-level or higher by placement at the top of poles. Add hooks, molding or screw channels to the panels and you can hang and re-hang your painted signs on this structure. If you add a roof with a protective ledge to the top of this structure and a Plexiglas front for each of the panels, you can use signs printed on poster-like paper. These are quicker and easier to prepare than hand-painted signs. Ask a professional electrician to add lights to the underside of the protective ledge for nighttime illumination.

▲ TRADITIONAL MARQUEE: Don't overlook the classic back-lit panel with letters hung on horizontal tracks—the kind of outdoor sign still used by movie theaters. Talk to a sign company about costs and options. The advantages of a marquee include ease of use, durability, and a traditional format that always says "show business."

▲ ROAD RHYMES: For supplemental signs to lead people along country roads to your theater, try the old, reliable Burma-Shave idea: A series of four small signs tacked to poles driven into the ground, spaced 50 feet or more apart, with each sign offering one part of a four-part rhyme. As people approach the theater they read the rhyme: *The theater's straight ahead / you're doing perfectly / so step aboard to watch our show / the musical, "Dames At Sea"!*

Wooden signs with an animated attachment attracts the eye. Add small pennants, flags or pinwheels, balloons, or an amusing whirligig. Check with local authorities to see if you're allowed to add battery-operated caution flashers.

See if your hardware store has paint that will reflect car headlights. Position the sign so it won't blind oncoming drivers.

The frames and boards of wooden signs must be painted with one or more coats of primer to seal the wood against the elements.

Sign design

A sign should announce the name of your group, the name of the show, production dates, and the phone number for tickets. For signs on the town green or along the road away from the theater, you might want to add the location of the theater.

For neat, readable letters, use stencils. Choose block letters with a sans serif face. Make the letters LARGE and keep the design simple.

An A-frame sign with essential information.

SUFFIELD PLAYERS

★ 38th Sensational Season! ★

☆ I'll Be Back Before Midnight! ☆
Oct. 18-19-20, 26-27 and Nov. 2-3 and 9-10, 1990

Thrills!

Just when you thought it was safe to go back to the theater, here's one of the scariest thrillers you've ever seen, featuring heart-pounding suspense and hair-raising special effects to put you in the proper mood for Halloween. Join us *if you dare!*

A Twisted Trilogy
Feb. 14-15-16, 22-23 and March 1-2, 1991

Chills!

An eerie evening of three one-act plays, each with a different director and cast, each with a special *twist* in the plot to surprise you--perhaps even to startle you just a little! Featuring *The Nightingale and not the Lark*, *The Audition*, and the classic tale of horror, *The Monkey's Paw*. Join us for this special showcase of Suffield Players talent!

Personals
May 2-3-4, 10-11 and 17-18, 1991

Cheers!

For our diamond jubilee 75th production, we present this hilarious musical comedy that explores the good, the bad and the ugly of modern dating through the *personal ads!* Join us for music and laughs!

All performances are presented at historic Mapleton Hall, on Mapleton Avenue in Suffield. Tickets are $5⁰⁰ on opening Thursday and Fridays, $10⁰⁰ for first Saturday night *(including after-show champagne gala)*, and $8⁰⁰ all other nights. Tickets go on sale three weeks before opening night. Reservations: (203)627-5749.

Coming your way
In 1990-1991!

MULTIPLE USES: This announcement appeared in the playbill, was distributed as a leaflet, and enlarged as a lobby billboard and poster. Note the different size and weight of type selected for emphasis and consistency of design.

Sign studies: A series of designs (above) created to add drama and fun to this theater's road signs. The individual show information would be painted over and the signs re-used by retaining the name of the group and its ticket reservation number. Yes, most of these designs were rejected as "too busy."

Below, the clearest design reworked with different lettering. The bolder, simpler lettering on the left is easier to read, and the phone illustration guides the eye to the all-important phone number. The marquee "lights" are painted with reflective paint to catch passing auto headlights.

Stick to one or two strong colors set against a contrasting background. Avoid complicated designs because people in cars, passing your sign as slowly as even 35 mph, can't take in much detail.

To paint multiple signs, first draw your design to exact size on a large piece of paper. Cover the design with a sheet of polyethylene, a stiff, clear plastic that has a shiny side and a dull side. It comes in rolls at art and hardware stores. Use a mat knife to cut away the lettering, leaving you with a reusable plastic stencil. Lay the stencil over your blank signboard, temporarily fix the stencil in place with masking tape, and use spray paint. You can quickly produce a series of beautiful signs this way.

Summary

- Publicity displays can entertain and educate your audiences.

- Use lobby displays to show memorabilia from past shows, creative materials from present shows, and posters announcing future shows.

- Don't overlook displays in bank lobbies, libraries, and store windows.

- Attractive, easily transported displays can be assembled on bulletin boards and set up on an easel. Keep bulletin board displays simple and organized-looking.

- Place signs in front of your theater and on roads leading to your theater two or three weeks before opening night to promote your production and help visitors find their way.

- Check out the possibility of a free billboard with your local sign company. If you ask, you might receive.

- Prime wood signs and use stencils to produce neat, readable lettering.

- Use LARGE lettering and keep your signs uncomplicated for quick reading from passing cars.

The Power of The Playbill

Chapter 15

- Mining promotional gold
- Making money and influencing audiences
- A useful layout system
- Advertising & billing
- Timetable and production tips

The playbill, or program*, is an often overlooked promotional tool.

In the hands of a wise publicist, the playbill can educate the audience about the performance, impress readers with the theater company's history of excellence, recruit new members, solicit financial support, flatter area merchants, and get everyone talking before the show, during intermission and after the curtain closes.

Oh, it offers one other tiny, little benefit: a playbill can make money!

It really makes me feel sad when an usher hands me a playbill that is a mere four pages long—a single sheet of letter-sized paper folded in half and consisting of a crude drawing on the cover, a list of cast and crew members typed on a hiccupping typewriter, and a brief greeting from the director on the back page.

This saddens me because it suggests one of two things: Either the publicist or playbill editor lacks imagination, or the poor soul has no one to help mine this mountain for its mother lode of promotional gold. With just a little more effort, what a piece of publicity this humble playbill could become!

This chapter will tell you how to enrich your promotional efforts with the playbill—step by step—and I'll even tell you how you can convince someone to take on the job so you won't have to.

This last promise is critical, because a super playbill that brings in super money involves super details and can be the cause of super headaches. (Please don't be supercilious. I'm super-serious!)

A necessity, not a luxury

On the question of elaborate playbills, there isn't much choice these days; either you produce a professional-looking playbill or disappoint your audience. This is because today's audiences are sophisticated people. Those who attend community or school theater often patronize professional theater as well, so they're used to seeing an attractive playbill with many pages filled with information and advertising.

Secondly, when amateur theater charges more for an evening's entertainment than a first-run movie house, audiences expect something for their money.

Finally, with the proliferation of computers and word processing applications in every aspect of our lives, it's no wonder that today's public isn't satisfied to see printed material poorly designed.

Make no mistake about it: if you don't know someone in town who will typeset your playbill at no charge, you should expect to include the expense of typesetting in your promotional budget as a legitimate cost of doing business.

Offer a commission

Let's get one worry out of the way: If your playbill produces sufficient advertising revenue, you can afford to hire a typesetter. (Check with a public accountant to determine what income taxes your theater group needs to pay on advertising revenues.)

---

*Throughout this book I avoid the word *program*. *Program*, meaning "the printed agenda of an event," may be confused with other meanings of the word, such as the event itself.

The Power of the Playbill 15.1

Playbill:
20 pages (5 sheets, 8½ x 14", folded in half, printed both sides); 1,000 copies

Cost of printing:
$.45 per playbill; $450 to print 1,000 playbills.

Price of ads:
$100 full page, $55 half page, $35 quarter page

Amount of advertising brought in:
13 pages of advertising, including 4 full-page ads, 6 half-page ads, 20 quarter-page ads, and 4 free quarter-page ads (you can always expect a few of these service-in-trade deals), for a total revenue of $1,430.00.

15 percent commission after printing costs:
$147.00

Profit for theater:
$833.00

You can bring in advertising revenue by assigning one person to do this and only this task for your group. You can convince someone to be your playbill advertising manager by offering a *commission*. In the world of advertising, the offer of a commission lures ambitious salespeople.

You or your theater's board of directors can set the terms: After the salesperson brings in a minimum amount of revenue (say, enough to cover the cost of printing the playbill) the salesperson can take a percentage (15 percent, for example) of all additional sales. The example (left) shows how this works.

This is my idea of a happy ending: the salesperson makes a happy profit, the theater has extra money, and you can afford to produce a handsome-looking playbill with several pages of information paid for with advertising revenue.

Seasonal advertising

Without raising advertising prices, you can increase your profit in one simple way: sell the advertising for your entire season at the beginning of the season. Your advertisers can be billed per show as long as they sign a contract for the entire year. Then you can go to your printer and print the majority of your playbill pages—those with advertisements—all at once for the whole year. This will cost less than printing just what you'll need for each show because you're printing in volume.

The most sought-after pages in the playbill are the most visible pages: the inside front and back covers, the back of the playbill, and the page opposite the list of actors and scene synopsis. You may wish to charge 10 percent extra for these pages. Offer these prestige pages to your most prominent merchants first.

All right. Have we got the financial worries out of the way? Before I leave this topic and move on to the creative part of putting together a playbill, let me suggest some tips for good customer relations:

How to pitch advertising

1. The Advance Notice: Mail letters to merchants to say that you'll be coming by their offices soon. Include a page from the playbill and a brief introduction about your group and its beneficial relationship with the community.

2. The Greeting: Call on customers in person. Nothing is as persuasive as a smiling face and a reassuring handshake.

3. The Introduction: Bring along dramatic photos and favorable news clippings about your theater and a recent production. Be prepared to relate a brief history of your group—but keep it *brief*.

4. The Preview: Announce that the purpose of the visit is to let the merchant know about your advertising program.

5. The Incentive: Mention how many people you're expecting to attend performances—i.e., how many people will see the playbill's advertisements. If you draw audiences from several communities, mention this (gather demographic information through audience surveys). Merchants are always trying to draw new business.

6. The Enticement: Show samples of your playbill or, if this is your first season with a new format, a mock paste-up of a proposed playbill to give the customer an idea of what the playbill looks like. On one of the pages, show a full-page ad featuring the customer's business.

7. The Pitch: Show a price sheet, printed on your theater group's letterhead, with your name and phone number at the bottom of the sheet. The sheet includes prices, dimensions of ads, deadlines for submission of to-be-composed and camera-ready ads, and scheduled playbill and performance dates.

8. The Lure: Show a second sheet with advertiser rewards: one free theater ticket for buying a quarter-page ad, two free theater tickets for a half-page ad, four free tickets for a full-page ad.

9. The Request: Ask for the sale. Get an agreement. in writing with a formal (but simple-looking) contract. Determine the payment schedule and agree on dates in writing.

10. The Closure: Thank the customer for listening. Leave the customer with information about the group, the price and reward fact sheets, a copy of the contract (if the customer signed), a flier about the coming show, and finally a coupon good for a free, nonalcoholic drink at your theater's refreshment bar if the customer comes to a performance.

Follow up for good relations

Once the sale is made and the contract is signed, get the advertiser to proofread the final version of the ad as it will appear in the playbill. Mail the advertiser information on how to reserve free tickets that come with the ad for the performance desired. Include a map to the theater and information about the show.

Once the playbill is printed, mail a "tear sheet" to the advertiser—the actual page from the playbill with the advertiser's ad—along with a thank-you note or a friendly reminder that payment is due.

At the end of the season, send a thank-you letter to all advertisers for supporting your theater throughout the season, and express your hope that the support will continue next year. Include a preview of next season's lineup of shows.

Getting organized: personnel

To put together a dramatic playbill, you'll need the skills of a sales manager who may also serve as billing agent (to make sure merchants pay), a typesetter, and a paste-up artist to prepare the playbill for printing.

In Chapter 12 on **Posters**, I list several ways to locate an artist. A good artist will not only paste the pieces of the playbill together, but also create a design that, used throughout the playbill, will give it a theme and a unified look.

Creating a theme

In a playbill for a production of my adaptation of *Dr. Jekyll & Mr. Hyde,* Victorian gas lamps appeared on the information pages along with diagrams of the brain from a medical book. For a Dracula play, the playbill featured bats in the corners of the pages.

In the playbill for a murder-mystery play that I co-wrote, *Decidedly Deadly*, the actors' biographies were accompanied by pairs of front and side mug shots, complete with number plates held under the chins.

You can convince someone to be your playbill advertising manager by offering a commission.

Playbill Informational Material	
Page	**Item**
1	cover
1	title page
3/4	actor and scene list
1/4	audience notes: smoking, exits, camera prohibition
1/2	list of songs
1	production crew list
1/4	theater company board of directors or top school officials
1	list of supporting patrons
1/2	clip & mail coupon to become a patron
1/2	history and philosophy of the theater company or school
2	actors' biographies
1/2	message from the director
1/2	history of the play
1/4	preview announcement of next show
1/2	list of awards or excerpts from recent reviews

For the musical *Is There Life After High School?* the playbill was designed to look like a yearbook, with actors' biographies listing "favorite subject," "activities," "nickname," and "voted most likely to —." You can easily go overboard with this total-theme approach to playbills; so, easy does it. Wait for a special show to come along that seems to beg for this treatment. Also make sure that the treatment ties into the poster graphic for a unified theme.

A word about actors' biographies: Resist with all your heart the tendency of many bios these days to be too cute or ridiculous. Don't allow an actor to say in a playbill's bio, "I'd like to thank Melvin, my pet snake." The biography format may be creative occasionally, but the content must always be informative and professional.

Contents of a playbill

To calculate how many pages of informational material (that is, everything that isn't an advertisement) you'll need in your playbill, you should begin by making a list of items and then estimating how much of a page you expect each item to use up. To make advertising pay, limit the total page count of informational material to about one-third to one-half of the playbill.

Appendix C has a blank form you can copy and use to itemize and tally. In the left margin on this page is a list for a 20-page playbill:

Readers doing rapid calculations will note that the list of information items totals 10 ½ pages out of a 20-page playbill. This threatens to cut into our profit margin, particularly if, taking the figures from the previous example, we need to fit 13 pages of advertising. The ads come first because these pay the bills. Therefore, three and a half pages of information must be eliminated to meet our goal of keeping the total amount of informational pages to no more than one-third of the playbill's 20 pages.

Let's consider the value of the listed informational items: Some of the items provide standard information that audiences look for, such as who the actors and crew are, what scenes and songs to expect, and who gives money to the group.

Providing a history of your theater group and listing theater festival awards is a way of familiarizing newcomers with your organization. If you've received favorable reviews, it's nice to blow your horn a little and reprint key words of praise along with the source of the quote. If you want to reprint more than a brief paragraph or two, you should get permission from the source.

An announcement about your next show does more than inform theatergoers to make plans; it also alerts potential actors and crew members to consider auditioning and joining your group. More than once I've heard of an audience member asking an usher if the theater company can use particular costumes or props for a show previewed in the playbill.

My friend Lyle Pearsons, a long-time member of the Suffield Players in Connecticut, came up with this idea while managing advertising for a playbill: He takes a half-page in every playbill to list the names of all businesses who have bought ads. He precedes the list with the request, "Please support our business patrons." In another playbill, the message reads, "Please welcome these new advertisers to our family of supporters." Advertisers see this as a free, extra mention in the playbill. This builds goodwill. This also teaches a fundamental lesson in good business: Always give customers something extra.

So far, all the informational items appear necessary, yet we must cut three and a half pages. Almost always, you'll find that your list of informational items exceeds your budget, leaving you with the obligation to cut the list. In our practice example, let's say that the show is a straight play; that allows us to eliminate the need for a half-page list of songs. We can try to put the actors' biographies all on one page instead of two since it's a small cast. For the same reason we can cut the actor and scene lists to a half-page.

It may begin to become clear to you that informational items for a big musical tend to take up more playbill space than for a straight play. True, true. You are also probably aware that musicals cost more to produce than straight plays. So, if you've passed over *The Iceman Cometh* for *Man of LaMancha*, plan on selling more ads to pay for the bigger playbill and the bigger show.

Let's cut the list of awards from the playbill and, instead, enlarge the list to poster size and display it in the lobby—perhaps above a table where patrons will find forms to put them on the theater's mailing list.

What's left? Still one more page to cut? All right, let's skip the history of the group for this issue and run it in the next playbill—another half-page savings. If we can list the members of the board of directors on the same page with the crew list, we'll find ourselves down to just a quarter-

FOR YOUR SAFETY AND ENJOYMENT

This production will have one 15-minute intermission.

There is NO SMOKING in the theater.

Absolutely NO CAMERAS or other recording devices may be used during the performance without the house manager's permission.

Emergency exits are in the rear of the hall, and through the doorways to the left and right of the stage.

Please silence pocket beepers and watches that may distract your fellow audience members during the performance.

Please see one of our ushers if you have any questions or special needs.

If you enjoyed the performance, please tell your friends. If you did not, please tell us!

ITEMS in an effective playbill may include cautionary and helpful information for the audience (above)...

VAMPIRE LORE

Do You Know How to Recognize A Vampire?

* a VAMPIRE has bright red lips
* a VAMPIRE has protruding, sharp pointed canine teeth
* a VAMPIRE has an ashen complexion
* a VAMPIRE can be seen only between sunset and sunrise
* a VAMPIRE can read minds
* a VAMPIRE never eats
* a VAMPIRE can hypnotise its victims
* a VAMPIRE casts no reflection in a mirror
* a VAMPIRE is extremely strong
* a VAMPIRE has red, diabolical eyes
* a VAMPIRE has pointed ears
* a VAMPIRE has foul breath
* a VAMPIRE is icy cold to touch
* a VAMPIRE can dissolve in a mist
* a VAMPIRE has animals at its beck and call
* a VAMPIRE can assume the shape of any animal - usually a bat or wolf

Do You Know How to Ward Off a Vampire?

* Sprig of Hawthorne
* Iron implements
* Religious pictures
* Silver
* A cross worn around the neck
* Holy Water
* Garlic or the scent of garlic
* Batswort worn on the person
* Thorns, esp. of a rose
* Avoid looking into its eyes

...information about the history or other background of the show to stimulate discussion, or (below) an extra thank-you for patronage.

Please Support Our Business Patrons

Aecon Design Builders
Agawam True Value Hardware
Ahrens, Fuller, St. John & Vincent, Inc.
Lawrence Albert, D.D.S., P.C.
American Offset Printers
Ronald Bauerle, D.D.S., P.C.
Billy's Pizza Restaurant
Enfield Federal Savings
First National Bank, Suffield
Gail's Flowers & Gifts
Gardner Holdridge Travel
Geery's Fine Arts
Get Nailed
Heritage Funeral Home

Inside Outlet
Mark Drug Co.
Milton Bradley Company
New England Bank & Trust Co.
Old Sykes Mill
Pioneer Telephone Answering Service
Norman G. Streeter, CPA
Suffield Bank
Suffield Medical Center
Suffield Sentry Hardware
Swim Center One
Travel Pros International
Zeke's Pump Service

A fundamental lesson in good business: always give customers something extra.

page over our seven-page limit for informational items in our 20-page playbill.

Suppose we ask the director to include a few brief details on the history of the play in his half-page message to the audience?

We did it! Even before we lay out the playbill, we can be confident that everything will fit because our numbers add up. Now...

How to lay out your playbill

To decide where to place ads and informational material, you should make a dummy program with blank paper. Number the pages and staple them together in the middle. Roughly sketch in the locations for your ads and information items.

Some guidelines: avoid placing two full pages of advertising facing each other. Advertisers know that readers looking through the playbill will simply turn the page without pausing if they see a two-page spread of nothing but ads, and advertisers won't want to give you their business under these conditions. The solution to this advertising glut is to *scatter your informational material throughout the playbill.* When you do this, you not only get audiences to read the ads while they're reading your message from the director, your list of awards and the names of contributing members; but, also, your readers don't feel overwhelmed by the imposing sight of several pages of non-stop informational items all jammed together.

"Oy," I heard a man lament as he looked at eight pages of information in the middle of a playbill; *"if I wanted to read a book, I'd have stayed home already!"*

There are two more pieces of advice about balancing ads and information:

▲ Place the page that lists the characters and scenes where the information will be easy to find—near the beginning or right in the middle of the playbill. This is the first page people look for because it tells them how many intermissions to expect.

▲ If your pages have a two- or three- column format, always place your informational items in the outside column, farthest from the center staple and nearest to the thumbs of the reader paging through the playbill. This is a natural position for information because the eyes always look first at the upper, outside corners of a page.

Once you have arranged your pages the way you like in your dummy playbill, pull out the center staples and spread out the pages. Notice how the pages are numbered in apparently mismatched pairs:

Sheet 1: pages 1 & 20 appear on one side, and 2 & 19 appear on the reverse side.

Sheet 2: pages 3 & 18 and 4 & 17

Sheet 3: pages 5 & 16 and 6 & 15

Sheet 4: pages 7 & 14 and 8 & 13

Sheet 5: pages 9 & 12 and 10 & 11

After you've laid out a few playbills, you'll find it quicker to map out the pages on a single chart of miniature pairs of pages. This will be especially helpful when you have some pages pre-printed for the entire season. You can indicate these pages quickly on the chart and fill in the rest with ease. **Appendix C** has a blank Playbill Page Map to copy and use.

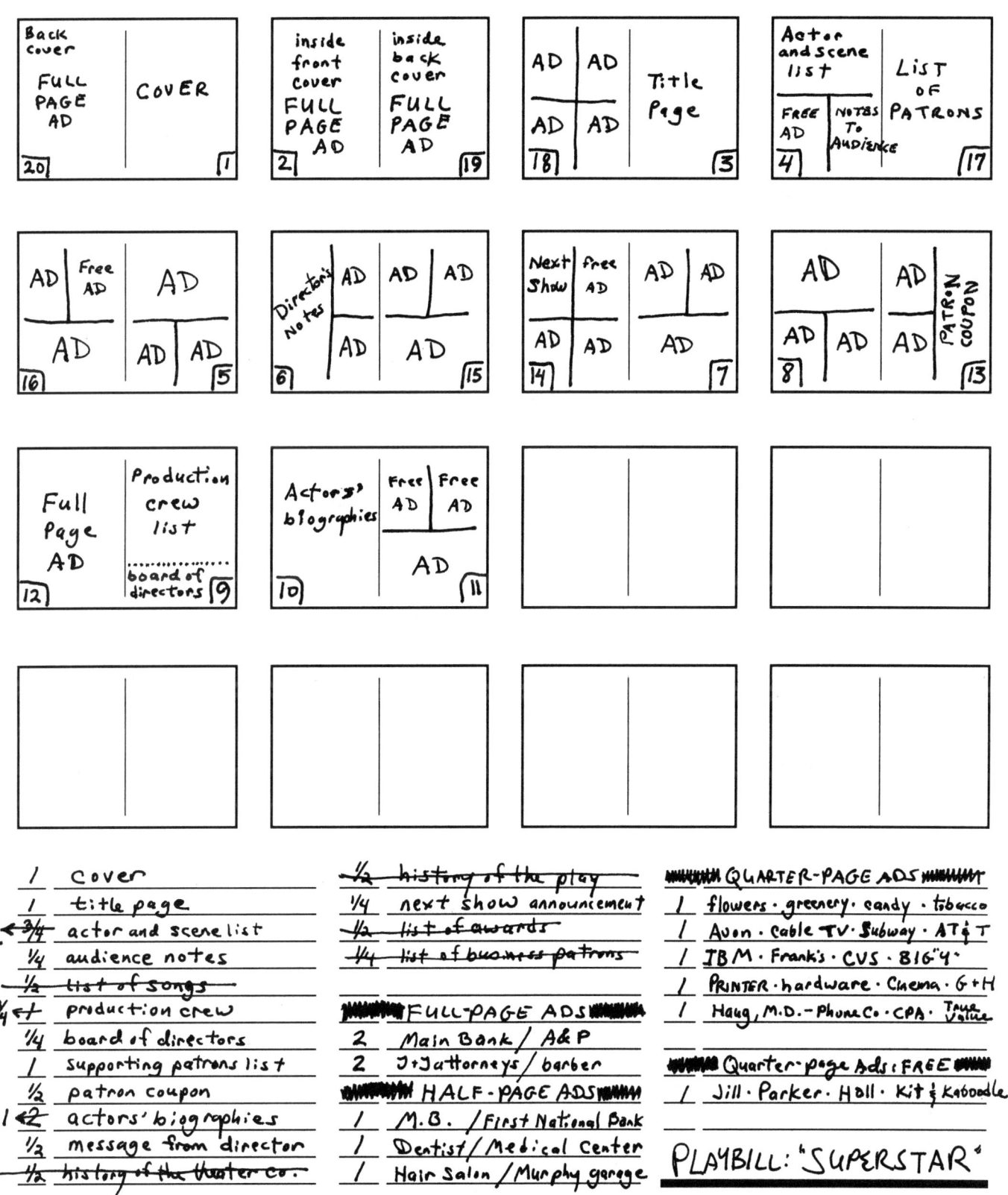

How to map your playbill pages: number the pages, map out placement for advertising, and fill in the remainder with editorial material. A blank map is in Appendix C.

Avoid placing two full pages of advertising facing each other.

Of course, if you have a competent layout artist, you can stop after the tally sheet and let the artist lay out the pages. I just thought you'd like to know how it's done. Now you know, and don't you feel so smart that you just want to burst?

Final design tips

Whether your playbill is only a few pages or a monster 40-pager like David Ladderbush produces five times a year for Lewiston/Auburn's Community Little Theatre in Maine, you should employ design principles to organize the ads and editorial information.

Create a set number of columns on each page and use this pattern throughout the playbill. Designate a series of specific sizes for all ads and stick to these measurements. If a page is laid out with two columns and divided into quarters for a maximum of four ads per page, a one-third-page ad will ruin the organized look of the playbill.

Select a series of borders (artists call these "rules") for your ads — no more than six or eight simple borders—and use only these borders. Avoid rococo frames and ribbon candy borders that look garish against other ads on the page. Make exceptions now and then for special occasions or insistent clients, but beware the helter-skelter look. Full-page ads can get away with wilder borders because they don't compete with anything else on the page.

Select a standard border or other design technique to help readers distinguish informational material from ads. I like to use a 1-point double rule for informational items. No ad is allowed to carry the same border as the informational material. For a less formal design, put borders on all ads, but no borders on informational material. Still another choice: highlight informational items with a light gray background (20 percent screen).

Some theater companies print their playbill cover and inside center page on color paper. The inside center page has the major information on cast and crew, song titles, scene listing and biographies. All other information is scattered throughout the playbill's white pages, and mixed carefully with advertisements.

Collect playbills from other theater groups and decide for yourself what appeals to you.

A final tip: Put a date, including the year, on your playbill's title page. It's an easy thing to overlook, but the omission will drive future theater historians crazy.

Working with printers

See Chapter 11 on this topic to learn about selecting paper and inks, previewing your design with the printer, and ways to save money.

Timetable and production tips

See the **Master Battle Plan** in **Appendix A** for a complete production timetable and steps to follow from collecting advertising to delivering playbills.

Meanwhile, here are a few tips that will help you avoid schedule and financial problems:

▲ Begin with an early deadline for placing all advertising orders. You need to know what you're working with to lay out your playbill. Ads that come dribbling in right up until the day before

~~~ Merry Monster Puppet Theater ~~~
PLAYBILL *style sheet*

TO TYPESETTERS AND DESIGNERS:

Playbills for the Merry Monster Puppet Theater will conform to the following format to ensure uniformity in style from one issue to the next, year to year:

Page size:	7 x 8 ½" (from 8 ½ x 11" sheet folded in half)
Margins	½" on all sides
Columns:	two: 2 ¾" each with ½" gutter
Borders:	hairline double-rule with squared corners for all informational material; advertisements may have single hairline, 1-, 2-, 3- and 4-pt., and combos such as 1-2 pt., 3-1 pt., and 1-2-1 pt., with round or square corners, or top-and-bottom-only format.

Informational Material

Display type:	28-pt. Helvetica Medium, U/L case, 2 pt. letterspacing.
Subheads:	16-pt. Helvetica Light, U/L case
Text:	10/11 x 14 Modern Times Roman, justified
Captions:	9/10 x 12 Modern Times Roman Light Italic, justified
	Advertisements may not use these fonts.
Photos:	hairline rule set out from photo edges by 1 pt. of leading

HERE'S WHAT CRITICS SAY ABOUT PLAYER PRODUCTIONS:

"The Suffield Players have big ideas and a big reputation..."
—The Hartford Courant

"The Suffield Players, one of the best groups in local community theatre, work moments of magic..."
—Springfield Daily News

"The Suffield Players, probably the most accomplished amateur community theatre in the area...set a new standard... Community theatre doesn't get any better."
—Manchester Journal Inquirer

"On a purely dramatic level, it makes for the most enjoyable and satisfying evening of playgoing that you're apt to see in a long, long time."
—Southwick-Suffield Advertiser News

"A polished theatrical gem...a visual feast! Applause, applause..."
—Westfield Evening News

"Costumes, lighting, and audio-special effects...grab your attention...a rousing success..."
—Agawam Advertiser

"When the job is done, the play's the thing...The Suffield Players often do original productions. Their most recent, the winner of several awards at the Association of Community Theatres Festival..."
—The New York Times

PLAYBILL POWER: A style sheet (above, left) guides typesetters to maintain a consistent look from one issue of the playbill to the next. Newspaper quotes (above, right) communicate quality and pride. Lines from a clever script (right, from Noel Coward's *Hay Fever*) give audiences an appealing preview and a fun reminder of their evening at the theater.

"Cowardly Quotes"

"You've always brought us up to be very free about things."

"They're a very Bohemian family, I believe."

"We're an independent family..."

"Swearing doesn't help."
"It helps me a lot."

"I should stay if I were you — it would be more dignified."

"I'd love to be beautifully poised and carry off difficult situations with a lift of the eyebrows—"

"The great thing is to get an obscure word."

"I'm always rude to people I like."

"Don't be statuesque."

Put a date, including the year, on your playbill's title page. The omission will drive future theater historians crazy.

the playbill is due at the print shop will drive you insane. Don't permit this.

▲ Let everyone know that you have an iron-clad deadline for advertising. Ask to speak to the assembled cast and crew, and encourage everyone to bring in advertising from their family, friends and neighbors. Request that they coordinate their efforts with the playbill's advertising sales manager.

▲ Get an agreement with the general manager, director, stage manager, and all designers: No one may offer free advertising in your playbill in exchange for services without your permission. Be stingy in allowing free ads, or too many generous souls will bankrupt you.

▲ Inform the general manager, director and stage manager that your playbill has editorial deadlines. That's right—more than one deadline. The first deadline, which comes at the same time as the deadline for advertising, should be about four to six weeks before opening night. At this time you should have the names and roles of the actors, the list of scenes, the names of the director and designers and principal musicians, the history of the play (you'll probably have to look this up yourself) and actors' biographies. Use the biography form in **Appendix D,** which will also help you write your news releases. Check the royalty contract for publicity requirements.

▲ The only informational items you won't have until the last few days before the playbill goes to the print shop is the list of *production crew* and, possibly, the updated *list of patrons*. Alert your typesetter to expect these two lists to arrive for immediate typing about two weeks before opening night. Ask the general manager to place a large sign-up sheet in the construction area so that crew members can record their own names if they want to be listed in the playbill. Provide the general manager with an outline list of crew members with spaces to fill in as the production weeks pass. Say you'll pick up the completed list two weeks before opening night. Prepare a line at the bottom of the crew list that says "Grateful thanks to all others whose names were not available at press time."

▲ Edit informational material as soon as it arrives. Don't wait for it to accumulate. Offer the typist a choice of receiving the edited material and ads a little at a time or all at once.

▲ Create a *style guide* that will give consistency to your playbills year after year, no matter how many times you change typesetters. The guide establishes the size and style of headline and body copy typefaces, margins, columns and borders. Ask your paste-up artist to help you develop the style guide.

▲ You can save money by asking the printer not to collate or staple playbill pages. Buy a long-mouth stapler and set up the pages assembly-line fashion backstage or in your rehearsal space (you'll need spoons for creasing the center fold and a box to store finished playbills). Arrange for a crew to assist with

THE BUSINESS OF SHOW BUSINESS: Promotional brochure (left) lists prices of playbill advertising, sponsorship, membership, and incentives for each. Two kinds of playbill covers (right): one emphasizes the production, the other promotes the name of the group.

There are three ways that you can become part of **StageWorks III**.

I. Season Subscription: See all three shows for $20.00. Season Subscribers are guaranteed the best seats in the house, save $3.00 off the regular ticket price and will only have to make **one** purchase for the entire season.

II. Advertiser / Sponsor: One payment buys you ad space in all **three** of our show programs *and* you will receive a variety of special ticket packages:

Ad Prices

Size	Cost	You Receive:
Full Page	$250	4 Season Tickets
Half Page	$150	2 Season Tickets
Quarter Page	$ 75	1 Season Ticket

Sponsor Rates

Category	Cost	You Receive:
Stage Door Johnnies	$ 25-99	1 Season Ticket
Stage Hands	$100-249	2 Season Tickets
Stage Managers	$250-499	6 Season Tickets
Stage Stars	$500 +	10 Season Tickets

-- Sponsors will be listed by name in a special section of the Program --

III. Membership: Join StageWorks. We are always looking for new people, both on stage and off. We need actors, singers, dancers, musicians, carpenters, painters, and a wide range of behind the scenes personnel. If you've ever wanted to get involved with theatre, now's your chance. A first year membership in StageWorks is $25.00, with $10 for each year after.

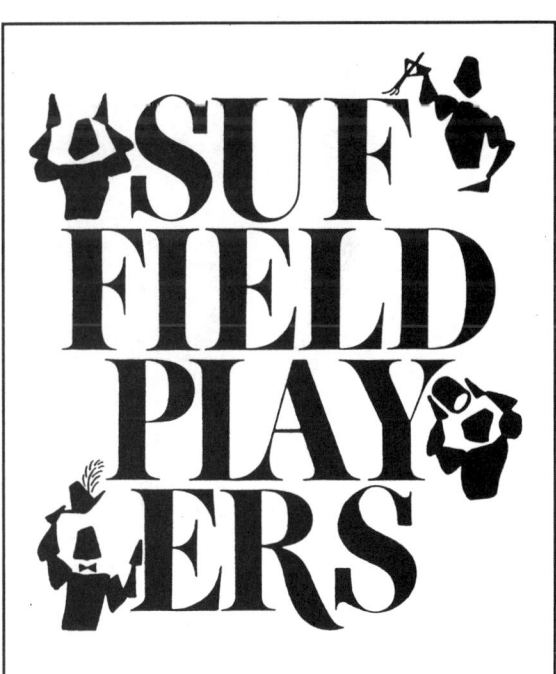

assembly, put an eager volunteer in charge, and busy yourself with some other project.

▲ If your show has several performances, you don't need to risk killing yourself and your volunteers by trying to assemble all the playbills before opening night. Assemble enough each night for that evening's needs plus 20-40 percent to get ahead on the next night's assembly.

▲ Save samples of the playbill for the advertising manager and for your group's history files.

SUMMARY

☛ Playbills can offer a wealth of information to help audiences appreciate the performance as well as the theater group. Today's audiences expect a well-designed playbill. Anything less risks making your group look unprofessional.

☛ Playbills should not just pay for themselves with advertising revenue. They should make a profit for the theater company.

☛ Motivate your salesperson with the offer of a commission.

☛ Make a tally sheet before laying out pages to determine your playbill's space needs. Informational material should not exceed the number of pages devoted to advertising.

☛ Organize your playbill. Design a column format for your pages and stick to it to give your playbill a uniform appearance.

☛ Mix informational material with ads to avoid "info-glut" and "ad blur," but create a design format that distinguishes one from the other.

☛ As with anything else in publicity, allow enough time to complete the steps needed to produce a playbill.

Advertising

Chapter 16

- Advertising's role
- Location & timing
- Calculating costs
- Measuring success
- Design for newspapers
- Ads for radio and TV
- Reality-check

The easiest kind of publicity in the world to do is advertising. You hand someone at the newspaper or the radio station (or if you have real money, the TV station) a wad of money and tell 'em to make an advertisement and "put it where people will see it." Advertising is almost always the most expensive kind of publicity, too, because you're paying someone—the business end of the news media—to do your job.

Yes, advertising is the easiest kind of publicity to do—but it's as hard as anything else to do well.

A poorly designed newspaper ad won't attract people. In fact, it may change people's high opinion of your organization. A poorly performed ad on radio or TV will do this, too. We all can think of corny commercials badly put-together for a local business. They look cheap, but the cost in lost prestige and public embarrassment is expensive! Finally, a great advertisement will accomplish nothing if it isn't properly placed—if the ad runs too infrequently, or on the wrong day, or time of day, or on the wrong page.

Effective advertising means knowing at least a few of the fundamentals that will prevent these errors. This chapter has the information you need.

Advertising's role

I hesitate to recommend a heavy emphasis on advertising to help school and community theaters achieve full houses for this simple reason: most amateur groups don't have a lot of money to buy advertising. For non-profit organizations, advertising should be considered a promotional tool of last resort. You should try all other techniques in this book first before buying ads. That's why I've left this chapter until now.

With that said, advertising may be just the thing to come to your rescue when audiences are sparse.

Advertising puts you on a par with your competition. Your ad, side-by-side with an ad of the same size (or same commercial length) placed by the Equity theater in town, makes your theater company look professional. Just be sure the quality of your production is acceptable or people will feel cheated.

Advertising lets you pick the exact time and place to announce your news, which a news release can't do.

Location and timing

Which is the right place for a newspaper ad? While the largest amount of advertising appears in Sunday and Wednesday editions, these are not necessarily good days for advertising your show.

It's true, Sunday is a big advertising day because, even if people don't buy a newspaper during the week, most everyone buys a Sunday paper. Advertisers know this and put their money in the Sunday paper.

Most people in the United States get paid on Thursday or Friday, and most people save their major shopping until they are paid. Advertisers know this and time their mid-week advertising to tempt people to spend a portion of their paychecks as soon as cash is in hand.

However, when do most people think about going to the theater? Usually on Thursdays, as they begin to think about the weekend. Also, Fridays and Saturdays, which are chief theater-going nights.

Possible Display Ad Campaign For "Pippin"

Production dates: Thursdays, Fridays and Saturdays

Oct. 22-23-24 & 29-30-31

Key: * = Production dates, A-J = Priority ad dates

OCTOBER

SUN.	MON.	TUE.	WED.	THUR.	FRI.	SAT.
				1	2	3
4	5	6	7	8 C	9	10
11	12	13	14	15 A	16 G	17 H
18	19	20	21	22 * B	23 * D	24 * E
25	26	27	28	29 * F	30 * I	31 * J

Advertising lets you pick the exact time and place to announce your news, which a news release can't do.

Newspapers know this, which is why most newspapers in this country print a special section on Thursdays that features arts and entertainment news. It follows that businesses and organizations involved in leisure-time activities are right to aim for publicity as well as advertising to appear on Thursdays. Friday and Saturday issues of the newspaper are fine, too, if you have extra money in your advertising budget. If not, at least get your ad into the Thursday newspaper's Weekend section.

What about Sunday? If your shows are staged Thursday through Saturday, a display advertisement (that's an ad with large lettering and displayed in a box, in contrast to a classified ad in the newspaper's Help Wanted section) in the Sunday paper is too soon or too late to have much effect on most people. Aim instead to get your show listed at no charge in the Sunday newspaper's weekly calendar of events.

Let's look at a calendar to consider possible dates to advertise a show in a daily newspaper. In the calendar at the top of this page, production dates are marked with asterisks. The letters A-J indicate how I would prioritize dates for advertising, with A (the Thursday before opening night) having the highest priority, and J, the lowest.

If I had money only for one ad in one newspaper and my show was opening on a Thursday night, I'd buy my one ad in the previous Thursday newspaper's Weekend section. This is because it's better to give readers a week's notice than to announce your show is opening on opening night.

Keep in mind that the display ad supplements a free calendar listing in that same Weekend section. If you sent out your news release in time, your event should be listed. The display ad only intensifies reader awareness of your show.

Back to the calendar. After taking out ads on opening night and the Thursday before opening night (A and B), my next priority, marked "C," would be for the next earliest Thursday—two weeks before opening night. With these three ads, you're in the Weekend section for three weeks in a row—a strong beginning to a longer campaign if you wish. The plan works especially well if your opening night is a Friday.

Assuming that most audiences don't decide sooner than two weeks before opening night to order tickets for a school or community theater production, the next two most important issues of the newspaper to place more display ads are the issues coinciding with the first Friday and Saturday night performances (D and E). This takes advantage of the possibility that people may look in the newspaper on impulse on these days and decide immediately to see that night's show. Just as importantly, however, advertising on these two days serves as notice for people planning their activities for the following weekend.

From here, I rank advertising on the last Thursday (F) as much more important than the last Fridays (I) and Saturday (J) of the production. This is because the last two days are nearly too late for advertising to do much good, except that these days might prompt a last-minute ticket sale. The name of the game is to promote *early* ticket sales.

So, next in priority, after the Thursday following opening night, I would choose to advertise on Fridays and Saturday before opening night (G, H).

Of course, if you are considering advertising in more than one newspaper, your budget will be stretched thinner. Still, I've given you the logic I use in deciding to advertise in any daily newspaper. The same priority method can be applied to several newspapers.

Calculating costs

Most newspapers sell display ads by the advertising column-inch. When you call a newspaper's display advertising department for prices, you should ask for the "cost per column inch" or PCI. You calculate the cost of your ad by multiplying the unit price by the number of columns wide and the number of inches deep you want your ad to be.

For example, in a newspaper with two-inch-wide columns and a PCI cost of $20.00, a display ad measuring one column wide and four inches deep is called a one-by-four-inch ad and will cost you $80.00—that's $20.00 per inch, per column. If you wanted your ad to be two columns wide and three inches deep, this would be called a two-by-three-inch ad and it would cost $120.00 (2x3=6; 6x$20 PCI=$120.00).

Ask if the newsaper offers a "buy one ad, get a second one in the same week at a discount" deal.

The day has not come when all newspapers have standardized column-widths, and even within a newspaper the editorial column widths vary from section to section and even on a single page. This is why you need to ask for the measurement of an advertising column width when calling your newspaper. When you get the measurements for each newspaper and compare the PCI price to the column width, you will discover that some newspapers offer a better advertising space price. Factor in a comparison of circulation before deciding what advertising to buy.

Most audiences don't decide sooner than two weeks before opening night to order tickets for a school or community theater production.

If you or an artist with your theater group is preparing the paste-up of your ads to be camera-ready for the newspaper, you will want to prepare your ads to fit within the advertising column width. When designing an ad that will be more than one column wide, remember that there is a "gutter," or narrow column of space between advertising columns. Ask for the exact width of a two- or three-column ad.

How big should your ads be? Look at others on the page. Your ad must be large enough to carry basic information about your show (see the section on "design" on the next page) without the print being too small. You don't want your ad to be the smallest one on the page because that will make your show look small. On the other hand, you probably can't afford the largest ad on the page (which is most likely a movie ad from a multi-screen cinema complex). Pick a size in-between the smallest and the largest that you can afford.

Advertising experts debate all the time the question of whether it's better to buy one or two big ads on key days or run several small ads. It's a delicate balance full of pros and cons. Trust your instincts. Still not sure? Ask the opinion of the advertising sales agent at the newspaper for an opinion. Set an amount that you want to spend, pick priorities by the logic we've examined in our calendar example earlier in this chapter, and see what the salesperson recommends.

Here is a rule of thumb: As long as the individual ads are of a minimum respectable size, frequency has an edge over size. However, if your ads are too small to be noticed, running one a day for two weeks won't do much good.

Ask your newspaper's advertising salesperson to explain the process of insertion orders, the policy for pulling ads in the event of sell-out shows, and contract rates for co-op advertising with other productions.

Measuring success

How do you know your ads work? There are two basic methods of determining this: Surveying your audience and placing a "tracer" in the display ad.

Conscientious theaters poll their audiences once a year to find out how they liked a show or the season of shows, how they rate the theater staff, what kinds of shows and services they would like to see, and how they learned about productions. Surveys may ask audiences specifically which newspapers they recalled seeing that carried advertisements about a production.

Surveys are helpful but of limited value when it comes to measuring advertising. My experience convinces me that most people have fallible memories and a tendency in surveys to say what they think the pollster wants to hear; so, I don't trust surveys as much as tracers.

An example of a tracer is a coupon either built into a display ad or designed as the entire ad. Somewhere on the ad, usually in a corner, the advertiser puts a number or letter code that is specific to the date and newspaper in which the ad appears.

When people show up at the box office with newspaper coupons offering $1.00 off a ticket on opening night, or a two-for-one offer for a preview show, the coupons reveal people's reading patterns. Here, for example, are the results of coupons handed in on an opening night:

> **Tracer Tally:** "Plaza Suite" opening night coupons
>
> **Opening night:** Friday, May 21
>
> **Coupon run:**
> Daily Herald (DH)   Thursdays May 13 & 20
> Weekly Bugle (WB) Tuesdays, May 11 & 18
>
> **Coupon results:**
> DH13 -   4 coupons
> DH20 - 16 coupons
> WB11 - 12 coupons
> WB18 - 19 coupons

The tracers tell us that during the week *preceding* the week of opening night, three times as many people clipped coupons from the weekly newspaper (12) as the daily newspaper (4). During the days leading to opening night, the weekly newspaper again drew more coupon clippings (19) than the daily (16). However, the number of coupons clipped from the daily newspaper on the day before the show's opening (16 coupons from May 20) was nearly as high as the weekly's (19 coupons from May 18), and four times as much as the previous week's daily coupon total (4 coupons from May 13).

This suggests that bargain-hunters may prowl the weekly news more than the daily newspaper, or it may mean that most people clipping coupons did so within three days of opening night. To save money next time, it might be frugal to eliminate advertising on the previous Thursday in the daily newspaper since it drew only four coupons.

Ad design for newspapers

Your newspaper ad isn't a billboard. It isn't a prospectus. It's a brief announcement that you are putting on a show. Like a poster but even more so, the simpler your ad is to read, the more impact it has.

Your newspaper display ad should include: The name of your theater company, the name of the show (and perhaps the playwright's name), location of the theater, production dates, and a phone number to reserve tickets. Consider the importance of three other bits of information: types of payment accepted, availability of air conditioning, and accessability of the theater for persons with physical impairments that affect their mobility.

Prioritize the information: Which is better known and more likely to attract the interest of potential customers in the community reading the newspaper ad—the name of your group or the name of the show? Whichever one of the two provides the stronger audience draw, put this in large, bold letters.

Organize the dates for people to understand: March 3-4-5 and 10-11-12 communicates two weekends of three consecutive nights each. March 3,4,5,10,11,12 comes out as a blur to the reader's eye. March 3-5 & 10-12 could be confused as just four dates. March 3-12 implies a show every night from March 3 through March 12.

Keep the wording minimal. Don't write, "For tickets please call: 987-7777." Say simply, "Tickets: 987-7777."

If you use graphic art, be sure it is clear and bold. Use the same graphic that appears on the poster. Reducing a complex line image or a photograph to one quarter of its original size causes a lot of detail to be lost, so select a symbol that's simple and bold. Silhouettes work very well for newspaper ads. Study movie ads in the newspaper and emulate the best ones.

Like a poster, the simpler your ad is to read, the more impact it has.

Advertising on radio

If your budget is flush and you need to fill a large theater, or if your audiences have been running thin, go ahead and try radio advertising. Use a stopwatch to write a 30-second script that can be read at a moderate speed. If you've never tried this, you'll be shocked at how little information fits into a brief commercial.

Naturally, you should pick an actor with an articulate, resonant voice. As a rule, I don't like to use the DJ's at the radio station to do the narration for a commercial; they read too fast, they "punch" the wrong words, and the dramatic tone is almost always off.

When you negotiate for air-time costs, avoid buying scattered time slots throughout the day. Most people listen to the radio between 7 and 9 a.m., at noontime, and 5-6 p.m. It's tempting to buy commercial time right on the hour or to sponsor the news, but you can save money by buying :30 spots *just before* or *after* the news broadcasts that come every half-hour in the morning. You don't need to run a lot of commercials all day long; just buy a couple in strategic slots, such as near the news, and run your commercials in those slots for a straight week.

Type your radio script in all capital letters, double-spaced, on one side of a sheet of paper. Keep your lines no wider than six inches (so that the eyes don't loose their place when jumping to the next line). Indicate directions for voice, music or sound effects in parentheses. Leave your ticket phone number for last.

Once you have a script you like, call the marketing manager at a radio station and make an appointment to come in and negotiate prices. Ask the marketing manager for advice about the script. If you want to use a DJ's voice, the manager will play taped samples for you to choose from. At this meeting you can also schedule the time to sit in with the DJ or audio engineer to listen to your commercial being recorded. You want to be there during taping to be sure that the commercial sounds the way you intend. The first try probably won't be what you want. Be prepared to ask the announcer to try again; after all, you're paying for the commercial.

The radio ad in Example 1 is an easy commercial to produce: one announcer and no tricky voices, and no other sound except, maybe, a little of the theme music from the show playing in the background. It's possible to record and include snippets of songs from the show sung by your cast members for a radio ad—use of licensed music for publicity is permissible as long as the use of any selection is less than 30 seconds—but remember that it's a lot of work to bring people into the radio studio for this. Plan on half an hour of standing around and testing microphones, half an hour of recording, and an hour to mix and edit sound in the studio.

In the radio ad in Example 2, the actors need only rehears the script before coming to the studio. Once in front of microphones, they recite their

Simple but effective display ads using a bold graphic, title, dates and ticket number.

16.6 Full House

Radio Ad Example 1

:30 AUDIO for "Guys & Dolls"

ANNOUNCER: SPOTLIGHT THEATER OF NEW BRANFIELD HAS NEWS FOR ALL YOU GUYS AND DOLLS: THE MUSICAL "GUYS AND DOLLS" IS COMING TO JULIA JAMES HIGH SCHOOL THIS FRIDAY AND SATURDAY AND AGAIN NEXT WEEKEND—FOUR CHANCES TO SEE NATHAN DETROIT PLAN A BIG DICE GAME, HIS GIRLFRIEND ADELADE PLAN THEIR WEDDING, SKY MASTERSON PLAN TO WIN A BET, AND BIG JULIE FROM CHICAGO PLAN TO CHEAT EVERYBODY. COME ON, PLAN TO SEE "GUYS AND DOLLS": 444-4344.

# # #

---

lines rapid-fire style and the only editing needed will be mixing the music underneath the voices. This use of several voices in character dramatically exploits the "you are there" quality of radio. The music can be provided by your audio technician or the radio station.

Television advertising

While many radio stations won't charge you to make your commercial, provided you buy sufficient airtime, television stations are more likely to charge you a studio production fee.

Radio Ad Example 2

:30 AUDIO for "Dr. Jekyll & Mr. Hyde

(OMINOUS MUSIC IS BARELY AUDIBLE UNDER VOICES AT FIRST, THEN BUILDS TO CLIMAX AT END OF COMMERCIAL.)

ANNOUNCER (OMINOUSLY):	SOME CALL IT A HABIT —
DR. JEKYLL (CALMLY):	WE ALL HAVE OUR OBSESSIONS.
ANNOUNCER	SOME CALL IT A WONDER DRUG—
VICTORIA (DEFENSIVELY):	IT DID RELIEVE HIS PATIENTS' DEPRESSION...
ANNOUNCER:	OTHERS CALL IT BLASPHEMY —
DR. LANYON (TERRIFIED):	HELL HAS DESECRATED EDEN!
ANNOUNCER:	— AND THE SUFFIELD PLAYERS CALL IT "DR. JEKYLL AND MR. HYDE." WINNER OF 11 AWARDS FOR THEATRICAL EXCELLENCE, THE SUFFIELD PLAYERS' "DR. JEKYLL AND MR. HYDE" OPENS MARCH EIGHT FOR JUST THREE WEEKENDS.
DR. JEKYLL (PANICKING):	TOO LATE! HYDE'S COMING!
ANNOUNCER:	FOR TICKETS, CALL 627-5749.

# # #

Like radio advertising, the effectiveness of TV ads depends not only on the quality of the ad but also on its placement. The salesperson at the TV studio will tell you that the lowest prices will scatter your TV advertisement "throughout the day" whenever there is an open slot. You may find most of your ads running at 2 a.m., however, and what good is that?

It's better to buy your TV time as specifically as possible. While prime time, between 6 p.m. and 9 or 10 p.m. EST is great, there are other time slots that will be nearly as effective but not nearly so costly. Look at the cost of buying time *just before* the 5 p.m., 5:30 p.m. or 6 p.m. news. This delivers the audience of viewers tuning in a minute or two before the evening news broadcast without paying the higher price of a slot within the news program.

Don't waste time in a TV ad reciting phone numbers and the address of the theater. Ask the video engineer to "super" (short for "superimpose") this information on the screen. Also, remember that studio time is costly, and an MTV style of editing with numerous, rapidly changing scenes may significantly raise the cost of producing the commercial.

Remember to keep your TV commercial visual: Costumes, makeup and action scenes can look great on TV. Dialogue can sound hollow if the tie clip microphones are too far away from the actors' mouths. Insist on rehearsing the commercial several times with the camera people before rolling tape—especially in an action scene where actors make sudden moves.

Approach a local college where TV production courses are taught. Ask if some aspiring students will direct, shoot and edit your commercial.

See the notes earlier in this chapter describing frequency and timing of radio and print advertising. These principles apply to TV, too.

Reality check: Before you advertise...

Certain conditions will not be helped by advertising. Other conditions cry out for advertising to give you a level playing field. Ask yourself:

▲ Is your theater's capacity too large? That is, are there more seats to fill than there are people to bring in? Back in Chapter 4 (**Getting Started**), we examined how to measure your publicity mountain. These days, even a talented theater group operating in the middle of a medium-sized suburb will have trouble filling a 400-seat theater every night for a week with a straight drama.

Filling a theater as big as this and as often as this may require an unrealistically large segment of the population to show up, especially these days when there are so many options for comfortable entertainment right at home. You may find that you'll be better able to fill the theater by moving to a smaller hall or closing-off rear and side seating in your present hall.

▲ Are you offering the wrong kind of production? Survey people at the local shopping centers and diners. Are you offering only a solid diet of dramas when people prefer a few comedies? Are you producing only small plays when people are screaming for an occasional big musical?

▲ Are your ticket prices too high?

Insist on rehearsing a TV commercial several times with the camera people before rolling tape.

▲ Are you failing to serve the comfort needs of customers? Do hard seats or poor temperature control make your audiences uncomfortable? Are you located too far out of town or does your theater need better exterior lighting and other security measures to make customers feel safe in your neighborhood?

▲ Are your shows timed badly? Are conflicting dates causing you to lose audiences to bigger events in town, such as county fairs, the circus, and productions by other theater companies? No amount of advertising is going to improve attendance at your theater if this is the case. You're better off selecting dates more carefully.

▲ Is there too much competition and too few outlets for promotion? If you are one of a dozen school, community and professional theaters located in a big city with only one or two newspapers that have limited room to run photos and pictures, you may find that advertising can buy the space you can't win through free publicity.

Summary

☛ Advertising is almost always the most expensive kind of publicity. You're paying someone to do your job.

☛ An effective advertisement is not just creatively designed; its timing, location and frequency are strategically chosen.

☛ For non-profit organizations, advertising should be considered a promotional tool of last resort. First try all other techniques in this book before buying ads.

☛ In print ads, frequency has an edge over size.

☛ Surveying your audience and placing a "tracer" are two methods of checking the effectiveness of your advertising.

☛ Advertising won't help much if your house capacity is too large for your total potential audience, if prices are too high, if plays aren't selected with your audience in mind, or if you've timed your shows to compete with other attractions in town that are more popular.

☛ Advertising will help you if theater news space in newspapers is too limited or if competition is fierce in a busy marketplace.

Publicity Stunts

Chapter 17

- Creating legends—not jokes
- Working with police and journalists
- Tying into your production's theme
- Evaluating risks

Great publicity stunts become the stuff of legends. Magician David Copperfield is world-famous for making the Statue of Liberty disappear and walking through the Great Wall of China.

Politicians—especially those running for president of the United States—turn to publicity stunts to attract the attention of the public.

To be effective, the message communicated in your publicity stunt must be connected to what you're trying to promote. Actors dressed as the Marx Brothers, giving away animal crackers on the steps of city hall, may be a perfect publicity stunt if you're promoting the stage version of the comedy *Animal Crackers*. The same actors handing out pretty boxes of chocolates won't convey the point of the stunt as well.

Two actors in costume, walking down opposite sides of Main Street and repeatedly shouting "To be...!" and "Or not to be...!" back and forth to each other, can call attention to a local production of *Hamlet*. To get the point across, however, you'd probably want to push the idea a little further. Perhaps the actors are in costume and handing out fliers about the show to passers-by. Perhaps the actors stop every few minutes and vary the routine: "Well?" one shouts to the other actor across the street. "Well? What's it to be?" the second actor replies defiantly. Pause. "Well?" says one, and "Well? Answer! What's it to be?" says the other. A crowd is collecting. They've observed a variation on the theme. Then the actors can begin again: "To be...!" and "Or not to be!" with renewed vigor, up and down Main Street.

It's a nutty but *calculated* way to get attention. That's what publicity stunts are all about.

CAUTION!

Please remember that a publicity stunt is not a practical joke. The audience—the public and journalists—must not feel badly used. They should be made to realize quickly that the stunt is meant to draw attention to your show.

DOUBLE CAUTION!

Take care to not endanger anyone during a publicity stunt. Don't become a public nuisance, tie up traffic, deface property, frighten people, or break the law.

If actors are promoting *Oklahoma!* in full Western get-up, they'd better not stroll into stores packing pistols. Even if they're toy pistols, store security guards won't like it one bit. For the same reason, for mercy's sake, don't go into banks wearing weird makeup or masks.

Work with the police

Alert the local constabulary before doing anything unexpected (such as walking up and down Main Street shouting Shakespeare) so that they are aware of the stunt and won't interfere.

Work with the news media—sort of...

What to tell the news media ahead of time depends on the stunt. If you're promoting a production of *The Pied Piper* that features a parade of 50 children invited to follow a costumed actor around the town green and up to the theater for an opening matinee, you'll probably want to call TV and newspapers.

A publicity stunt is not a practical joke.

On the other hand, if you're doing the play *Abraham Lincoln*, you may want to send elegant stationary embossed "from the White House," inviting teachers, shopkeepers and reporters to attend a speech by "The President of The United States." Curiosity will get the best of most editors who will assign a photographer to "check out this item—just in case there's a story." If you include your phone number and people respond, you can simply say, "All I can tell you is that Jansen Jester Theater Company has arranged for the president of the United States to arrive at the memorial fountain in Crandall Park at 11 a.m. Saturday morning. We hope you can attend."

This gives just enough information for the news media to suspect what's going to happen without saying anything that can be used in a quote. Most news media will play along, realizing that the *real* president won't be in town. Of course, a city official and the police will be in on the stunt and sworn to secrecy. (If you haven't guessed, the "president" who will appear at the memorial fountain will be the star of your play in the guise of Abe Lincoln.)

Here's another kind of stunt you can try: I mailed in a check and a request for a classified advertisement to run in the "items wanted" section of a local newspaper. The ad read:

> **WANTED IMMEDIATELY:** Stilettos, bludgeons, harpoons, machetes, crossbows, double axes and other instruments of pain and death. All for a good cause. Call 545-4000.

I "accidentally" mailed the request to the editor of the arts page of the newspaper, who immediately tried the phone number to find out who in the world wanted these gruesome items. The man who answered the phone cheerfully explained that he was directing a community theater group's production of Ira Levin's murder-mystery *Deathtrap*, and he needed to borrow some weapons to dress the stage. The newspaper not only ran the advertisement, but also published a news story on the wacky stunt. Score: Two-for-one!

I checked to be sure that it wasn't illegal to advertise for these things, too—just in case.

TRIPLE CAUTION!

Another word of caution about publicity stunts. The element of surprise is lost if you cook up a stunt for every show your theater group presents. Save the publicity stunt as your secret weapon, to be used only when you have a special show to promote. It could be an anniversary production, the premiere of an original play, or a show that is not well known and may need a little extra promotional boost.

Think things over carefully and ask: Who would be harmed by misinterpreting this stunt? What could go wrong? What will people think? Is the point of the stunt clear? Is it harmless?

Is it harmless?

Is—it—harmless—?

More ideas

▲ A charity baseball game starring the cast of *Damn Yankees*.

▲ A historical lecture and tour of the local graveyard by the director of *Spoon River Anthology* (the play is set in a cemetery).

▲ Discount tickets offered to professional marriage counselors attending *Private Lives*, Noel Coward's comedy about spouses who divorce, remarry, and then run off with their first spouses.

▲ Costumed actors offer to whitewash a needy school's fence to promote *Tom Sawyer*.

▲ An actor playing an impish Mozart is allowed to "conduct" the school orchestra for a few moments during a concert scheduled a week before the school's drama club presents the stage version of *Amadeus*.

By now, I hope that your creative juices are working. I'll leave you with one more publicity stunt. It was an elaborate scheme that I admit was a little risky. But, after all, life is full of chances.

A mystery mailing

You can create a little mystery with news kits by leading up to the mailing in a creative way. I'm about to give you an example, but please understand that this technique should be used sparingly—perhaps only once a decade. The uniqueness of this idea quickly vanishes and you may annoy a journalist if this stunt is not done well.

A few years ago I looked for a way to promote *Orphans of Eternity*, an original play about Dracula, written by local writer Konrad Rogowski. I wanted to communicate the suspense and drama of this character (Dracula, not the playwright), yet suggest humor, too, because, after all, it's fun to see a play with vampires and bats and howling wolves—especially if the play is timed for Halloween.

A week before I planned to mail the news kit, I mailed key reporters and editors a red, invitation-sized envelope with no return address. Inside the envelope was a white card with a red border, and on the card I stuck a Band-Aid with two tiny red dots in the center (to simulate a vampire's puncture wounds). Above the Band-Aid I wrote in red pen, *THE MASTER IS COMING...*

Two days later, I mailed a second anonymous card with the same red-ink inscription, but this time I drew a silhouette of a bat on the card. A day later, I mailed a third small envelope with the identical inscription, but then I added *OCT. 19* to it (this was the date of the opening night of the show). On this third card I glued a rectangular

Save the publicity stunt as your secret weapon, to be used only when you have a special show.

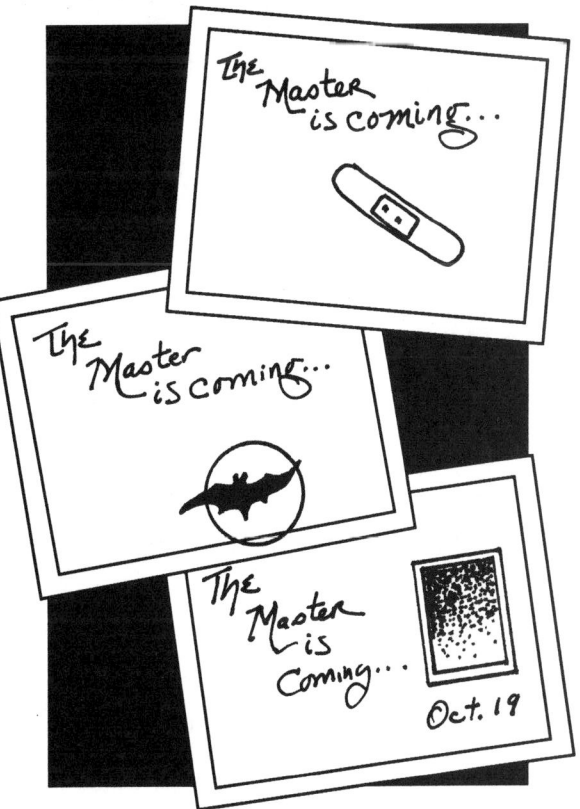

A mystery mailing leading up to the arrival of a news kit: a publicity stunt whose efforts were in vein — but not in vain!

piece of tin foil and drew a picture frame around the foil to simulate a tiny mirror (onto which, of course, vampires are known not to cast a reflection).

These three messages were carefully prepared so that they had a professional, artistic appearance. Each card gave a clue about the subject of the coming show without being direct. You can imagine that after the first two mailings, reporters' curiosity peaked at the arrival of a third red envelope. Newsrooms must have been buzzing with theories about the source and meaning of these mailings.

I let two days pass before mailing a bright red 9-by-12-inch envelope containing the news kit for the Dracula play. In the upper left hand corner of the envelope I stuck a white label with my name and address. On the label, above the typed address, I wrote in red ink, *THE MASTER HAS ARRIVED!* The kit contained the standard information about the show but also had a letter from me. I apologized for keeping the reporter in suspense, explaining how I wanted to communicate the feeling we hoped our audiences would experience in the theater as they waited for the "Master of the Undead" to arrive on stage. My brief letter then invited the reporter to look over the enclosed information about the show and to call me if she or he wanted to "have an interview with a vampire." (This was about a year before Anne Rice came out with her now-famous book with this title!)

You can bet I got calls from reporters! They felt the suspense that I tried to convey by the mysterious mailings, and the resulting publicity was quite satisfying.

QUADRUPLE CAUTION!

Again, be very careful about doing this kind of a mystery mailing. Any hint of danger or warnings could get you a visit from federal agents who don't like people using the mail to threaten people! If you have any concerns about how a mailing like this will be received, think things over again.

It may look as if I took a big chance of angering a reporter with this Dracula stunt, but the risk was calculated to be minimal. I knew from past dealings with the reporters who received my mailings that they had good senses of humor. Good luck and happy planning!

Summary

☛ Publicity stunts help draw attention to your production, but use them sparingly. The element of surprise is lost easily if you're known for pulling stunts all the time.

☛ Don't endanger people during a publicity stunt. Don't become a public nuisance, tie up traffic, deface property, frighten people, or break the law.

☛ Get clearance from the police before trying a publicity stunt in public.

☛ Evaluate the risks carefully when planning a stunt. Imagine everything that could go wrong. Consider whether your group can afford the risk of the public not appreciating your efforts to surprise and amuse.

School Promotion

Chapter 18

- Taking advantage of the system
- The problem of recruitment
- Organizing and teaching

In community theater, the producer, the director, the costume designer, set designer, box office manager and the publicist are often separate people. In elementary and secondary schools, the principal expects the responsibilities of all these people to come wrapped up in one frantic, superhuman body: the drama coach.

God bless 'em (the drama coaches, I mean). They stage substantial productions using large groups of inexperienced actors and dancers, singers, crew members and administrative assistants. They must work with a meager budget and obtain props, costumes and stage construction materials, deal with fragile egos, and train everyone: lighting, sound, costume and makeup workers, ticket-takers and ushers, and the all-important publicity volunteers.

Even the president of the United States has a cabinet of advisers and an entourage of assistants to get the job done. The school drama coach often feels very much alone.

Taking advantage of the system

Of course there are a few things drama coaches have in their favor, the most important of which is the built-in audience: the school's students and families, teachers, and administrators. These are the key audiences for the school show as well as the key sources of performers and crew members.

The school newspaper, daily home room announcements, parent call-in hot lines, and bulletin boards in classrooms, halls and lounges are just a few of the many places news of the school show can be posted.

Look for opportunities to present a scene or two from the show at a school assembly or a room tour, for example.

Pictures in the school paper should show students having FUN, even if the show is *Death of a Salesman*. Show students laughing while working together on set construction. Pictures are also effective if they show students in positions of responsibility, such as running the light or sound board.

The most effective pictures of student actors show them expressing strong emotions. If there's a romantic embrace, a fight, a breakdown or a side-splitting laugh, photograph this carefully for maximum impact and send it to the school newspaper, or post blow-ups of these pictures in the cafeteria for everyone to see. These subjects will get plenty of attention because they will communicate to students and adults that the school show is alive and charged with energy.

School tool: T-shirts

If the school dress code permits, a popular promotional tool is the T-shirt. Once a logo or poster design has been created for a show, T-shirts can be silk-screened for students working in the show to wear to school. Costs can be kept low if the T-shirts can be made in the school or in a local college art class where silk screening is taught.

Students wearing the T-shirts to classes, in the halls and cafeteria, and everywhere else in school become walking billboards for the show weeks in advance of opening night. If the design is truly eye-catching, the popular T-shirts can even become a fund-raising tool.

Pictures in the school paper should show students having fun.

The T-shirt can be a powerful promotional tool if students can be convinced to wear them to school (and if officials allow them).

T-shirts with the show logo do three other things:

1. Like uniforms or team emblems, they instill a spirit of teamwork and comeraderie among the students in the show.

2. They communicate a message to others that the student wearing the T-shirt is a joiner and a worker - someone committed to a school project.

3. They spark a little envy among other students who may become inspired to join the show — perhaps to help out with publicity!

There are also three major stumbling blocks to watch for:

1. The cost of T-shirts must be kept low and some provision for impoverished students must be made. What a shame if an eager, talented student is discouraged from working on the show because he can't afford to buy a shirt like his friends. Actually, the shirts can be considered a legitimate advertising and promotion expense. If the show budget can't absorb the entire cost of the shirts, perhaps it can subsidize the price.

2. To have time for the T-shirts to generate the maximum promotional punch, they must be ordered early and arrive several weeks before the show opens.

3. Students must be encouraged to wear their T-shirts to school. Keeping T-shirts in a closet at home won't do the show any good publicity-wise. The drama coach has to make this clear to the students, who may not realize that one of the purposes of the T-shirt is *advertising*.

Use school technology

Some of the greatest changes in American schools in the last 10 years have been technological, motivated by the need to communicate more and more information to a diverse and dispersed population. Efforts to promote the school show should include taking advantage of all technology.

Certainly news about auditions, organizational meetings, rehearsals and ticket sales can be made during the morning announcements issuing from the principal's office. If this is an audio announcement transmitted by intercom, consider using radio techniques — music, sound effects or dramatic voices doing a brief exchange of lines from the show — to dramatize your message. Remember folks, this is theater. We're expected to be dramatic!

For example, an announcement for *A Christmas Carol* might have the actor who plays Marley's Ghost rattle his chains and moan a little before informing enraptured listeners where they can buy tickets — perhaps from The Ghost of Christmases Yet to Come who will be found dressed in a long black robe seated in a graveyard of styrene headstones outside the cafeteria during lunch period. For a production of *Grease*, a few bars of 1950s' rock n' roll music can introduce an actor urging students to attend auditions if they really want to be, like, cool, man.

If students can be booked on a local radio talk show program, arrange to give away school show tickets on the air while the students are being interviewed. People tuning in are already interested in the school show and are therefore likely to phone in and try to win a pair of tickets. For more tips on giving away tickets, see Chapter 10, **Media Relations** for a look at working with radio and television.

TV or MTV — that is the question...

Some technologically advanced schools now have a student-produced daily news program that originates in a school video studio and viewed via cable and TV monitors to every home room in the school building. If your school has this technology, use it effectively. Fully exploit the creative possibilities of video: dramatic MTV, not sleepy ZZZ.

For example, if in-school TV exists, don't have a straightfaced student sit at a desk and read an announcement about rehearsal. For crying out loud, use the visual power of the medium and put someone in costume and acting in character in front of the camera. Work with the studio ahead of time to tape a compelling commercial.

Look back at Chapter 10 to review the section about working with TV. Yes, you can have the student news anchors interview the drama coach or the lead actor, but how about showing students at work? With a little planning and rehearsal the student TV program can present a costume design assistant exhibiting drawings and books to quickly show the research process—but then bring in two or three students to model the costumes. This kind of visual promotion packs a lot in only 60 seconds and, unlike the sit-down-and-read-the-news-straight format, it's dramatic and educational.

Even if there isn't an in-school TV system, you can videotape a documentary or an outright commercial and show it in the school cafeteria while students wait in line.

You get started on the documentary by assigning a team of responsible students (or advertising in the school or at a nearby college for a team of video or communications students) to make a video documentary of rehearsals, construction, and design and publicity efforts, intercut with interviews of people involved with the show. As long as another adult is supervising the student documentarians, the drama coach and/or publicist can attend to other details of the production.

Jim Stidfole, a high school drama coach in Waterford, Conn., is an enthusiastic believer in the power of electronic publicity. He notes that most large communities have a cable TV station that offers a community access channel. His advice is to seize this great opportunity to inform the community by using the station's resources to produce and air a 30-minute documentary about the making of the school show.

Again, you don't have to direct the documentary yourself. You can farm out the project to a team of responsible students in the high school or local college, or to adults taking video workshops at the cable company. Let them do the planning, shooting and editing with the help of the station's equipment and personnel. Just be sure to sit in (or have another adult connected with the show sit in) on the final edit to ensure that the program to be aired will help and not injure ticket sales.

Schedule the video to appear one week before opening night. If the video airs closer to opening night than this, people don't have time to

Use school equipment or work with a local cable TV station to produce a 30-minute documentary about the making of your school show.

plan to attend. If it airs ten, twelve or more days before opening night, people tend to forget to buy tickets and then wind up missing the show.

Report cards, bills and other computer stuff

Report cards are now computer generated. See if you can get an announcement about the school show printed at the bottom. The same for bills and library notices. Many schools have a hotline where parents and students can phone in to check what homework is assigned. Arrange for a cheery reminder about the school show to be included with these messages.

Contests

Students love contests. Over the morning announcement broadcast, play three seconds of a song from the soundtrack of the school musical, and offer free tickets to students who correctly name the song; students enter the contest by depositing a slip of paper with their guess in a clearly-marked entry box in the school office.

Run a mail-in trivia contest about the show in the school newspaper (note the statement declaring who is elegible to win). Another contest idea: offer prizes (donated by area businesses) to students who sell the most tickets.

Parental connections

Parents of students in a school show want lots of people in town to attend and see their prized child perform on stage. Survey your students to find out who has parents who can help promote the show:

▲ You say that Heather's father runs a restaurant? Perhaps she can ask her dad to put tent cards

---

ZOUNDS! HOW NOW, HAMLET?
Here's your chance to brush up on your Shakespeare and win a free ticket to Secora High School's production of *Hamlet*. Twenty winners will be selected from among correctly answered entries. Be sure to indicate your name and home room number below and drop off your entry in room A-43 no later than 3 p.m. Friday, Nov. 21. Good luck!

1. Which is the correct quote from **Hamlet**, *Act V?*
        a. Alas! Poor Yorick, I knew him well!
        b. Alas, poor Yorick, fare ye well!
        c. Alas! Poor Yorick. I knew him, Horatio.
2. Which item does not appear in **Hamlet***?*
        a. A poison drink
        b. A poison ring
        c. A poison sword
3. Which ghost appears to Hamlet in the first scene?
        a. His father
        b. A witch
        c. Yorick

Name_____ Home Room_____

Winners will be announced November 16.
Plan to attend the school production of *Hamlet* November 28, 29 and 30 in Radding Auditorium at 8 p.m. Tickets are available at the *Hamlet* information booth in the cafeteria:
$3.00 for students with school I.D., $4.00 senior citizens, $6.00 adults.
      Cast, crew, and others associated with the production are ineligible to win tickets.

or printed placemats on tables for customers to see (see Chapter 14 on **Signs and Displays**).

▲ Did we hear that Tyrone's mom works for an insurance company that runs radio ads in town? Maybe he can ask her if the company will add a 10-second tag to the radio spot, reminding the public to attend the school show.

▲ A parent who works in a flower shop or nursery can display a humorous model of the hungry plant from *Little Shop of Horrors*, or may be enticed to subsidize a discount coupon for the show with every customer receipt the shop hands out.

Look for ways to get parent-connected businesses to underwrite or support the school show as a community service.

Cooperative ventures: combine and conquor

Check the school calendar and with key faculty, administrators and students to find out if anything else is going on at school during the week leading up to and during the school show. A popular sport event, field trip, concert, or speaker may conflict with your show's schedule and draw audiences away.

Instead of fighting over a date, try to combine appropriate events for mutual benefits: A spaghetti dinner fund-raiser held by the senior class can be scheduled the same night as the play and billed as an optional dinner theater evening with a discount offered for buying tickets to both events.

Parents have to get a baby sitter for only one night, and wind up getting a dinner and a show. *Be sure the combination is appropriate,* however: You don't want dinner theater for a production of *Sweeney Todd*, do you? (The musical features customers at a popular café eating pies made with a secret recipe—stray animals and people—ugh!)

The problem of recruitment

On the face of it, the large number of students in any school would suggest that recruiting publicity help shouldn't be as tough as it often is. However, kids today are likely to be as busy as adults. Moreover, the young people who show up to work on a school show are often the same ones involved in the band, chorale, dance, the literary magazine, yearbook and school newspaper. No wonder kids' favorite activities are eating and sleeping! School drama coaches are lucky to get a half-hour a day from these energetic but perpetually exhausted marvels.

However, building a publicity crew is absolutely critical in school theater because the drama coach, as manager of the entire production, can't devote all her or his energies to publicity alone.

It's two words: Show-Business.

To successfully manage publicity, the drama coach must recruit adequate help. By adequate help, I mean that other adults must be brought in to help supervise student volunteers. Try the business education teacher. Recruit parents or other adults in the community. This is the business end of show business: managing human resources.

Adult assistance may be found in a number of places, including many mentioned in Chapter 6,

Look for ways to get parent-connected businesses to underwrite or support the school show as a community service.

Set a detailed schedule and clear deadlines for volunteers

The Publicity Team. Briefly, don't overlook senior citizens councils whose members have time on their hands and a wealth of experience. Consider contacting the local college to find students majoring in marketing, communications, journalism or English. Graduation requirements may include internships-for-credit in which they practice their classroom skills in a real-world situation.

Parents brought in to assist with publicity can be a blessing or a curse, but it's worth the risk of winding up with a half-dozen stage parents if you find one or two organized, generous, talented people with natural management skills.

Begin by sending out letters to parents. Invite them to a brief get-together, featuring attractive refreshments, to talk about the show and what needs to be done to make the show a reality. A paragraph in the weekly or monthly bulletin from the principal isn't good enough; you need a *sales letter* like the ones magazines send to lure subscribers. For an example, see the letter on the following page promoting *The Music Man*.

No matter how many or how few parents show up, sell them on how much fun and how easy it will be to donate a few hours in the afternoon or evening. Plan a second meeting where each person who showed up for the first meeting is encouraged to bring a neighbor or friend.

These volunteers will be glad to help sell tickets later on, too, since they've invested their time and energy in the show. Like the students, however, the adult volunteers will need direction.

Training the publicity team

Working with students presents a special challenge. Young volunteers are immature. Often, they do not show up for work and rehearsals because they have not developed the steady habits of adults. They need to be shown how to do everything because everything is new to them. They can be alternately amazingly patient and also easily discouraged.

Mary Norris, a drama coach in Norwich, Conn., with seven years of experience working with high schoolers and 19 years with community theater, recommends setting a detailed schedule and clear deadlines for volunteers. "Set small, goal-oriented jobs that kids can follow, such as giving one student the task of writing the radio PSA by following an example from a previous show," she says.

Breaking down the large job of publicity into brief tasks that take only 30 or 45 minutes a day is critical when coaching young people. If they see an assignment that looks like it'll take hours to do, young people may become overwhelmed and run. A half-hour may not seem like much time at all when there's a lot of work to do, but two students working together on publicity four days a week, 30 minutes a day each, amounts in six weeks to 24 hours of effort. Get them to come in for just two hours on weekends and you've doubled the output.

Run a tight but pleasant ship. Be sure all the equipment the publicity volunteers need to work with are on hand. Computers with word processing software are musts. Perhaps you can arrange with your business education teacher or your librarian to allow computer time for your volunteers. Or ask the head of a local community or professional

The Willow Glen School

Orlando D. Free
Principal

Shirley U. Gest
Superintendent

January 5, 19—

Dear Parent:

Happy New Year to you. Willow Glen students are starting off the new year on a happy note - actually, several evenings filled with many happy notes - as they begin preparing the musical "The Music Man" for three performances on April 3, 4 and 5.

It's a lively show with dancing and marching, imaginative and colorful costumes, a run of hit songs including the fast-talking "Trouble" (with a capital "T"!), the rousing "76 Trombones," and the hauntingly sweet "Till There Was You." It's the story of a con man who shows up in town one day and winds up giving his heart away - but not without some hijinks and hitches along the way.

More than three dozen student actors will appear on stage, another fifteen will perform in the orchestra, and a score or more will work hard behind the scenes helping actors change costumes, put on makeup, construct the sets, sew costumes, run the lighting and sound equipment, sell tickets, usher, write news releases, design posters, and help out in so many other ways.

For many young people, participating in a school show will bring some of the happiest and enduring memories they will retain from their time at Willow Glen High. The joy of teamwork and the experience of rehearsing and planning over the next few weeks will present valuable life lessons. The lessons of "The Music Man" will also touch those watching the show.

I urge you to become part of this experience. Your participation is important for the show to succeed. Your involvement will make it possible for these life lessons to help shape the hearts and minds of the students on stage, backstage, and in the audience. Please consider giving just two or three hours of your time a week over the next few weeks to help me guide the students toward that all-important and all-exciting opening night.

To learn just how easy and enjoyable a little volunteering can be, please join me next Tuesday, January 15 at 7 p.m. for a brief get-together in band rehearsal room M-12. Hot tea and coffee and some fresh baked goodies will be served. You'll meet other parents and get a sneak-preview of the show's costume and set designs. Mr. Michael Dulac, the school band conductor, will play a few tunes from "The Music Man."

If you have any questions, by all means call me at home after 6 p.m. at 737-3737. Together we can make "The Music Man" a show to remember!

Best wishes,

Amanda B. Reckonwith

Amanda B. Reckonwith
Drama Coach

DIRECT APPEAL: Invite parents to a brief get-together to talk about what needs to be done to make the show a reality. This sample letter gives a plot synopsis, a list of student activities, the benefits to all participants, a request for a specific time commitment, and a clear agenda for an informative meeting. Note the promise of entertainment and refreshments.

Breaking down the large job of publicity into brief tasks is critical when coaching young people.

theater. Appeal to this person's sense of duty to help prepare the next generation of theater people.

Like any community theater publicist, a school drama coach needs to prepare a three-ring binder with photocopied examples of news releases, PSAs, ads, posters, playbills and other publicity ideas. They'll need fact sheets and background material (history, criticism, set and costume designs) on the current play, as described in Chapter 6 on building *The Publicity Team* earlier in this book. With young people, however, the fact sheets and other written material may need to have pertinent data highlighted to help them discern key ideas.

Students and adult volunteers should be able to see posted on a bulletin board or in a handout what tasks await them for the entire rehersal period so that they understand (1) they are needed and appreciated because tasks won't get done unless they show up, (2) individual publicity tasks add up to a successful plan the way bricks stack up to make a building, and (3) in general, planning is a superior method for getting things done than last-minute improvisation.

Finally, here's a secret weapon to boost your volunteers' energy and motivation: consider keeping on hand a supply of juice, bread, peanut butter and jelly—the equivalent of rocket fuel for teenagers and those young at heart!

Summary

- ☛ The school drama coach should not be expected to manage publicity without adequate help —adults who can help supervise the student volunteers. Publicity is too important and too detailed a set of tasks to leave entirely in the hands of the same overworked person who is directing as well as producing the show.

- ☛ Use the school's established systems of communication—school newspaper, daily home room announcements, parent call-in hot lines and bulletin boards—to recruit help with publicity and to sell tickets.

- ☛ Set the right tone. Publicity used to recruit help should show volunteers having FUN. The mood in the office, room or corner set aside for publicity volunteers should communicate excitement and FUN. No one wants to volunteer for w-o-r-k.

- ☛ Consider the power of T-shirts, contests, video and any new, emerging technologies to promote the school show.

- ☛ Create a detailed schedule and clear deadlines for volunteers. Set small, goal-oriented jobs that are easy to follow. Prepare a three-ring binder with examples of publicity projects: news releases, fliers, posters and invitations.

- ☛ Review Chapter 6 on building The Publicity Team.

Building Group Recognition

Chapter 19

- The value of name recognition
- Elements of an identity program
- Developing a communications plan

McDonald's golden arches. MGM's roaring lion. Prudential Insurance's piece of the rock. Batman's black and yellow Bat Signal. The Pillsbury Dough Boy. Greyhound bus line's racing dog. Land O Lakes' kneeling Indian maiden.

These are effective corporate symbols* because they are familiar and well-tailored to the image the company wishes to communicate about itself. When you see or merely think of one of these symbols, you easily recall the company name, its products and its reputation.

The best corporate symbols, backed by a strategic publicity campaign, also invoke an emotion: The Bat Signal creates a mood of danger, mystery, and adventure. Prudential's Rock of Gibraltar suggests stability and dependability. The MGM lion proclaims pride and superiority.

The value of name recognition

Like a well-known brand of, well, anything—hot dogs, jeans, perfume or automobiles—your theater company can acquire a reputation for quality that the public will recognize and respond to the moment it hears your group's name. There is great marketing power in achieving instant name recognition in your community.

When people hear that your company is putting on a show, many of them will immediately note the performance dates and make plans to attend—even if they don't recognize the name of the play or know what the show is about.

Name recognition spurs advance ticket sales and reduces the need to spend money on advertising. It makes fund raising easier because people tend to support organizations and causes with which they are familiar. Name recognition improves a theater group's relations with journalists, who are more likely to pay attention to a news release from a well-known group or individual than to an unknown one—*provided the group continues to reach for high standards.*

A well-known and well-respected theater company is more likely than a lesser-known group to attract new actors, directors and crew members when auditions are announced. Members of a theater group that has taken time to analyze and strategically promote its identity will take pride in being part of the company, and group loyalty plays an invaluable role in an organization's stability and growth.

Moreover, should the slings and arrows of outrageous fortune strike—a fire, theft, or an emergency need for a critical but hard-to-find prop, for example—the public is apt to respond quickly with generous assistance to a known, respected organization. People are also willing to pay a little more for tickets to a show presented by a popular theater company. In theater, "well known" often translates into "well loved" and, thus, "well attended."

For these reasons, it's important for a publicist to look beyond the promotional needs of the current production towards building the group's long-term image.

---

* The names of corporations, their slogans and their symbols which appear as examples throughout this chapter are protected trademarks. All rights reserved under international copyright laws.

Building a group's identity takes a plan of action—in fact, a series of related, coordinated actions.

Steps toward identity and recognition

How does a group acquire name recognition? It's natural to assume that a theater company that has its act together and consistently presents quality productions will eventually achieve notoriety by word of mouth. However, that can take a long time and this method alone is not always certain to succeed. The truth is, a little marketing strategy is also needed to move a group along the road to fame.

Building a group's identity takes a plan of action—in fact, a series of related, coordinated actions designed to communicate a message to the public about what the organization represents. These activities and the overall message are developed in a logical, progressive way.

Here is how a professional identity or marketing consultant might approach a communications plan for a theater group. You should follow these steps in order:

1 Analyze the group: its history, activities, resources, membership and audience.

2 Determine what the group's defining philosophy is and study its mission statement. It should be clear, simple, short, and consistent with its audience's needs.

3 Develop a company symbol and a slogan.

4 Designate key places and occasions to heighten public exposure of your group's existence.

Analyzing the group

A group first must examine itself and determine what it is and why it exists. The theater company's most successful shows (and, in the opposite sense, also it least successful shows) offer important clues about its identity. The background of its members and the audience it serves also tell much about a group's chief characteristics.

One theater group I know formed with a specific goal—to practice and perform improvisational theater. Another group specializes in presenting dramas on contemporary adult themes such as AIDS, feminism and prison reform. A third group performs only musicals. Another theater company, made up of primary school teachers, produces children's theater. Still another troupe, made up of devout Christians, presents a repertoire of religious plays. A high school drama club's plays consist of classics by outstanding foreign playwrights.

These theater groups have different missions, or reasons for their organizations to exist. Their audiences are likely to have different values, tastes and interests. These differences will affect the look and sound of publicity. A parochial school's approach to promoting *A Christmas Carol* would likely emphasize the play's reflections on the redemptive power of contrition, while a lay group's publicity might play up the production's ghostly theme and special effects "that haunt the dickens out of the audience with a spirited performance."

An important part of a theater publicist's job is to know the history and character of the company and the nature of the audience. Normally, audiences of an

BUILDING GROUP RECOGNITION: Company symbols range from traditional to whimsical, each reflecting the personality of the organization. The mission statement and history appear in playbills and brochures to reinforce the group's image.

the windsor jesters

MISSION

The Suffield Players are dedicated to providing opportunities for as many area residents as possible to participate in the creative process and the fellowship of quality, live theatre, and thereby to enjoy the social, artistic, and educational benefits of this enriching form of expression.

HISTORY

Since incorporation in 1952, the Suffield Players have presented more than 50 theatrical productions ranging from Molière to Noel Coward. In drama competitions with other community theatre groups, the Company consistently wins awards for its costumes, set design, acting, directing and technical wizardry. This string of successes and curtain calls culminated in the Players' capturing Best Connecticut Production four years in a row. The Players perform in Suffield's historic Mapleton Hall, two minutes from the Massachusetts border and twenty-five minutes from downtown Hartford. The Company sponsors workshops, theatre trips to New York and Boston, and competitive drama festivals for its members. The Company's role in supporting civic activities, establishment of the Robert Alcorn Memorial Drama Scholarship, and donations to many charitable organizations demonstrates the Players' concern for Suffield's history - and future. The Suffield Players depend almost entirely on the generosity of Contributing members to finance the operating budget. A devoted core of Active Members provides the intensive labor needed to continue to provide quality programming and excellent productions. The Suffield Players continually strive for growth and artistic achievement.

Won't you consider supporting your community theatre? Please send your tax deductible donation today!

THE SUFFIELD PLAYERS
P.O. BOX 101
SUFFIELD, CT 06078

A theater publicist's job is to know the history and character of the company and the nature of the audience.

established theater group are composed largely of a faithful core who regularly attend every production, along with a smaller number of the semifaithful who may come to half the shows, and a few newcomers who may become members of the faithful or semifaithful. The publicist must learn what it is about the theater group and its offerings that current and potential audiences find appealing, and then shape promotion accordingly.

A publicist should interview the members of the theater group that have been with the group longest to learn how and why the group was founded, what traditions have been established over the years, and where and why those traditions started. Young people and newcomers can give valuable insight into the contemporary needs of the current and next generation of members. Members who have been with the group only a few years have a valuable perspective to offer on how the theater company is changing for better or worse.

After I learned from newcomers to the Suffield Players in Suffield, Conn., that they enjoyed the many opportunities offered them to learn lighting, sound and construction skills (the group's technical crew was one of the company's strengths), I used this in a recruitment campaign: "We offer on-the-job training. Join us!" This theme has become a key part of the group's identity and has helped attract many more people who will develop into this theater company's new leaders in a few years.

In the same way, the opinions of audience members can alert a publicist to which details in a production are likely to attract loyal theater-goers. When I designed a brief audience survey (and this is the trick: limit the number of questions or audience members will feel overwhelmed and invaded), the survey revealed that the majority of patrons came back year after year because each season offered a variety of productions: musicals, comedies and costumed dramas. The next season's brochure used the word "variety" and "choice" several times, and the box office noticed a marked increase in advance ticket sales.

Audience relations is often overlooked by theater groups too focused on getting through the current show. The penalty for this oversight is often the loss of customers. From the moment people call a box office for tickets, they receive impressions of how much thought an organization has given to the care and feeding of its audience:

▲ Are customers greeted—on the phone or in person—in a professional and friendly manner? Can personnel answering phones describe the play and give directions competently and quickly? (Provide a fact sheet with answers—see Chapter 4.)

▲ Are all theater personnel trained to properly assist persons with disabilities who come to your theater either as audience members or volunteers? (Your local human services agency can offer advice.)

▲ Do all theater personnel dress appropriately and do they behave professionally when audiences are in the theater?

Ask yourself whether theater company members view ticket holders as de facto members of the company or faceless hoards of paying customers. Do members view the theater group as a responsible partner in the community, or a private organization that owes nothing to its neighbors?

This subject may seem to be a diversion from the main interest of a publicist, but in fact these questions are very much a part of a publicist's concern for overall good public relations. If you and your group's governing board don't ensure membership satisfaction in all aspects, then your ability to promote a show is weakened before you begin.

The opinions you receive from surveying the cast, crew, management and audience members should help you and your theater's governing board check on whether the group is remaining consistent to its established long-term goals, or *mission*. If a survey reveals that the membership is not happy with a group's activities, this may indicate that the group is merely unfocused. However, wide dissatisfaction or apathy reflected in a survey often heralds a shift in the original mission of the group—or a change in the composition of the audience.

For example, let's assume that for two decades Center City Theater has offered 1940s and '50s musicals to a population of middle-and upper-income people between 40 and 60 years old. This core audience has attended shows faithfully for most of the last twenty years, but recently the city's population has changed: The core audience has aged and moved to the suburbs, and fewer and fewer of the same upper income population remain in the city after offices close to attend theater. Today the urban center is populated mostly by younger, lower income people who are attached to more contemporary themes in their entertainment choices. Noting the population shift, Center City Theater management is faced with a choice: continue offering the same kinds of shows it has for 20 years and wait for death to come, move to the suburbs, or change its offerings to appeal to a new population with different needs.

There is a difference between a mission and a marketing plan. A *mission statement* (explained in more detail in the next section of this chapter) defines the purpose of an organization, including its long-range philosophical goal. A *marketing plan* defines strategies to achieve specific, short-term goals that are consistent with the group's overall mission.

In the above example, if Center City's mission has been to perpetuate America's early years of musical theater, then the governing board might respond to its changed neighborhood by deciding to change its mission to offering contemporary urban American issues. After establishing its new mission, the group should develop a marketing plan to reach its new audience. The plan may include discussions in schools, appearances at block parties, and ticket give-aways.

The choices a group makes to define its identity and appeal to its membership are inspired by its mission.

The mission statement

A mission statement helps focus a theater company's identity and guides the publicist in designing promotion. Knowing that a group is dedicated to presenting classic American plays, or to offering opportunities for local people to develop dramatic arts skills, or to exploring contemporary issues facing

GET IN THE ACT

If you enjoyed tonight's performance, here's a dramatic idea: JOIN US!

You don't need a college degree or a resume, and don't worry about "talent." If you have enthusiasm and interest, that's what we need.

Can you usher or tend the snack bar one or two evenings? How about helping prepare the theatre before audiences arrive?

The Suffield Players offer "on-the-job-training" in backstage skills, lighting and sound, set building and dressing, costume making, makeup and, yes, acting, too!

Spend a Saturday helping at Mapleton Hall and we *guarantee* you'll meet a dozen friendly folks, make friends, learn a theatre trick or two, and come away feeling downright dramatic!

Interested? Want to know more? Ask one of our ushers, actors or crew members. Come on! Join in the fun!

SUFFIELD PLAYERS

SUFFIELD PLAYERS

Audience Survey

We're glad you're here! To show our appreciation, we'd like to know your wishes for the Suffield Players' future. Please take 5 minutes to fill out this brief survey and hand it completed to any usher. Thanks for your help.

1. How many plays (community or professional) have you attended in the last 12 months?
   [ ] 1-2 plays
   [ ] 3-4 plays
   [ ] 5 or more

2. How many different Suffield Players productions have you ever attended?
   [ ] 1-2 plays
   [ ] 3-4 plays
   [ ] 5 or more

3. How did you learn about this show? *(Check as many answers as you wish.)*
   [ ] newspaper article *(which newspaper?)* _____
   [ ] radio   [ ] direct mail
   [ ] poster   [ ] word of mouth
   [ ] other _____

4. What one improvement to audience *comfort* would you like to see at Mapleton Hall? _____

5. How can the Suffield Players make it more *convenient* for you to attend our productions? _____

6. What made you want to see *this production*? _____

7. What productions or types of productions would you like to see performed by the Suffield Players? _____

Your town: _____ Today's date: _____

Please note below any other suggestions you have for the Suffield Players.

ABOVE: An audience survey that asks a few key questions without burdening those asked to complete the questionnaire. Note the mixture of multiple-choice and open-ended questions.

LEFT: A playbill stuffer designed to build active membership, using the theater company's mannequin mascot to build group identity.

society—such clearly defined missions give a publicist a theme to work with. A theme, carried through news releases, fliers, posters and other promotion, gives a theater company a consistent image that the public can easily recall.

Avoid the trap of working with a mission statement that is so broad ("dedicated to excellence in theater") that it fails to make your group distinct from other companies. A mission statement is not a bragging platform, either. It is a snapshot that reveals, not merely flatters.

Publish your mission statement in your playbills and newsletters, and post it in large letters in the theater. Publish the statement by itself on a separate sheet of paper and include it in news kits.

Consider including the mission statement in your news releases. The statement should appear in a way that distinguishes it from the rest of the words on the page. For example, the statement might be printed in small type and placed in a box at the bottom of the first page. You could print the mission statement in the same color as your letterhead when you have your stationery printed. In any case, take care that the placement of the statement is never intrusive when it appears on stationery. It should seem to say "By the way..." not "Hey, look at me!"

Seeing is believing

The aim of building group identity is to inspire loyalty: "Look," you want people to say; "The Gibson Grenadiers are putting on a show. I've heard great things about them. I'll get tickets and see for myself."

However, to get your theater group's name recognized, people have to *see* the name. Look at your posters, playbills, fliers and news release letterhead. Is the name of your group prominently and strategically displayed? Is the name *graphically* distinctive?

Your poster should read "Picklepuss Playhouse" or "Picklepuss Playhouse presents—" followed by the name of the show. People will more easily remember a group's name if it is the first item they read in an announcement. Also, the name of your group should be large enough to read from at least ten feet away on an 11-by-17-inch poster.

How crucial it is to place your theater company's name prominently and strategically on road signs becomes obvious when you stop to observe your potential customers whizzing by signs at 45 miles per hour!

Now, please, don't go overboard: The name of your theater group should be prominent, but it should not overwhelm your signs and posters. *The name of the show* should still be the largest word(s) in your announcements.

Symbolic logic

It helps, too, to design a logotype and a symbol for your group. A *logotype* is a distinctive lettering style, or typeface, associated with your group's name whenever it appears in promotional materials. Think of the distinctive cursive typeface used whenever Coca-Cola Classic soda appears on a label, or the sans-serif lettering for Mobil gasoline where the "o" is always a lighter color. The names Kodak, Levi's, L'eggs, Nabisco, Hershey's, Bic, Memorex, Eveready, Firestone,

A mission statement defines the purpose of an organization, including its long-range philosophical goal.

Revlon, Lord & Taylor, Yves Saint Laurent, GE, RCA, Hoover and Black & Decker always appear on their products, each with its own distinctive typeface to help people recognize not just the sound but also the look of the company name.

Logotypes are often accompanied by a *symbol*. The symbol can be integrated with the logotype, such as the kneeling Land O Lakes Indian maiden framed by the "O", the owl eye that dots the letter "i" in Wise potato chips, and the overlapping twin circles that always accompany the name MasterCard. Symbols can also appear alongside but separate from the corporate name. They may even become so familiar that they can stand alone: the Texaco star, McDonald's golden arches, the Playboy bunny, and Pocket Books' kangaroo are examples of instantly recognizable symbols.

Some companies select a distinctive color or combination of colors with which to associate their symbols and logotypes: green for John Deere; red for Rubbermaid; red and blue for Milton Bradley's MB symbol.

Designing an identity

Your logotype and symbol should not be selected casually. The history of your theater group, the shows it presents, the community in which it operates, and the spirit and mission of the group must all be taken into consideration. A theater group that specializes in innovative approaches to drama would communicate the wrong message to the public if it selected as its symbol the classic top hat and pair of white gloves. On the other hand, a traditional quill or a silhouette of an actor with an Elizabethan ruffled collar might be appropriate symbols for a company of Shakespearean actors.

Selecting your symbol should not be left to people with no experience with the subject. Don't hold a contest to let people vote for the best design; the average person has no knowledge of the psychology and marketing strategy involved with graphic art. A contest might elect an inappropriate design that you'll be obliged to use for years.

Instead, seek out an experienced graphic designer or advertising agency who might be willing to create your logotype and symbol as a pro bono assignment—that is, at no charge, as a public service. Promise that if the design is accepted by your theater company's governing board you will recognize the designer's name and efforts in playbills, news releases and during a special ceremony on opening night of the first play of the next season. Do the designer a favor, too, and promise not to reveal that the designer's fee was donated, or a hundred other organizations may hound the designer for free work.

The symbol and logotype must be designed with its uses in mind: it must be adaptable for use on letterhead, envelopes, business cards, reply cards, name tags and badges; posters and signs; and T-shirts, coffee mugs, key chains and other merchandising you and your group think up. It must look good enlarged to banner size or reduced to fit a small display advertisement. When reduced, thin lettering and artwork shouldn't lose detail and become illegible.

After your designer interviews key members of your theater group and develops one or more concepts, the designer should be invited to make a formal presentation before the governing board. The proposed logotypes and symbols should be displayed as they would appear on sample letterheads and envelopes. The board should hear how the designer came to decide on the designs. Then, after discussion, the board should vote on the design.

If there is more than one design to consider, it's not a bad idea to take a month to consider them before voting. You might try displaying the proposed designs around the theater personnel's work areas—the rehearsal space, office, meeting room or snack area—to see which design draws the most appeal over time (the designs should not be displayed for the general public to see, however; only the final choice should be revealed). You must not rush the decision to accept something as long-lasting and deeply defining as a symbol that will represent your theater group for years to come.

Once you have a design, you'll want to display it proudly everywhere, but don't. Avoid pasting the new identity in too many or inappropriate places, or you'll diminish the impact of the symbol and weaken its value. Fight the temptation, for example, of painting the symbol on every one of your theater's chair pads, doors and toilet seat covers.

Developing a communications plan

The Master Battle Plan delineates and coordinates all your publicity efforts for a specific show. Similarly, a theater company needs a communications plan to outline and coordinate all efforts to promote the overall image of the group.

The first half of the plan covers the general image of the group. The plan should say:

▲ How the name of the group should appear in communications. (Mumblemime Theater Co.? The Mumblemime Theater? Mumblemime Theatre?*)

▲ How the symbol and logotype should be used. (Are they restricted to certain colors? May they appear separately or always together?)

▲ How and where the mission statement should be used.

Also consider what key messages, incorporated in your group's mission statement, should be communicated to the public.

The communications plan's second part governs activities:

▲ What specific promotional goals should be achieved in the next year, three years, five years, or however long-term you wish the plan to cover. Examples: change the image of the group; broaden the company's name recognition in specific communities or among a particular age group.

▲ What specific activities will be carried out to achieve the goals of the communications plan. A wide or targeted direct-mail campaign? Door-to-door visits? Identity advertising or PSA's (see **The News Release** chapter) in specific news media? Public lectures? An

A communications plan outlines and coordinates all efforts to promote the overall image of the group.

---

* For a discussion of the spellings *theater* and *theatre*, turn to the introductory page called **The Spell of Theater** at the front of this book.

open house? Messages in the playbill and theater company newsletter? Displays in the theater lobby, libraries, or bank windows?

Meaningful activities

A group should develop strategic ceremonial opportunities to celebrate, reinforce and advance the identity of its theater company. Anyone can throw a party. A theater company should hold events with a theme that advances its mission statement.

A group's mission should not stop at promoting theater. Organizations are expected to contribute to the welfare of the community as well. Whenever possible, the two concepts should merge.

For example, it's satisfying to hold an annual costume party where proceeds benefit the local soup kitchen, orphanage or other charity. A party like this with a distinct purpose has a better chance of getting publicity, too.

Other community activities that can promote the image of a group include: contributing funds to a library each year to buy books about the dramatic arts, holding theater workshops for the public, contributing entertainment to the annual town fair, holding an annual reception or open house with previews of the coming theater season, volunteering to staff civic projects, answering phones during public television fund raising, and lending theater space to other non-profit groups.

Not all the activities in your communications plan must be noble and selfless, but all activities should clearly communicate whatever your mission statement says about your group—beginning with the message that your group practices the dramatic arts.

Summary

☞ Promoting your theater company's name will result in many benefits: increased ticket sales, better fund raising, smoother media relations, improved membership recruitment, heightened group pride and loyalty, more assurance of public assistance in times of adversity, and more acceptance of higher ticket prices—all provided your group produces quality work, of course.

☞ To achieve group identity and name recognition, follow these four steps in order:

1. Analyze the group: its history, activities, resources, membership and audience.

2. Make sure the mission statement is clear, simple and consistent with the audience's needs.

3. Develop a company symbol.

4. Designate key places and occasions to heighten public exposure of your group's existence.

The One-Person Publicity Shop

Chapter 20

- Setting priorities
- Basic equipment
- Acquiring skills
- Keeping organized

Throughout this book I have stressed the need to build a team of volunteers because publicity can be such an involved, highly detailed job.

However, I realize that often there is no one else to help with publicity. I know the feeling because I've been there many times. People may offer to help but when the chips are down you can find yourself alone with a lot of publicity to handle in a critically short time.

So, whether you are the sole person doing publicity for a theater company, or the publicist for your own one-person traveling show, a few streamlined strategies will get you through. Here they are:

1. Set priorities

It's three weeks before opening night and publicity until now has been nonexistent.

The quick-fix solution is to *analyze the market*. Where is your audience and what news media do they pay attention to? If you don't have time to compile an extensive mailing list, identify only the key newspapers, radio and TV stations that have *the greatest chance to draw your audience*. For reliable advice on which media are key, ask the person behind the counter at a local restaurant, the town librarian, or the mayor's publicity manager. Hit the key news outlets fast and hard.

THE NEWS RELEASE: You have time for just one news release, so write a good one with a direct lead sentence: "Puppeteer Marcy Desautels will bring her Noodlerama Puppet Theater to Garfield Memorial Library for a free show Wednesday, March 28 at 3 p.m...." Include visual details but limit your release to two pages.

Include a fact sheet that lists the words *who, what, when* and *where* on the left half of the page, and brief answers to these questions on the right half. This gives busy news editors the information in an organized form that can be quickly and easily inserted into the weekly calendar listing of town events.

PHOTOGRAPHY: Include a photograph. If your show is a set production that you take to various locations, you should have a stack of publicity photos made up ahead of time. In a pinch, call the local high school principal or college office of student activities to locate the school's photography club president. Beg or bribe this amateur photographer to snap your picture with black and white film and sell you some prints in 24 hours. Bring a few props, dress in costume and—smile!

An alternative that can work when you're in a rush to make a newspaper's deadline is to set up a fast photo session at the theater and then bring the undeveloped film to the editor of the local paper. Present your news release, apologize for the last-minute notice, offer the roll of film and ask whether the editor would consider using any of the pictures if they're judged to meet the newspaper's standards for quality. Often, small newspapers will hand the roll of film to the staff photographer for developing. I wouldn't recommend showing up at the newspaper and asking the editor to assign someone to take a picture, however. That's asking too much.

RADIO: Call the station and ask if there's a morning program you could be booked on for just a few minutes to let people in town know about your show. Hand-deliver or mail to the radio station (with a brief cover

When you're the sole publicist, identify the key newspapers, radio and TV stations that have the greatest chance to draw your audience.

letter) the fact sheet you produced for the newspapers and request that the station inform its listeners about your show.

TELEVISION: Mark your calendar and call the key TV station(s) three days before opening night. Ask for the assignment editor (this is the person who assigns stories to the camera crews). Briefly introduce yourself and launch immediately into the purpose of your call. Emphasize the visual aspects of your show: costumes, color, action, laughing children in the audience—things that will look good on camera. Invite TV to look in on a rehearsal.

HANDBILLS: Print up handbills that can double as posters. For quick, inexpensive typesetting, drop by the computer lab of your local high school or college. Present the information you want on your handbill neatly written out. Collar a bright-looking student and offer free tickets, gift certificates or a little bit of cold cash in exchange for a rush typesetting job. Young people are notoriously impoverished and are known to respond to bribes.

If your traveling show is performing at a school, ask the principal or the teacher in charge whether a few dependable students can be recruited to help post handbills in town. Supply rolls of tape and ask the teacher to suggest key places where handbills should go. Offer to deliver a special lecture to the teacher's class or the PTO in exchange for this help.

Always make it sound like you're offering more than what you're asking for in return. Then back up your offer with a truly valuable gift of your talent or your theater company's talent.

2. Collect basic equipment

Always have on hand plenty of stationery, coils of stamps and a sponge in a shallow dish to apply the stamps, fresh film in the refrigerator, a working 35mm camera and flash, a typewriter with spare ribbons, note paper, tape, pens and opaque white correction fluid to cover your mistakes, an up-to-date telephone directory (a good library has directories for the entire county and perhaps all the directories for the state), a working telephone (a telephone answering machine is an absolute must for busy publicists), a dictionary, a thesaurus, a writing style guide (see Chapter 4 on **Getting Started** for details on these items), stock publicity photographs and hand-drawn clip art, and a drawing board and T-square/triangle set acquired from the local art supply store.

A computer was once a luxury item, but it has quickly become a necessity. You'll need word-processing software that lets you write and store news releases, and print mailing labels. In an emergency, you can rent time on a typewriter or word processor at most large libraries and all college libraries.

The only other basic equipment you'll need is this book, and you already have it!

3. Acquire skills

Read books on graphic design at the library and ask the local school system and town adult education program to offer a course on basic layout and paste-up skills. Look for an introductory course in black and white photography. To become truly self-sufficient, learn how to develop your own pictures (almost all camera stores and high schools offer this training). Most amateurs with limited space set up their darkroom in the bathroom.

At the library, study the arts and entertainment sections of local and big-city newspapers. Learn from these how to write better news stories and captions, and how to pose interesting photographs. Photocopy and file stories and pictures that you want to emulate.

Collect brochures and other handouts that you find appealing. Store these in a drawer or a box marked "ideas."

4. Keep organized

You'll need a large wall calendar. Draw one on a large sheet of paper and mark your "to do" and "deadline" dates.

Work out your own version of the **Master Battle Plan** (Chapter 5) and post this where you can see it. Check your plan and calendar every day.

Organize your working space. Get a milk crate and fill it with file folders. Label the file folders "news releases," "photos," "mailing lists," "clip art," "correspondence," "receipts," etc. If you're promoting several performances in different locations, as in the case of a traveling show, file information on each show in a separate folder.

Keep stock publicity materials neatly arranged on shelves: tickets, stationary, standard releases and fact sheets, photos, reprints of newspaper reviews. Put these in individual boxes or trays and label the sides. Stack your information books to one side for quick reference: phone books, guide books, dictionary. Don't haphazardly throw pens and paper clips into a desk drawer: Store pens, pencils and markers in a cup. Store clips, stamps, erasers, fasteners and other small items in handy containers.

Before going to bed each night, make a list of the things you need to do tomorrow. If the list is long, prioritize the tasks by noting an "A" (priority), "B" (secondary) or "C" (if there is time) beside each item on the list. Each weekend, reevaluate what needs to be done in the coming week and adjust your calendar and Master Battle Plan.

During slow periods, get ahead on routine tasks. Stuff envelopes with standard publicity material.

5. Plan for next time

Read the next chapter to learn how to exude confidence. Be constantly on the lookout for volunteers. Recruit passionately. Let others know you're looking to build a crack publicity team.

Summary

- When you're the sole publicist, streamline your campaign. Identify only the key newspapers, radio and TV stations that have the greatest chance to draw your audience. Hit these key news outlets fast and hard.

- Make a news release work for you by keeping it short and including a fact sheet.

- Use resources at the local high schools and colleges to arrange for quick photography and typesetting.

- Barter services for assistance.

- Seek out courses and library books to acquire publicity skills, including graphic design and photography.

- Stock your work space with proper tools and keep your work space organized.

Self-Promotion

Chapter 21

- Getting recognition you deserve
- Being—and looking—prepared
- Get credit by giving credit
- Inform, reward and cheer others

It doesn't have to happen, but it does: The publicist may do a great job of bringing in an audience but not get a word of thanks from the cast, crew or administration.

Imagine! The show has been a great success and the theater company declares a profit. The local newspaper published lots of news and ran a favorable review. A record number of audience members signed up to put themselves on the theater's mailing list.

At the cast party there is wholesale slapping of backs among the cast and crew. The theater company's president or the director stands up and toasts the production manager. A few gifts are exchanged among the crew. The cast basks in the glory of a marvelous production as everyone sits around the television to watch a videotape of the show.*

And in one corner, the forgotten publicist sits and stews. We don't ask for much, just two minutes of embarrassing praise, some mock hero-worship, and perhaps the key to the city or a replica of an Oscar. (Well, no one accused publicists of being shy or lacking imagination!)

Seriously, a publicist can be so busy promoting everyone else that it's easy to forget to conduct a little self-promotion. The principle that something UNSEEN and UNTOLD is UNSOLD applies to the publicist, too. In this case, however, a publicist who goes unrecognized soon feels unappreciated and disheartened.

Besides, a publicist needs to drum up a little appreciation for the job so that when budgets are assigned, the publicity budget will retain a healthy allocation of funds. The bottom line is, the bottom line's at stake!

So, take heart. Here are a few ideas you can try that won't sacrifice your natural tendency to remain humble yet can win you the small share of applause that's your due:

1 Present a budget: As soon as you learn about the new show you'll be called on to promote, sit down and calculate a budget (see Chapter 7 on **Budgeting and Money Management**). Develop a proposal for a publicity stunt if you wish, and estimate the additional cost. Then, when the next board meeting comes around and the harried general manager suddenly turns to you and says "Uh, I'm gonna need some kind of estimate for publicity. Can you work up some figures for me? I'd like to know by Friday," you can calmly turn to your file of papers in front of you, pull out your budget and say "Here you are. Have a nice day." People will be impressed.

2 Present a Master Battle Plan: In the same vein, develop your publicity schedule right away. Line up your assistants and deliver preliminary assignments. Type up the information and, at the first organizational meeting, wait for your turn to speak.

Clear your throat and pause for dramatic effect; people will think you've been caught unprepared. Then slowly rise and distribute papers to the general manager, the director, the stage manager and other administrators, saying in an

---

* Most royalty contracts forbid videotaping performances, but nearly every group I know tapes its shows for private use anyway. I'm not advocating breaking the contract, but merely reporting what I know goes on.

unassuming manner, "Here is a list of the members of the publicity team, along with their assigned areas and the phone numbers. Please call them or call me. Chet has agreed to design the poster, Janet is already working with Beth on getting ads for the playbill, Kelly will lay out the playbill, Dana is helping me with the news releases, and we're going to try a new method of distributing posters. If the idea succeeds, we'll cover town in just one morning.

"On this second sheet of paper is a fact sheet about the show. Donna, I think this will help the box office people because most of what they need to know about the show is here.

"On this third handout you'll see the schedule of deadlines I'll be following to get publicity done. Owen, you can see that I'll need biographies from the actors and from you in about two weeks. We should have posters in four weeks.

"And, finally, on this last handout are details on my proposal for the publicity stunt I mentioned earlier. The one snag in the plan is getting Arthur up on a horse, but I think I can talk to someone at Wilson's riding stables about giving him a few lessons. If it doesn't work, we'll go to plan B."

Then add hesitantly, "Um, I think that's all for now." Sit down and fold your hands in front of you. Look humble—never smug. People will be impressed.

3 **Give credit and thanks:** At subsequent meetings, when everyone is watching and listening, give a progress report that is not too detailed but not too skimpy either. Look for opportunities to give credit and thanks: "Thanks to Chet, who came through two days early on the poster design, we're ahead of schedule; the poster is already at the printer's. Dana wrote all the hometown news releases you see here and, I think, he's done a great job. Konrad came to the rescue—thanks, Konrad—and we have publicity photos right out of the dark room to look at tonight. Oh, and Kelly is doing her usually bang-up job with the playbill. It looks like smooth sailing."

At the cast party, thank each member of your publicity team and acknowledge the assistance of anyone who helped. Say, "I especially appreciate the patience of the cast members who sat through the photo sessions, drafted biographies for the playbill and, in Lisa's case, even took time out from work to go on the radio. That's teamwork." When you praise other people for helping you—even if they were simply doing their jobs—people will be impressed.

4 **Project confidence:** It's become a joke with my theater group. "How's publicity going?" someone will ask. "Everything's under control," I'll respond dramatically. Someone else asks, "How goes the battle?" and my answer is "The enemy doesn't stand a chance." When someone asks "Have you solved that problem?" I say, "There are no problems, only peculiar challenges."

Exude confidence, even when you're running in five directions and feel like you're losing your mind. If you're falling behind and need help, calmly turn to the general manager or the theater company president and say, "Listen, Gwendolyn, who do we have that can lend a hand for a few days—just to help run off copies and stuff, stamp and address envelopes?" Don't apologize or beg forgiveness for being up to your armpits with work. Seek out opinions from others, thank them, and project confidence.

When the publicist looks worried, people begin to suspect that the publicist isn't capable. Look capable. Sound capable. People will be impressed.

5 Display the fruits of success: When articles begin to appear in the newspapers about your show, clip them, identify the name of the newspaper and the date, and make copies. Post a copy on a bulletin board in the rehearsal hall. Give copies to the director, the general manager and the theater company president. If a good-sized article appears with pictures, take this to a quick-copy print shop and enlarge it to twice the original size. Post this on the bulletin board.

Don't make a big deal, don't wave the article around and yell "Lookit! Lookit!" Just keep posting the articles, add the poster when it arrives, put up a few spare publicity photos and copies of the news releases—all to subtly let everyone know that you're on the job. Soon the bulletin board will be filled. Add a neatly lettered banner that says "Peabody Town Players In The News." People will be impressed.

6 Keep people informed: When a newspaper photographer or reporter is coming to rehearsal, ask the stage manager to make the announcement to the cast and crew (this lets the stage manager take the floor and feel important). When the reporter arrives, have your news kit ready and introduce the reporter to everyone. When you know a story is going to appear in the newspaper about your group, tell key people and let them spread the word. When the story appears in print, people will think, "Well! We were told that the story would appear today, and here it is. The publicist sure knows what's going on!"

At the last meeting before opening night, report some statistics. Report the number of news releases mailed out, the number of phone calls made by you and your publicity team, the number of posters distributed, the number of photos mailed out, the number of newspapers announcing your show. Don't brag. Recite the numbers modestly with a "just thought you might like to know, that's all" tone of voice.

Tell people what's going to happen, tell people what's happening, and then tell 'em what happened. People will be impressed.

7 Reward volunteers: Before the work begins, pass out some small gift to your publicity team helpers—a nice pen, an attractive notebook, a few candy bars wrapped in a bow with the message "I hope these give you a little extra energy when you find you need some!" Midway through the promotion campaign, have a pizza party and pick up the tab. After the show closes and the cast party is done, invite your helpers to a victory brunch. Ask their advice on how to do things better next time, ask them to stay on for another show, and hand out little gifts with a personal message. The gifts shouldn't be extravagant by any means. A $1.00 gift certificate for the local hamburger stand is fine. It really *is* the thought that counts.

People will be impressed.

8 Be the cheerleader: Watch the others in your group. When they seem down, put your

Exude confidence, even when you're running in five directions. Look capable. Sound capable.

hand on a shoulder and listen to their problems. Don't offer a solution unless you're specifically asked. Most of the time, people just need to know that they're not failures and that the world doesn't hate them. Lend a sympathetic ear.

When you meet your co-workers, look as if you're happy to see them. Ask people about their families. Look for people who need recognition—the carpenter who's been at it all afternoon making three sets of stairs, the young stage hand who's trying to grow out of awkwardness and has just helped move some flats, the old timer who's seen it all and just wants to tell the old stories one more time, and the shy newcomer who is standing at the doorway, wondering whether to come into the hall or turn around and run (the business of theater work can be pretty scary to novices).

Be friends to all these people. Greet them, listen to their stories and woes, compliment them on their work. Say "nice job." During a break on construction day, don't let people eat alone. Look for the new person who's not included around the snack bar and bring them into the conversation. Learn people's names.

People will be impressed.

Summary

- ☞ Don't let people take your work as publicist for granted. Find modest but effective ways to remind them that your work is valuable.

- ☞ Be ready before being asked to present a budget and publicity plan.

- ☞ Be generous and kind. Give credit and thanks to those who assist you. No deed is too small to praise. Reward volunteers.

- ☞ Project confidence. Be the cheerleader. You'll get your way more often and build alliances.

- ☞ Don't hide your success under a bushel basket. Display favorable news clippings for everyone to enjoy. Keep officials informed.

Final Words

Chapter 22

- Why we do what we do.

In Chapter Eight, I mentioned that people involved in the arts, including theater publicists, often harbor the misconception that the majority of the public is interested in the arts.

If the majority of people in the United States were easily and passionately supportive of the arts, every community would have one or more thriving arts centers drawing capacity audiences to exhibits, screenings, workshops and performances. Every community would raise funds to build theaters as readily as the public contributes to new halls of fame for sports.

The hard reality is that, when budgets get tight, the very first programs to be cut from our schools, governments and businesses are the arts. The daily evidence before us is that newspapers give twice as much space to reporting sports as they give the arts, and radio and TV devote ten times as much attention to athletic competition as they do to the healing power of the arts.

At any college or university, the humanities go begging while science research and athletics bring in the big bucks from enthusiastic donors. Businesses phone college athletic departments and professional teams, eagerly offering great sums of money to support these events in exchange for a chance to advertise their wares and services to audiences. Most of the arts go hat-in-hand to businesses, hoping to squeeze out enough financial assistance to keep their programs alive for one more year.

The world is starved for art, only most people don't know it. They think that the unsettling feeling in their stomachs and the vague emptiness in their hearts is only the normal boredom that comes with modern living. What's really gnawing at them is their souls aching for nourishment.

The fact is, the world doesn't need hockey. People would get along fine without (insert any baseball team you want here). A hundred years from now most people on this planet won't remember a single tennis match that took place in the previous century.

But the world will quote Shakespeare. New generations will rediscover Georgia O'Keeffe. People will return again and again to witness *The Nutcracker*, and the music of Louis Armstrong will never die. Young people around the globe will continue to study *Antigone* and *Tartuffe*, *Uncle Vanya* and *Hedda Gabler*. *The Marriage of Figaro* will fill arenas and theaters with laughter and move hearts to beat stronger and faster for countless years to come. These works will remain alive and give lasting meaning to people's lives long after golf clubs and basketballs are buried in time's shifting sands.

What's most exciting is the thought that all the greatest pieces of theater may not—probably have not—been written yet.

The theater publicist practices a noble trade, then, for just as the playwright pens (or, these days, keyboards) great thoughts and the actor gives life to these thoughts, it is the publicist that calls out in a great voice the good news for hungry souls: Nourishment is at hand; joyful and heartfelt stories of human greatness are near; lasting lessons about the meaning of our lives are within reach.

However, the theater publicist must have a strong voice in today's modern, noisy world, and that voice must speak clearly and with skillful brevity so that each word is carefully chosen, and so that each poster and display is thoughtfully designed to stir the public from its lethargy and preoccupation with the world's distractions.

Perhaps one day the arts will get as much attention as they deserve. Perhaps everyone one day will know the thrill of attending the opening night of a play.

You and I should work for that day. I hope very soon you will find yourself walking into your theater and finding the director embracing you with tears, exclaiming in amazement, "Your publicity worked! We have a full house!"

APPENDIX A:
Master Battle Plan

Master Battle Plan

Publicity schedule for _____
NAME OF PLAY

Show dates: _____, 199____

Tickets go on sale: _____

Playbill ads sales close: _____

News Releases & Photographs: _____
PERSON RESPONSIBLE

_____ - Mail audition notice to newspaper, TV and radio calendars [4 weeks before event].

_____ - Secure services of photographer to shoot publicity photos, including dress rehearsal; remind photographer to order any special film [10 weeks before opening night].

_____ - Mail Show Dates Set listing (including times, location, ticket and ordering information) to news media calendars [7 weeks before opening night].

_____ - Take black and white head shots and publicity photos: group actors by home towns [7 weeks before opening night].

_____ - Mail Cast Selected announcement to newspapers; order photos from contact sheet [6 weeks before opening night].

_____ - Mail Tickets On Sale announcement with photos [5 weeks before opening night].

_____ - Mail Feature Stories with photos [4 weeks before opening night].

_____ - Mail Home Town Actor announcement with pictures [3 weeks before opening night].

_____ - Call arts editors or regional reporters of major newspapers; pitch story ideas and photo opportunities [2 weeks before opening night].

_____ - Mail reminder photo and caption to newspapers [2 weeks before opening night].

_____ - Take photos during last rehearsals and develop immediately.

_____ - If necessary to spur final sales for second weekend performances, send another reminder photo or notice of tickets still on sale [right after first weekend].

_____ - Retrieve pictures from display boards and file in archives [after show closes].

Coding For News Release Distribution Guide

Type of Release	Timing	Distribution
1. Auditions	4 weeks before event	A B C D E F G
2. Show dates	7 weeks before opening	A B C _ E F _
3. Cast selected	6 weeks before opening	A B _ _ _ _ _
4. Tickets on sale	5 weeks before opening	A B _ D E F G
5. Feature stories	4 weeks before opening	A B C _ _ _ _
6. Home town news	3 weeks before opening	A B _ D? _ _ _
7. Reminder photo	2 weeks before opening	A B _ _ _ _ _
8. Added reminder	right after 1st weekend	A B? _ _ _ _ _

Coding For Releases & Contacts

A — Daily newspapers (may or may not include Sunday newspapers).

B — Weekly papers, including shoppers and community bulletins.

C — Quarterly publications (entertainment newsletter listings, including state and local arts commissions, tourism bulletins).

D — Local high school and college newspapers.

E — Area community theater, high school and college drama groups.

F — Dance & music schools, magic stores, costume and makeup shops.

G — Radio stations and TV bulletin boards.

Fact Sheet: _____
PERSON RESPONSIBLE

_____ - Gather fact sheet information [8 weeks before opening night].

_____ - Distribute fact sheet to publicity team, playbill sales manager, box office manager [7 weeks before opening night]. Reviewers: _____

_____ - Call editors to secure preliminary interest and names of reviewers. Mail invitation letters and news kits [4 weeks before opening night].

_____ - Make follow-up calls and reserve seats [3 weeks before opening night].

_____ - Put spare news kits in box office along with late-news information packets for reviewers [1 week before opening night].

_____ - Confirm that reviewers are coming [2 days before opening night].

_____ - Collect news clips, distribute copies to director, general manager and theater president, post reviews in the theater, and file copies [within 24 hours of publication].

Electronic News Phone Calls: _____
PERSON RESPONSIBLE

_____ - Call radio and TV talk shows to book guests [3 weeks before opening night].

_____ - Send info to TV news [1 week before targeted rehearsal].

_____ - Make follow-up call to TV news [2 days before target].

_____ - Targeted rehearsal date.

Posters: _____
PERSON RESPONSIBLE

_____ - Get specifications from general manager and director and give to poster artist [10 weeks before opening night].

_____ - Review artist's design. Get director's and general manager's approval [8 weeks before opening night].

_____ - Proofread poster galleys and make corrections [7 weeks before opening night].

_____ - Take completed paste-up to printer [6 weeks before opening night].

_____ - Pick up posters from printer [4 weeks before opening night].

_____ - Distribute posters [3 weeks before opening night].

Displays: _____
PERSON RESPONSIBLE

_____ - Prepare list of locations and secure permission; make list of materials needed for displays [5 weeks before opening night].

_____ - Assemble materials and arrange on boards, take paste-ups to printer, and make other preliminary arrangements [4 weeks before opening night].

_____ - Set up displays [3 weeks before opening night].

Membership Fliers & Invitations: _____
PERSON RESPONSIBLE

_____ - Mail audition notices to members [2 or 3 weeks before auditions].

_____ - Mail opening night invitations to patrons and VIP's [4 weeks before opening night].

_____ - Mail reminder of show dates to membership mailing list [2 weeks before tickets go on sale to general public].

Playbill: _____
PERSON RESPONSIBLE

_____ - Deadline for all advertising orders and editorial copy [7 weeks before opening night].

_____ - Deliver copy to typesetter [6 weeks before opening night].

_____ - Proofread typeset galleys, give one hand-corrected set to artist and another to typesetter for corrections [5 weeks before opening night].

_____ - Deliver final galleys to artist. Proofread later that week [4 weeks before opening night].

_____ - Deliver paste-up to printer [3 weeks before opening night].

_____ - Pick up playbills from printer [1 week before opening night].

Road Signs: _____
PERSON RESPONSIBLE

_____ - Design road signs and locate materials [5 weeks before opening night].

_____ - Paint road signs [4 weeks before opening night].

_____ - Post signs [2-3 weeks before opening night].

_____ - Take down, store signs [morning after show closes].

Radio Give-Aways: _____
PERSON RESPONSIBLE

_____ - Get approval from general manager to give away tickets [7 weeks before opening night].

_____ - Contact station promotion manager [6 weeks before opening night].

_____ - Prepare information packets for winners [5 weeks before opening night].

_____ - Send radio station information packs to mail to winners; alert box office to set aside seats [4 weeks before opening night].

_____ - Listen to radio to hear tickets being given away [2 weeks before opening night].

_____ - Obtain list of winners from radio station. Deliver list to box office manager [1 week before opening night].

_____ - Review list of winners who showed up [after opening night].

Advertising—Radio and Newspapers: _____
PERSON RESPONSIBLE

_____ - Gather information on advertising prices [7 weeks before opening night].

_____ - Plan campaign and get budget approved [6 weeks before opening night].

_____ - Design newspaper display ads and radio ads. Place insertion orders [5 weeks before opening night].

_____ - Deliver newspaper ads [4 weeks before opening night].

_____ - Sit in on radio advertising recording [3 weeks before opening night].

_____ - Monitor advertising [radio: 2 weeks before opening night; newspapers: 2-3 weeks before opening night].

APPENDIX B:
Publicity Budget Work Sheet

Master Publicity Budget

Publicity budget for _____
NAME OF SHOW

News releases—postage and printing

\#___ general release(s) **x** #____ mailings **x** $_____ postage per piece = $_____

\#___ feature story(s) **x** $_____   = $_____

\#___ hometown releases **x** $_____   = $_____

\#___ reminder releases **x** #_____ mailings **x** $_____   = $_____

\#___ letters inviting reviewers **x** $_____   = $_____

\#___ news kits @ $_____ **x** $_____ postage per piece   = $_____

photocopying charge: #_____ copies @ $_____   = $_____

\#___ mailing lables (_____-count per pack) @ $_____   = $_____

- Total   = $_____ $_____ $_____
Estimate   Final

Photography and displays

\#____ rolls of B&W film for press pictures   = $_____

$____ cost of developing film **x** #____ B&W rolls   = $_____

\#____ regular-sized reprints @ $____ each   = $_____

\#____ enlargements @ $____ each   = $_____

\#____ rolls of color slide film @ $____ each   = $_____

$____ cost of developing slides **x** #____ rolls   = $_____

$____ cost of bulletin board materials   = $_____

- Total   = $_____ $_____ $_____
Estimate   Final

Road signs and banners

white opaque base paint, colors   = $_____

cost of wood $_____; cost of cloth $_____   = $_____

- Total   = $_____ $_____ $_____
Estimate   Final

B.1 Full House

Playbill

typesetting $_____ per hour x _____ hours = $_____

printing #_____ copies of #_____ original pages = $_____

-- Total = $_____ $_____ $_____
                                                          Estimate Final

Posters

#_____ posters printed x $_____ (unit cost) = $_____

cost of added materials if hand-decorating = $_____

-- Total = $_____ $_____ $_____
                                                          Estimate Final

Fliers

printing: #___ mailings x #_____ per mailing @ $_____ per copy = $_____

postage: #___ total copies @ $_____ each = $_____

-- Total = $_____ $_____ $_____
                                                          Estimate Final

Newspaper and radio advertising

_____: #___ ads @ $_____ each = $_____

_____: #___ ads @ $_____ each = $_____

_____: #___ ads @ $_____ each = $_____

_____: #___ ads @ $_____ each = $_____

_____: #___ ads @ $_____ each = $_____

-- Total = $_____ $_____ $_____
                                                          Estimate Final

Invitations

printing (including envelopes, RSVP cards) = $_____

postage: #___ invitations x $_____ each = $_____

-- Total = $_____ $_____ $_____
                                                          Estimate Final

Tickets

printer's estimate:_____

-- Total = $_____ $_____ $_____
                                                          Estimate Final

Miscellaneous *(other regular or special publicity costs)*

radio give-aways (printing materials, mailing)   = $_____

publicity stunt:_____   = $_____

tent cards, bank stuffers, handbills, special displays, others

_____   = $_____

_____   = $_____

_____   = $_____

_____   = $_____

--- Total   = $_____ $_____ $_____
                                                                    Estimate   Final

Phone Calls

long distance charges_____

--- Total   = $_____ $_____ $_____
                                                                    Estimate   Final

Totals	Estimate	Final
News releases	$_____	$_____
Photography and displays	$_____	$_____
Signs, banners	$_____	$_____
Playbill	$_____	$_____
Posters	$_____	$_____
Fliers	$_____	$_____
Advertising	$_____	$_____
Invitations	$_____	$_____
Tickets	$_____	$_____
Miscellaneous	$_____	$_____
Phone calls	$_____	$_____
Total Publicity Budget	$_____	$_____

APPENDIX C:
Playbill Tally Work Sheet

Playbill Tally Sheet

Production Name: _____

Indicate estimated, revised and final amount of room needed, measured in fractions of pages, for each item in the playbill (Note: Not all information items may apply to the production):

Estimated Pages	Revised Estimate	Final Count	
_____	_____	_____	cover
_____	_____	_____	title page
_____	_____	_____	list: actors, director, settings, scenes
_____	_____	_____	list: production and administrative staff
_____	_____	_____	house rules, safety notice
_____	_____	_____	biographies of actors, director, chief crew members
_____	_____	_____	note from the director
_____	_____	_____	notes about history of the play and playwright
_____	_____	_____	list of donors/patrons
_____	_____	_____	clip and mail membership form
_____	_____	_____	history and mission of the theater company
_____	_____	_____	list: plays produced since company was formed
_____	_____	_____	preview of next play/next season
_____	_____	_____	_____
_____	_____	_____	_____
_____	_____	_____	_____
_____	_____	_____	_____

C.1 Full House

ADVERTISING [note ad size and business name]

Estimated Pages | Revised Estimate | Final Count

___ ___ ___   Free display ads _____ _____

                                                   _____ _____ _____

___ ___ ___   Ads paid for entire year:

                                                   _____ _____ _____

                                                   _____ _____ _____

                                                   _____ _____ _____

                                                   _____ _____ _____

___ ___ ___   Paid ads appearing in this playbill only:

                                                   _____ _____ _____

                                                   _____ _____ _____

                                                 _____ _____ _____

                                                 _____ _____ _____

                                                 _____ _____ _____

                                                 _____ _____ _____

                                                 _____ _____ _____

                                                 _____ _____ _____

___ ___ ___   **TOTAL PLAYBILL PAGES** [must be a multiple of 4]

Playbill Page Map

C.3 Full House

APPENDIX D:
Biography Questionnaire

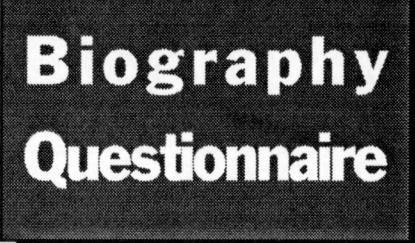

Biography Questionnaire

Publicity Questionnaire For Cast and Crew

Name of production: _____ Opening night: _____

> *Congratulations !*
>
> *...on being part of this production! Information that you provide about yourself on this form may be used for publicity in several ways: for a biographical sketch in the playbill, for a news release mailed to your hometown and to any business or club newsletter you might suggest, and in interviews with news reporters.*
>
> *Not all the information may be used, and you need answer only the questions you wish. Your street address and phone number will be kept confidential and used only if I need to reach you outside of rehearsals.*
>
> *Please take a moment to fill out this form and return it to me by _____ .*
>   DEADLINE DATE
>
> *Thanks, and very best wishes,*
>
> _____
>
> *Company Publicist (phone number: _____)*

1. Your name (as you want it to appear in publicity _____

2. Your address and phone number (day and evening numbers)
   _____

3. What role do you play in the production? _____

4. For quotation: What is it about the script that you find most interesting and challenging for you? Why do you think audiences will like this production?
   _____
   _____
   _____

5. Please list your theater experience that you wish publicized; the list need not be comprehensive. If you list an acting role, please indicate in the "role" column your character's name and if the role was a lead; otherwise, use the "role" column to indicate that you are describing experience as a director or production crew member:

CHARACTER/JOB	PRODUCTION NAME	THEATER GROUP/TOWN	YEAR
_____	_____	_____	_____
_____	_____	_____	_____
_____	_____	_____	_____

D.1 Full House

6. Please note any other theater experience you have:
_____
_____

7. Have you won theatrical awards? If so, please list them, the production, and the year the award was won.
_____
_____

8. Can you remember your first time on stage? Please describe this occasion briefly.
_____
_____

9. Where were you born/where did you grow up? (Journalists sometimes like to mention this; your response is optional.)
_____

10. Do you hold any academic degrees? Professional certifications? Have you served in the military (if so, what rank did you achieve and where have you served)?
_____
_____

11. Have you received any formal training in theater? Where and when?
_____

12. Please list any other hobbies or achievements you would like publicized.
_____

13. If you have worked with this theater company before, please indicate how many years and if you have served in any official administrative office:
_____

14. Please list hometown newspapers, club newsletters or employee newsletters that should receive news:
_____

15. Is there anything else about yourself that you would like mentioned in publicity?
_____

Please give your approval:

I authorize _____ to use the above information (excluding my street address and phone
            NAME OF THEATER COMPANY

number) in any publicity for _____, being produced _____
                                      NAME OF PRODUCTION   DATES OF THE PRODUCTION

through _____ 19____ , in _____ , _____ .
                                                                 TOWN   STATE

      SIGNED _____   DATE _____

Please return this questionnaire to _____ no later than _____ .
                                                                                                                                                                          DATE

"Break a leg!"

APPENDIX E: Journalism Style

Journalism Style

All professional journalists and publicists follow certain accepted rules of capitalization, abbreviation, punctuation and word usage. These rules help editors and reporters achieve a uniform way of expressing things in writing.

These rules are adopted from the Associated Press and United Press International stylebooks. The rules below are a partial listing of some of the most common style problems likely to trip you up writing news releases and other materials for journalists or the general public. A book on journalism (check your library) will give you a more complete listing. Any major book store can order a copy of the *Associate Press Stylebook and Libel Manual*, or you may write directly to the Associated Press at 50 Rockefeller Plaza, New York, NY 10020 for information.

My favorite book on punctuation is the very readable *Up Your Punctuation!* by Edgar C. Alward, available for $15.00 plus $2.00 postage from Pine Island Press, 69 Pine Island Lake, Westhampton, MA 01027.

1. Capitalization

1-a. CAPITALIZE books, plays, songs, poems, movies, TV shows, etc., and place in quotation marks: "The Great Gatsby" and "Inherit the Wind." The words *a, an, and, of, the* are capitalized only at the start or end of a title: "Of Human Bondage" and "I'm Getting My Act Together and Taking It on the Road."

1-b. CAPITALIZE the first word of a quotation making a complete sentence after a comma or colon: Shakespeare wrote, "All the world's a stage."

1-c. CAPITALIZE formal awards and honors: Emmy, Oscar (Academy Award), Tony, Pulitzer Prize, Medal of Honor. LOWER CASE rank and generic title awards: first prize, second place, honorable mention, the best actor award, the award for best stage design, blue ribbon.

1-d. CAPITALIZE formal titles preceding a name: Grangeville Theater Company President Jane Wallace. Chairperson Jose Gonzales. Use LOWER CASE when standing alone or following a name: Jane Wallace, president of the Goofus Players.

1-e. CAPITALIZE titles of authority before a name but LOWER CASE when following a name or standing alone: Producer Bill Beefeater. Bill Beefeater, the producer. The producer, Bill Beefeater. The producer.

1-f. Use LOWER CASE with occupational or "false" titles: The stage was constructed by carpenter Soon Kim with the help of attorney Jack Greene and chemistry professor Peter Gibbons.

1-g. CAPITALIZE titles of government officials when accompanying the name: Senator Helen Gilbert. LOWER CASE these titles when standing alone: Edward Jefferson, mayor of Barnfield.

1-h. CAPITALIZE U.S. Congress, Senate, House, Cabinet; Legislature when preceded by the name of the state; City Council. LOWER CASE when standing alone: The legislature is considering a bill to give $1 million to every community theater group in the state. The city is the *capital*; the building is the *capitol*.

1-i. CAPITALIZE political parties: Democrat, Democratic, Socialist, Republican. LOWER CASE democratic form of government, republican system.

1-j. Long titles follow names: Carl Carlson, secretary-treasurer of the Bang-Bang Playhouse.

1-k. CAPITALIZE names of states, cities and towns, names of companies and organizations, holidays, historic events, religious feasts, rivers, mountains and lakes, streets and roads, nations, continents, etc.: Colorado, Boston, First National Bank, the American Cancer Society, Thanksgiving, the American Revolutionary War, Passover, the Mississippi River, Mount Everest, Cold Spring Road, New Year's Eve, Belgium, Antarctica. LOWER CASE: we'll ring in the new year; the arctic winter.

1-l. LOWER CASE the plural of compounds: The intersection of Oak and Main streets.

1-m. CAPITALIZE specific regions: New England, the Midwest, the South, Southern California, the Panhandle, New York's East Side, the Far East, the South Pacific. LOWER CASE directions: winds headed east, rain fell in western South Carolina.

1-n. CAPITALIZE committee in full names only: the Long-Range Planning Committee. LOWER CASE the word "committee" standing alone. LOWER CASE subcommittee titles.

1-o. CAPITALIZE U.S. armed forces: Army (USA), Air Force (USAF), Navy (USN), Marines (USMC), Coast Guard, National Guard. LOWER CASE all foreign armed forces except Royal Air Force (RAF), Royal Canadian Air Force (RCAF), Royal Canadian Mounted Police, and French Foreign Legion.

1-p. CAPITALIZE trade names: Frisbee toy disk, Kleenex facial tissues, Xerox photocopy, Plexiglas plastic plating, Thermos vacuum bottle, Styrofoam polystyrene, Mace chemical spray, Dacron polyester, Sheetrock plasterboard, Novocaine anesthetic, Tabasco hot pepper sauce, Band-Aid adhesive bandage, etc.

1-q. CHECK CAPITALIZATION in the dictionary for proper names that have gained an independent meaning: brussels sprouts, dutch door, but Russian roulette, Spanish omelette.

1-r. CAPITALIZE formal documents: the Bible, the Declaration of Independence.

1-s. CAPITALIZE formal names of races and ethnic groups: Caucasian, Asian, Native American, African-American, Hispanic. LOWER CASE black, white, red, etc.

1-t. CAPITALIZE months: January, October. LOWER CASE seasons: spring, autumn.

1-u. CAPITALIZE names of organizations, expositions, etc: Girl Scout, Cub Scout, Buford County Fair. LOWER CASE scout and fair when standing alone.

2. Abbreviations

2-a. ABBREVIATE months when used with dates, but SPELL OUT months standing alone: Jan. 3, 1992. Abbreviations are: Jan., Feb., Aug., Sept., Oct., Nov. and Dec. SPELL OUT March, April, May, June and July. (Note: Do not add "st," "nd," "rd," or "th" in dates: write Jan. 3 and 4, not Jan. 3rd and 4th. *See also 4-g and 4-o.*)

2-b. (or, not 2-b) SPELL OUT days of the week: Monday, Sept. 29, 1993.

2-c. Mr. is only used with Mrs. or with clerical titles (except when quoting someone). Journalism style (except for a few newspapers like the New York Times which retain "courtesy titles") drop all titles: Lyle Pearsons will play the lead in "Count Dracula," a role Pearsons says he can't wait to sink his teeth into.

2-d. SPELL OUT first mention of organizations, clubs, businesses, agencies, etc., and then ABBREVIATE afterwards. Exception: AFL-CIO, NAACP, CBS network, and NCAA are examples of agencies so well known that the abbreviations are better known than the words they stand for; use these abbreviations in all instances. With names that are not well known, abbreviations should follow in parentheses on the first mention: The Associated Community Theaters of Connecticut (ACT-CONN) held its annual theater festival last weekend in Enfield. In its eighth year of sponsoring the festival, ACT-CONN held its largest gathering of community theaters last Saturday and Sunday.

2-e. ABBREVIATE St., Ave., Blvd., Terr. in addresses but not Circle, Drive, Lane, Place, Plaza, Point, Port, Road.

2-f. Lower case abbreviations usually take periods. If the letters without periods spell words, periods are usually needed: c.o.d.; a.m., p.m. *(See also 4-p.)*

2-g. ABBREVIATE time zones: EDT, CST.

2-h. Place B.C. after date, A.D. before: 300 B.C., A.D. 60.

2-i. ABBREVIATE versus as vs. (with period)

2-j. ABBREVIATE businesses: Milton Bradley Co., Warner Bros., Acme Hardware Inc., Amalgamated Pincushions Ltd. (Note that no comma is inserted before Inc. and Ltd.)

2-k. Standard state abbreviations (Note: These abbreviations differ from the two-letter abbreviations used by the U.S. Postal Service for addresses. Use postal abbreviations for mailing addresses only):

Ala.	Ariz.	Ark.	Calif.	Colo.	Conn.	Del.	Fla.	Ga.	Ill.
Ind.	Kan.	Ky.	La.	Md.	Mass.	Mich.	Minn.	Miss.	Mo.
Mont.	Neb.	Nev.	N.C.	N.D.	N.H.	N.J.	N.M.	N.Y.	Okla.
Ore.	Pa.	R.I.	S.C.	S.D.	Tenn.	Tex.	Vt.	Va.	Wash.
Wis.	W.Va.	Wyo.							

Don't abbreviate if six letters or less, except Texas. SPELL OUT Alaska, Hawaii, Idaho, Iowa, Ohio, Maine and Utah.

SPELL OUT names of states standing alone: She went to Alabama with a banjo on her knee.

Set commas before and after abbreviated states in mid-sentence: The play was first performed in St. Paul, Minn., where it met with critical success.

2-l. ABBREVIATE Canadian provinces following a city or town: Alta., B.C., Man., N.B., Nfld., N.S., Ont., P.E.I., Que. and Sask.

2-m. ABBREVIATE United Nations and United States in titles, but SPELL OUT when used as a noun: U.S. Department of Commerce, but United Nations peace-keeping forces.

2-n. ABBREVIATE and capitalize academic, fraternal, honorary and religious degrees, but use lower case when spelled: B.A., bachelor of arts, bachelor's degree; M.A., master of arts, master's degree; Ph.D., doctorate, doctoral degree. Use M.D. and D.D.S. only in formal titles and addresses: Mark Roy, M.D.; Dr. Jan Jaskiewicz, or Jan Jaskiewicz, D.D.S.—but never Dr. Richard Veilleux, M.D. Refrain from placing academic titles after names except in formal titles. Avoid writing this: "Sherry Fisher, Ph.D., will star in the musical "Mame." Instead, write this: Sherry Fisher, a psychologist with a Ph.D. from Temple University, will star in the psychological thriller "I'll Be Back Before Midnight."

2-o. ABBREVIATE titles and capitalize when immediately preceding a name but not after a name: Asst., Atty., Gov., Lt. Gov., Rep., Sen., Supt. Example: Gov. William Whitcomb and George Quibble, lieutenant governor *(See also 1-d.)*

2-p. DO NOT ABBREVIATE Christmas, association, detective, department, deputy, general manager, secretary, or treasurer.

3. Punctuation (A partial listing)

The Period

3-a. Avoid using the ellipsis (three periods in a row) to indicate a pause: Well... I really don't know. The ellipsis should be used to indicate an omission in a quote, such as to condense from a longer quote: "But, soft! What light... breaks?" (Romeo and Juliet, II,ii,1)

The Comma

3-b. Omit the comma before the last in a series unless the omission will cause confusion: If Jacques is so smart, why can't he add, subtract, multiply, divide—and spell "Quasimodo"? (The dash, rather than the comma, implies that Jacques should be able to do all those mathematical computations as well as "spell 'Quasimodo'.")

3-c. Do not use a comma before *of*: Lily Lucrece of Littletown, La.

3-d. Use the comma to set off attribution: The weapons, he said, will be used to decorate the stage.

3-e. Omit the comma before Roman numerals, company designations and family name successions: Samuel Bates III. Quality Control Inc. Sammy Davis Jr. *(See also 4-i)*

The Semicolon

3-f. Use the semicolon to separate phrases containing commas to avoid confusion. Use the semicolon to separate statements of contrast and statements that are too closely related:

The soldier, who was tall and muscular, was courteous; the sailor, short and tattooed from head to foot, didn't even try to mind his manners.

Theater jobs include publicity; back stage crew; set, costume and lighting design; lighting and sound engineering; set construction; ushering and bar tending; house and box office management; and fund-raising.

The Apostrophe

3-g. Use the apostrophe to indicate a contraction: it's means it is. Don't means do not.

3-h. Use the apostrophe and an "s" to show possession: Jack's crown. Omit the "s" but keep the apostrophe to show possession with a noun ending in "s": Moses' tablets.

3-i. Use the apostrophe for plurals of letters and numbers with the exception of years: Mississippi has four i's, four s's, and two p's. The year 1991 has two 1's and two 9's.

Do not use an apostrophe to indicate the plural of years: The 1980s were the Reagan years.

3-j. Use the apostrophe to indicate certain omissions of numbers and letters: She was in one show after another through the 1960s, '70s and '80s. The cockney chimney sweep said "Well, I'll 'ave t' think it over, gov'ner, an' let you know tomorrow."

3-k. For organization names, the use of the apostrophe follows the form of the official name: Actors Equity Association, the Suffield Players' new theater season.

The Colon

3-l. Use the colon to introduce something.

The Peter Pocket Players say they have 110 reasons why audiences should see their production of The Music Man: 10 hit songs, 25 hot performers, and those famous 76 trombones.

Quotation Marks

3-m. Use quotation marks in news releases for titles of books, plays, poems, songs, movies, TV shows, etc.

3-n. Use quotations marks to indicate "slang" expressions.

3-o. Alternate double-marks with single-marks to punctuate quotes within quotes. *(See the next example.)*

3-p. Periods and commas go inside quotation marks. Semicolons go outside: "I had no idea what a fine cast I had when we started," the director said; "but, by the end of the first week of rehearsal, I found myself saying, 'This is going to be a great show!' and wishing we could rehearse every night."

The Dash

3-q. The dash is used for sudden changes—no, make that apparent interruptions—in the stream of thought.

The Hyphen

3-r. Use the hyphen to form compound modifiers: This theater group, whose headquarters straddle the Bolton-Greenfield border, offers would-be techies some valuable on-the-job training using state-of-the-art lighting control panels.

3-s. Use the hyphen to avoid confusion in forming compound words: co-worker ("coworker" makes the reader see the word "cow"), re-cover (to cover again) and recover (to get over a surprise or illness).

3-t. The hyphen is repeated in a series of modifiers: Auditions will be limited to 5- and 6-year-olds.

3-u. Never use a hyphen with adverbs ending in "ly": the newly formed comedy team. A happily married couple. A heavily guarded secret. A long-desired return. A wrong-headed idea.

3-v. Use a hyphen for combination modifiers that precede the noun; after the noun, no hyphen: A well-done production. The production was well done.

3-w. Newspapers have abandoned the use of the hyphen in campuswide, worldwide, citywide, etc.

3-x. Use the hyphen to write out fractions and compound numbers: three-fifths of an hour. One-third the effort. Fifty-two cards. An eight-by-ten black and white photo.

The Exclamation Mark

3-y. Use it sparingly to convey only those rare moments of great emotion. Overuse will annoy readers and eventually cause readers to ignore your point. *Never* write three exclamation marks in a row.

4. Numerals

4-a. In general, spell below 10, use numerals for 10 and above: I saw 11 pipers piping, 10 lords a-leaping, nine ladies dancing, and eight maids a-milking.

4-b. Use figures in all human and animal ages.

4-c. Spell numbers under 10 for inanimate objects: three-mile trip, two blocks from City Hall. Exceptions: Fifth Avenue, Big Ten, Gang of Six.

4-d. Correct forms: 5-year-old boy, the boy is 5, she is 5 feet 2, 6-foot-2 doorway, Chicago won, 7-2. $15.00 shirt, nine-cent stamp, eight-hour rehearsal, five-day week, 85 cents, .38 caliber pistol. Attendance totaled 5,271. The 20th century had many wars, but the Twentieth Century Limited was a grand train.

4-e. Keep series simple: Here are three one-act plays, one 12-song musical, and 26 two-person scenes.

4-f. $8 million and eight million people.

4-g. 6th Fleet, 2nd Army, 3rd Division, 18th District

4-h. Spell casual numbers: Gay Nineties. A thousand thanks.

4-i. Roman numerals for historic sequence: Pope John Paul II, James J. Shea III (may prefer use of 3rd), King George V; but, Act II, scene 3.

4-j. Highways: U.S. 202, Interstate 91, Nevada 20.

4-k. Spell "cents" in amounts less than a dollar. A movie used to cost just 25 cents. Stamps used to be five cents.

4-l. Ranges: $10 million to $12 million, not $10-$12 million.

4-m. Fractions for the typewriter: 3 ½ (three and one-half), ⅞, 22 ¼.

4-n. Five percent. Use "%" only in tabular columns.

4-o. January 5, never January 5th.

4-p. Time: 7 a.m., 8:30 p.m., 9 a.m. to 3:15 p.m., 4-6 p.m.

4-q. Write: No. 1 choice, No. 2 candidate.

Suggested Reading

Theater

Theatre Management and Production in America: Commercial, Stock, Resident, College, Community, Theatre & Presenting Organizations, by Steven Langley. Drama Book, 1990. $37.50 cloth.

Writing in Restaurants, by David Mamet. Penguin Books, 1987. $6.95 paper.

Stage Directions (P.O. Box 1966, West Sacramento, CA 95691-9944). Magazine (10 issues a year) with articles on education, design, products and services, management, acting and directing, publicity and more. Especially suited for amateur theater.

Theatre Crafts (P.O. Box 470, Mt. Morris, IL 61054). Magazine (10 issues a year) with articles on sound, scenery, costumes and other design and tech news. Occasional news about promotion. Mostly suited for college and professional theater.

Writing

Associated Press Stylebook & Libel Manual: The Journalist's Bible, by The Associated Press, 1987. $10.95 paper.

The Elements of Style, by William Strunk Jr. and E.B. White. Third edition. Macmillan, 1979. $4.75 paper.

Up Your Punctuation, by Edgar C. Alward. Pine Island Press, 1988. $15.00 spiral-bound paperback.

Writing with Style: The News Story & the Feature, by Peter Jacobi. Lawrence Ragan Communications, 1982. $19.95 paper.

Promotion

Are They Selling Her Lips? Advertising and Identity, by Carol Moog. William Morrow, 1990. $18.95 cloth.

Do-It-Yourself Publicity, by David Ramacitti. AMACOM, 1990. $22.95 cloth.

Expose Yourself: Using the Power of Public Relations to Promote Your Business and Yourself, by Melba Beals. Chronicle Books, 1990. $18.95 cloth.

Getting Publicity: A Do-It-Yourself Guide for Small Business & Non-profit Groups, by Tanya Fletcher and Julia Rockler. Self-Counsel Business Service, 1990. $12.95

How to Get Publicity: (And Make the Most of It Once You've Got It), by William Parkhurst. Random House, 1985. $14.95 cloth.

How to Get Publicity in Newspapers, by Arnold Furst. Borden. $3.95 paper.

Ogilvy on Advertising, by David Ogilvy. Vintage Books, 1985. $15.95 paper.

Publicity Stunt: Great Staged Events That Made the News, by Candice J. Fuhrman. Chronicle Books, 1989. $12.95 paper.

You Can Spend Less and Sell More: The Advertising Book, revised ed., by William K. Witcher. Mark Publishing, 1987. $14.95 paper.

Photography

The New 35mm Photographer's Handbook, by Julian Caldoer and John Garrett. 2nd revised edition. H.C. Crown, 1990. $16.95 cloth.

John Hedgecoe's Complete Guide to Photography, by John Hedgecoe. Sterling, 1990. $24.95, cloth.

Professional Portrait Techniques. Eastman Kodak, 1987. $16.95 paper.

Photographic (6725 Sunset Blvd., Los Angeles CA 90028). Magazine with practical tips on lighting, posing, etc.

Popular Photography (P.O. Box 51803, Boulder CO 80323-1803). Magazine with news on new products and helpful ideas.

Graphic design

How to Understand & Use Design and Layout, by Alan Swann. North Light Books, 1991. $19.95, paper.

Problems: Solutions, Visual Thinking for Graphic Communications, by Richard Wilde. Van Nostrand Reinhold, 1989. $29.95 paper.

Index

Abraham Lincoln 17.2
action poses 9.13
actors' biographies 15.3, 15.5, 15.10
Actor's Nightmare, The 4.1
adult themes 4.4, 8.9
Advertising 2.6, 3.2, 4.6, 5.4, 6.1, 6.2, 7.4, 8.5, 8.8, 8.27, 16.1-16.10, 19.1
    free advertising 15.10
advertising agent 6.1
advertising revenue 15.1
Agnes of God 2.6
Albers, Joseph 1.4
Amadeus 17.3
Animal Crackers 17.1
Annie 8.26
anniversary 4.4, 9.8, 13.5, 17.2
Antigone 22.1
Aristotle 2.3
Armstrong, Louis 22.1
art shows 12.6
artist 6.1
arts bulletin 8.26
arts organization 4.2
assignment editor 8.7, 10.1
audience 2.1, 2.2, 2.3, 2.4, 2.6, 3.2
auditions 3.1, 4.3, 6.2, 8.7, 8.8, 15.4, 18.2, 19.1
authority 3.3
awards 13.5, 15.4

backstage pictures 9.14
bank stuffers 6.1, 13.1
banks 9.7, 13.8, 19.10
bids 7.4
big city newspaper 8.26
billboard 14.6
bills and receipts 4.6
biographies 4.6, 6.1, 9.8, 15.4
black and white film 9.6
box office 4.4, 6.2, 10.3, 10.8, 19.4, 21.2
Bride of Frankenstein, The 9.1
brochures 3.2, 6.1, 9.7, 9.15, 10.2, 13.1-13.8
budget 3.1, 4.6, 6.1, 6.4, 6.5, 7.1-7.6, 21.1
bulletin boards 11.1
Burns, George 10.9
businesses 2.4, 6.2

cable TV 8.6, 18.3
    community access 10.10, 18.3

calendar 4.3
calendar of events 16.2
caption 8.11, 9.20, 11.7
cast 6.3, 6.4, 8.7, 8.9, 8.10
cast photo 9.17
casting 3.1
catharsis 2.3
Cats 12.1
Chamber of Commerce 13.8
Chorus Line, A 12.1
Christie, Agatha
    Ten Little Indians 8.26
Christmas Carol, A 18.2, 19.2
civic groups 6.2, 9.7
college 4.3, 6.2
college theater 10.4
color 6.2
color photocopying 11.1
color photograph 9.6, 9.7
comedy 2.4
commercial 18.3
commission on the arts 7.1
communications plan 19.9
community access channel 18.3
community activities 19.10
community calendar 8.6, 8.9, 8.28
Conaty-Buck, Susan 7.3
contact sheets 9.6
contests 18.4
controversial material 2.6, 4.4
Copperfield, David 17.1
corporate newsletter 8.11
costumes 2.4, 4.2, 6.2, 8.10, 9.2, 9.7, 9.8, 9.14, 9.15, 10.6, 10.9, 13.5, 14.2, 14.3, 15.4, 16.9, 18.13
coupon 10.2
Coward, Noel 8.9, 17.3
    Private Lives 17.3
critics 4.4
Crucible, The 5.3
cutline 11.7

Dames At Sea 14.7
Damn Yankees 17.2
dancing 2.4, 10.9
deadline 8.27, 10.2
Death of a Salesman 18.1
Decidedly Deadly 15.3
Dickens, Charles
    Christmas Carol, A 18.2, 19.1
    Oliver! 8.27
dinner theater 18.5
directions 10.2
director 3.1, 8.7, 8.8, 8.10
disabilities 13.5, 19.4

Display Manager 6.2
Displays 3.2, 6.2, 9.7, 9.8, 9.14, 9.15, 10.5, 12.6, 13.4, 14.1-14.7, 15.5, 19.10
documentary 18.3
Dr. Jekyll & Mr. Hyde 9.4, 15.3
Dracula 15.3, 17.3
drama departments 4.3
dress rehearsal 9.6, 9.13
Durang, Christopher
    The Actor's Nightmare 4.1
duties 3.1

expenses 6.5, 7.2
    estimate 3.1, 7.2, 7.3, 7.4
    expense reports 3.1

fact sheet 4.4, 4.6, 10.2, 10.6, 12.8, 20.1, 20.3, 21.2
fax machine 8.11
feature articles 8.2, 8.10, 9.8
fliers 3.1, 3.2, 4.6, 6.1, 9.6, 10.8, 11.1-11.3, 11.5, 13.1, 19.7
Frankenstein 10.9
Freud, Sigmund 12.4
fund raising 9.14, 10.5, 13.4, 19.1, 19.10

general manager 3.3
Glass Menagerie, The 1.4
Grease 18.2
grip-and-grin shot 9.3
guest book 14.3

halftone 9.6, 11.5
Hamlet 17.1, 18.4
handbills 20.2
handouts 6.1, 13.1-13.8
head shot 6.2, 9.7, 9.8, 8.10
Hedda Gabler 22.1
high school 6.2
historical record 9.13
history 6.4, 10.6, 13.5, 15.2, 15.4, 15.5, 15.10, 15.12, 19.2
history file 4.4, 12.8, 12.10
home town stories 9.8
house manager 3.2, 9.15

Iceman Cometh, The 8.9, 15.5
interviews 3.2, 6.1, 8.6, 10.5-10.7
Is There Life After High School? 15.4
Jesus Christ Superstar 4.4, 8.26, 9.14

Index-1

Joseph and the Amazing Technicolor Dreamcoat 12.1
Julius Caesar 10.9
Jung, Carl 12.4

King Richard III 2.3

Ladderbush, David 15.8
leaflets 13.1-13.8
Les Miserables 12.1, 12.4
Lewiston/Auburn Community Little Theatre 15.8
library 4.2, 4.3, 6.3, 8.9, 9.7, 11.4, 13.5, 14.2, 14.3, 18.4, 19.10, 20.1, 20.2
light meter 9.18
lighting 9.16-19.20, 14.2, 14.3
lighting designer 9.14
Little Shop of Horrors 18.5
lobby 3.2, 6.2, 9.7, 9.8, 10.5, 12.6, 14.1, 15.5
logo 6.4, 11.8
logotype 11.8, 19.7

Macbeth 2.1
mailing lists 3.1, 4.2, 4.6, 10.1, 10.8, 14.3, 15.5, 20.3
makeup 8.10, 9.8, 9.15, 10.9, 14.3, 16.9
Man of LaMancha 15.5
map 10.8, 13.5, 15.3
marketing 3.2
marquee 14.6
Marriage of Figaro, The 22.1
Marx Brothers 17.1
Master Battle Plan 4.3, 4.6, 5.1-5.8, 6.4, 6.5, 21.1
mechanical 5.2, 11.8
Media Director 6.1
Media Writer 6.1
membership 14.3
membership solicitation 13.5
Miller, Arthur 2.3
    The Crucible 5.3
mission statement 19.2, 19.5, 19.9
money 4.1
Money Management 7.1-7.6
Moon For the Misbegotten 8.27
movie 4.4
Mozart 17.3
murder-mystery 10.9, 15.3

music 2.4
musical 2.1, 6.4, 8.9, 10.7, 14.4, 15.5
Music Man, The 18.6
mystery 2.4, 14.4
name recognition 19.1
negatives 9.5
news conference 10.10
news director 8.7, 10.1
news kit 6.1, 9.6, 10.2, 10.5, 17.3, 21.3
news media 3.1, 3.2, 4.1-4.3, 8.1-8.28, 9.1-9.22, 10.1-10.10, 17.1-17.4, 20.1-20.3
News Release 2.2, 3.2, 4.6, 6.1, 8.1-8.28, 9.21, 10.1, 10.2, 10.8, 10.9, 19.7, 20.1, 20.3, 21.2, 21.3
newsletter 19.10
newspapers 4.2, 10.1
    big city newspaper 8.26
    home town stories 9.8
    regional muckraker 8.25
    shopping news 8.25
    small town daily 8.25
non-profit 7.5
Norris, Mary 18.6
nudity 2.4
Nutcracker, The 22.1

offset printing 11.2
O'Keeffe, Georgia 22.1
Oklahoma! 8.26, 9.1, 9.2, 17.1
Oliver! 8.27
O'Neill, Eugene
    Moon For the Misbegotten 8.27
open house 3.1, 6.3, 19.10
organizations: arts and civic 4.2
original play 8.10, 14.2, 17.2
Orphans of Eternity 17.3
outdoor displays 14.4

pamphlets 11.4
papering the house 10.7
past productions 6.4, 9.7
paste-up 5.2, 11.9
Pearsons, Lyle 15.4
Personals 11.1
personnel 4.4
Peter Pan 10.9
Phantom of the Opera 12.1, 12.6
Photography 3.2, 4.6, 6.2, 6.6, 7.2, 8.11, 8.25, 8.26, 9.1-9.20, 10.2, 11.1, 11.5, 11.8, 13.5, 14.2, 14.3, 20.1-20.3
    action poses 9.13
    backstage pictures 9.14
    black and white film 9.6

Photography *(cont'd)*
    cast photo 9.17
    color 6.2
    contact sheets 9.6
    cutline 11.7
    film speed 9.17, 9.19
    flash 9.16
    grip-and-grin shot 9.3
    halftone 9.6, 11.5
    head shot 6.2, 9.7, 9.8, 8.10
    light meter 9.18
    negatives 9.5
    push processing 9.20
    slides 6.4, 9.7, 9.19, 11.1, 14.2
    triangulation 9.18
    tungsten 9.17, 9.19
Pied Piper, The 17.1
placemats 18.5
Playbill 2.4, 3.2, 4.6, 5.4, 6.1, 9.5, 9.6, 9.7, 9.8, 9.15, 10.5, 11.6, 12.8, 13.4, 15.1-15.10, 19.10, 21.2
playbill supervisor 6.1
playbills 3.1, 6.2, 10.5, 11.1, 11.4, 14.3
playwright 10.6
plot 3.2, 8.9
Poitier, Sidney 4.4
police 17.1
poster 4.6, 5.4, 6.1, 9.2, 9.15, 10.2, 11.6, 14.3
poster and flier manager 6.1
Posters 3.2, 4.6, 5.2, 5.4, 6.1, 7.2, 9.6, 11.1, 11.2, 11.4, 12.1-12.10, 14.1, 14.2, 14.3, 19.7, 20.2, 21.2, 21.3
press kit: see "news kit"
preview story 10.5
prices 7.1
printers 3.1, 4.6, 5.3, 7.4, 9.8, 11.1, 12.8, 15.10
printing 7.2
Private Lives 17.3
progress report 21.2
proofread 11.6, 12.9
props 2.4, 9.2, 19.1, 9.15, 15.4
PSA: see "public service announcement"
public service affairs 3.1
public service announcement 3.2, 6.1, 8.4, 8.28, 10.1
Publicity Stunts 17.1-17.4, 21.1, 21.2
Publicity Team 3.1, 6.1-6.6, 9.15, 21.2, 21.3
push processing 9.20

quote 13.5

radio   4.2, 6.1, 8.4, 9.7, 10.1, 10.7, 18.3, 20.1, 21.2
radio advertising   16.6, 18.5
radio script   16.6
radio techniques   18.2
Raisin in the Sun, A   4.4
receipts   3.1, 7.5, 20.3
recruiting   6.2
regional muckraker   8.25
rehearsal   9.15, 10.5, 10.9, 18.2, 18.3, 21.3
reimbursement   7.5, 7.6
reporters: see "news media"
reviewer   8.10, 9.6
reviews   2.3, 10.3, 13.5, 14.2, 15.4, 20.3
Rice, Anne   17.4
road signs   6.1, 9.2
Roccoberton Jr., Bart. P.   4.1
Rogowski, Konrad
    Orphans of Eternity   17.3
royalty contract   10.7
royalty credit line   12.8

sales tax   7.5
school newspaper   8.28
School Promotion   18.1-18.6
school theater   10.4
schools   4.3, 9.7, 11.4, 18.1, 20.2
script   2.3, 2.4, 4.4, 4.6, 6.3, 6.4, 8.9, 12.8, 14.2
season announcement   13.4
seating arrangements   8.9
seating style   3.2
Self Promotion   21.1-21.3
senior citizen   6.3
set construction   9.7, 9.15, 13.5
set design   9.15
sets   2.4
1776   1.4, 13.4
Shakespeare   2.3, 17.1, 19.8, 22.1
    Hamlet   17.1, 18.4
    King Richard III   2.3
    Julius Caesar   10.9
    The Tragedy of Macbeth   2.1
shopping malls   9.7
shopping news   8.25
show announcement   13.1
Signs   3.2, 5.4, 6.1, 6.2, 7.2, 9.15, 11.1, 14.1-14.7
slides   6.4, 9.7, 9.19, 11.1, 14.2
slogans   4.4
small town daily   8.25
spec sheet   11.4, 12.9
special effects   10.9

special promotions manager   6.2
Spoon River Anthology   17.2
stationery   4.6, 20.3
Stidfole, Jim   18.3
Subject Was Roses, The   2.6
Suffield Players   9.14, 15.4, 19.4
survey   7.1, 14.3, 16.9
Sweeney Todd   18.5
symbols   19.1
synopsis of the play   6.1

T-shirts   6.6, 18.1
table cards   14.4
talk shows   8.6, 10.1, 10.7, 10.8
Tartuffe   22.1
telephone   7.2
telephone bills   7.3
television: see "TV" and "cable TV"
tent cards   6.3, 14.4, 18.4
Thomas, Bob   9.8, 9.13, 9.16
thriller   2.1
ticket prices   3.2, 4.4, 6.4, 12.4
ticket reservations   4.4
ticket sales   3.2, 18.2
tickets   4.6, 6.1, 8.9, 13.1, 13.5, 14.7, 15.3, 20.3
    free tickets   6.2, 10.1, 10.3, 10.4, 10.8, 18.4
Tom Sawyer   17.3
Toulouse-Lautrec, Henri de   12.1
town hall   13.8
triangulation   9.18
tungsten   9.17, 9.19
TV   4.2, 6.1, 8.6, 9.7, 10.1-10.10, 18.3: see also "cable TV"
Twelve Angry Men   9.1
typesetter   6.1

Uncle Vanya   22.1
ushers   6.2, 6.3

videotape   18.3, 21.1
volunteer   6.1-6.6, 14.3, 18.1, 18.5-18.8

whammy   8.27
workshops   19.10
writing guides   4.3, E.1, Suggested Reading

About the Author

George E. Chartier has seen the inside workings of journalism as a newspaper reporter, and has combined this knowledge with fourteen years in advertising, public relations and community theater.

He is a public relations specialist for The University of Connecticut, and advises the renowned Ballard Institute and Museum of Puppetry there. He has worked in advertising and public relations for Milton Bradley Company, where the script he wrote for Playskool's Toy Telephone was used for a television commercial that ran several years nationwide. He has been consulted for promotional advice on town-level political campaigns, higher education, and numerous charities including the American Cancer Society, the Goodwill, and U.S. Savings Bonds.

As promotional advisor for Connecticut's award-winning Suffield Players, he has designed posters and publicity that have helped sell out entire productions — sometimes before opening night. He has twice won the theater company's annual President's Award for outstanding work in promotion and publicity team-building.

A graphic designer, he has created many posters and brochures for the Suffield Players and lectures at theater conferences on the psychology of poster design.

He has co-authored two plays, *Decidedly Deadly*, an audience-participation murder-mystery, and *Dr. Jekyll & Mr. Hyde*, a new adaptation of the classic Robert Lewis Stevenson thriller. *Dr. Jekyll & Mr. Hyde*, co-written with Lyle W. Pearsons, won an unprecedented 11 awards at the 1989 Associated Community Theaters of Connecticut drama festival.

George Chartier has also practiced theater and promotion as a stage magician.

Photo by Liz Galvin